THE
EUROPEAN
PARLIAMENT

Paula Scalingi

THE EUROPEAN PARLIAMENT

The Three–Decade Search for a United Europe

ALDWYCH PRESS · LONDON

ISBN: 0-86172-006-7

First published 1980

in Great Britain by Aldwych Press Limited
3 Henrietta Street, London WC2E 8LU

in the United States of America by Greenwood Press
A division of Congressional Information Service, Inc.
51 Riverside Avenue, Westport, Conn. 06880
as Contributions in Political Science, Number 37

Printed in the United States of America

10 9 8 7 6 5 4 3 2 1

to Ciro
and
Olive Scalingi

CONTENTS

PREFACE

In June 1979 the nations of the European Economic Community held the first European elections in history. For a brief few days, the news media on both sides of the Atlantic focused on the little-known European Parliament, the popular assembly of the Community. Without doubt the election of 410 "Euro M.P.s" by roughly half the 180 million eligible voters was extraordinary news. Journalists, however, with their penchant for stressing the big event— the surface rather than the substance—dwelled on the elections *per se*. The articles centered on the novelty of European elections, on the glamorous and/or highly respected candidates (such as Willy Brandt) who won or lost, and on the impact of the returns on the national politics of the various Community states. Ironically, the media ignored the most important element in the electoral postmortem: the three-decade struggle of advocates of a directly elected European Parliament to achieve their elusive goal.

Yet a thoughtful analysis of West European political integration since 1945 is crucial before one can assess the impact of a directly elected European Parliament on future federalization. The Europe of 1980 is not the war-weary continent of 1950. The aspirations of the early postwar Federalists, who dreamed of creating a genuine multinational legislature, have been replaced by the pragmatic considerations of self-styled realists who envision a loose association of European nations with limited federal institutions.

¶ for conclusion

I would like to emphasize that this study is not another pessimistic
assessment of the recent lack of progress toward further political integration. While the drive for unity certainly has lost the momentum of the
1950s, an investigation of the last thirty years reveals that *external* crises—
the Cold War-related events of great impact such as the Korean War and
the 1968 Soviet invasion of Czechoslovakia—revitalized the West European
nations' commitment to political unity. Conversely, *internal* crises—competition and dissension among Community members during periods of
relative security—have effectively stalled further integration. This stop-go
mode of progress has developed into a predictable cyclical pattern that
has determined the course of European unification and the development
of a real European Parliament.

At present, political integration is, to use a favorite Community term,
stagnating. In an era of détente, the election of 410 delegates to an institution that is not really a legislature at all has wide public interest but little
significance; hence the brief spate of articles on the Parliament during the
elections. But if the pattern of the past three decades continues, yet another crisis is in the offing. The European Parliament may indeed evolve
into a formidable power in the not too distant future.

In the preparation of this study, I received much appreciated assistance
from many individuals, especially the staff of the European Community
Delegation Library in Washington, D.C. I would particularly like to thank
Earl R. Beck, whose advice and encouragement I found invaluable.

THE
EUROPEAN
PARLIAMENT

chapter 1

THE FEDERALIST HERITAGE

The tug-of-war between proponents of the nation-state system and advocates of a united Europe based on supranational institutions has been a dominant theme of the post-World War II era. Today, the nationalists are on the ascendancy after more than thirty years of struggle. It is difficult to imagine that in the immediate postwar era, the concept of a "United States of Europe" had great allure for a large number of Europeans.

The most optimistic advocates of union were those who came to be called the "Federalists." Their approach was premised on the need to create a European government based on *supra*national, as opposed to national, institutions. The legitimacy of this new federal Europe would rest on a written constitution. Modeled somewhat on the American system of representative democracy, this United States of Europe would have an executive, a judiciary, and a legislature which was elected by universal suffrage. However, in the European fashion, the executive would be responsible to this legislature—a European Parliament.

While the Federalists represented the most idealistic among the pro-integration movement, there were those who espoused a more cautious, or "functional" approach to European unification. The Functionalists felt that intergovernmental cooperation through limited federal institutions in certain areas of common interest—for example, steel and coal production—would "spill over" into other areas such as agriculture, trans-

portation, and monetary policy. This process would inevitably involve
political cooperation on a supranational scale, leading to the creation of
a European federal state.

At the far end of the pro-integration spectrum were the "Confederalists,"
those Europeans who wished to retain the nation as the fundamental unit
of a new European order that would be based on voluntary intergovernmental cooperation.

Today, the distinction among these three approaches is quite blurred.
The terms *Federalist*, *Functionalist*, and *Confederalist* are no longer used.
Instead, the designation *European*—previously used interchangeably with
the former two terms—denotes advocates of intergovernmental cooperation. Thirty years ago, such was not the case. Although few in number,
the Federalists were a powerful force in the immediate postwar period.
Many of the original Federalists—government officials or intellectuals in
exile and members of the various non-Communist Resistance groups—
were to become the leaders of the resurrected European states after the
war: Paul-Henri Spaak, Jean Monnet, Robert Schuman, Alcide de Gasperi,
Johan Willem Beyen, Konrad Adenauer, Joseph Bech, and Altiero Spinelli.
Others such as André Philip, Henry Frenay, Hendrik Brugmans, Denis de
Rougemont, and Count Coudenhove-Kalergi, devoted their considerable
talents to the federalist cause.

Their crusade for a united Europe founded on a democratically elected
European Parliament had its immediate roots in the trauma of total war.
The horror and destruction caused by the Second World War explain in
large part the motivations behind this wholehearted repudiation of nationalism. The rapid collapse of the continental nations early in the conflict was horrible evidence of the inability of the national governments—
no matter what their ideological leanings—to provide adequate security
for their populations. Beyond this, the terrible vitality of the Nazi regime
was grim evidence of the destructive capability of a totalitarian nation
bent on world domination.

The history of the European nation-state system has been a chronology
of wars. World War I—the Great War—was supposedly the war to end all
wars. After 1918, scholars and statesmen wrestled with the unsolvable
dilemma of how states could insure future cooperation and peace. In the
early postwar period, collective security in the guise of the League of
Nations appeared a viable instrument through which to maintain peace.
International law prohibiting aggression, as typified by the Kellogg-Briand

Pact of 1928, appeared to be another effective means of discouraging national conflict. When both collective security and international law turned out to be failures in the struggle to maintain the precarious postwar peace, statesmen turned to the age-old technique of personal diplomacy as a last resort. It was at Munich on September 29, 1938, that the nation-state system failed most miserably and dramatically.

For a large proportion of the members of the Resistance movements in the states under Nazi or Fascist control, it was only logical that the war-prone nation-state system should give way to a new federation of European peoples in the immediate postwar era. Walter Lipgens, in his study of the World War II Resistance, observed that the Resistance leaders felt they were living "at the end of an epoch."[1] Whether the Resistance group in question was French, Polish, or Dutch, the recurrent theme in their copious writings was the same—only through the creation of a European federation within the broader framework of a world peace organization could Europe avoid war, escape totalitarian rule, and protect the human rights of its peoples. For the Federalists, the American-British concept of collective security which was to find its expression in the United Nations Charter was imperfect and hence insufficient in itself to maintain peace. One of the most fervent Federalists, Belgian statesman Paul-Henri Spaak, recalled later that Federalists saw the United Nations as flawed from the start. According to Spaak, by stressing the concept of "universality," the architects of the UN allowed undemocratic states with obvious imperialistic ambitions to join. He also noted that although the veto power exercised by Security Council members was less absolute than the unanimity of the old League of Nations, still the minority could tyrannize the majority. As a member of the San Francisco Conference and a delegate to the newly established UN, he was repelled by the disruptive behavior of the Soviet Union and the atmosphere of confrontation.[2]

The idea of a united Europe certainly was not the brainchild of Spaak and his like-minded fellow Europeans. The Greeks and Romans saw Europe as a single entity. (One may recall the myth of Europa.) The concept was emphasized and romanticized in the era of Charlemagne. The universality of the Catholic church during the Middle Ages linked the territorial and mythological concept of Europe with the idea of spiritual unity, while later would-be caesars such as Napoleon attempted to unite the continent by force. The last four centuries and especially more recent times witnessed the birth of myriad theories and schemes for a new European order, many of which centered on the creation of an assembly, diet, council, or senate—a European legislature of sorts.[3] Among the earliest and most famous of these plans was the Duc de Sully's "Grand Design" for an international association of heads of state. This plan was confederal in nature as was the abortive Concert of Europe established after the Napoleonic Wars.

It was the success of the United States that conferred a degree of respectability on a novel type of governmental system—representative democracy. However, in the intensely nationalistic atmosphere of the nineteenth century, federalism on a continental scale could hardly take root. Even when World War I first revealed the bankruptcy of the nation-state system, federalism was not viewed as a realistic means of insuring future peace. In the troublesome 1920s, amid premonitions of yet another European conflict, French statesman Aristide Briand's nebulous proposal for a European federation was embraced only by a few "crackpot" pan-Europeans such as Count Coudenhove-Kalergi.

World War II, however, radically altered the situation. With the national governments discredited, federalism emerged as the only real alternative in the eyes of many of Europe's future leaders. For some of these men, namely, Konrad Adenauer and Alcide de Gasperi, other considerations enhanced the desirability of a federal Europe. Such a system would ease Italy and especially Germany back into the family of European nations while dispelling the fears of France and the Benelux states concerning a German resurgence and reviving the destroyed economy of Europe as a whole and Germany in particular.[4]

The views of the Federalists were by no means shared by many of their colleagues who were also destined to determine Europe's fortunes in the 1950s and 1960s. For example, within the Resistance, certain right-wing groups (such as the Beck-Goerdeler group in Berlin and the Organization Civile et Militaire in Paris) were for economic integration only, preferring to retain some degree of national sovereignty in matters of foreign policy.[5] For certain leaders of governments in exile such as French General Charles de Gaulle, there was no alternative to the nation-state as the basic unit of any new postwar European order. According to de Gaulle, the duty of France's future leaders was to restore their nation to greatness.

Winston Churchill's attitude toward European unification was obscured by his politician's propensity to make sweeping statements designed to appeal to the aspirations of his audience. Churchill's views on federalism foreshadowed the British refusal to participate in the supranational experiments of the 1950s. For all his expostulations on the virtues of a United States of Europe, Churchill had no intention of including Britain in what he believed should be strictly a continental federation. An examination of his speeches on European unity and his foreign policy decisions makes this quite clear. A recurrent theme throughout his wartime and postwar addresses was the need to strengthen the ties between the United States and "Great Britain and the British Commonwealth and the Empire." Furthermore, "special associations within the circle of the United Nations" would aid rather than hinder the UN. As he expressively phrased it, "Like the great unity of the British Empire and Commonwealth, a United States of Europe . . . will unify the Continent in a manner never known since the fall of the Roman Empire. . . ."[6] In his famous Zurich speech on September 19, 1946, Churchill called for the establishment of "a kind of United States of Europe." "There is no reason why a regional organization of Europe should in any way conflict with the world organization of the United Nations. . . . There is already a natural grouping in the Western Hemisphere. We British have our own Commonwealth of nations." Churchill also observed that the only way to "re-create the European family" was through Franco-German cooperation. The "first step" to this end was the creation of a "Council of Europe."[7]

However, as revealed by his foreign policy and that of the Labour government which succeeded him in August 1945, Britain's traditional goals—maintenance of the balance of power, protection of the Empire, and retention of naval and economic preeminence—remained the basis of British foreign policy. Churchill's willingness to divide the world into Soviet-Western spheres of influence was evidence of his continued faith in great power politics. As he noted in a letter to Roosevelt on February 2, 1943, through the sanctity of a "world organization" comprised of "blocs," Britain and the United States would police the world.[8]

The attitude of the United States to the concept of a European federation underwent a remarkable transformation from hostility in the wartime years to enthusiastic acceptance after 1947.[9] In the first two years of the war, for example, regional European economic cooperation was seen by U.S. policymakers as a threat to an anticipated world security organization. However, by the spring of 1944, leaders in the Roosevelt administration and Congress were expressing the desirability of some form of European confederation to integrate defeated Germany back into

the European economy. However, fear of Soviet objections to this idea
and apprehension over the possibility that such an association of European
states would "gang up" on the United States tempered this new foreign
policy direction. An additional fear, voiced by the Council on Foreign
Relations in November 1944, was that Britain would attempt to create
an anti-Soviet, British-dominated West European bloc for her own security.[10]
Churchill's repeated references to a United States of Europe seemed to
indicate this direction in British foreign policy. Furthermore, and more
fundamentally, Roosevelt saw the postwar era in terms of Soviet-American
cooperation, as seen in the decisions made at the Tehran and Yalta conferences. The "four world policemen" (the United States, the Soviet Union,
Britain, and China) would deal with the realities of power politics while
the new world security organization would provide the necessary sanction
of world public opinion for their policies.

American distrust of European unity disappeared rapidly as the friction
between the United States and the Soviets increased. Western Europe, in
the throes of political and economic chaos, appeared destined to fall under
Russian domination. According to future Secretary of State Dean
Acheson, through the winter and spring of 1947 most of President Harry
Truman's chief advisors shared a growing belief that communism would
engulf Western Europe unless something was done to get the European
states back on their feet. This consideration was chiefly behind the United
States' sudden conversion to a pro-federal European policy which found
its first expression in the Marshall Plan. As Policy Planning Staff head
George Kennan described the U.S. plan for European economic recovery,
"By insisting on a joint approach, we hoped to force the Europeans to
begin to think like Europeans and not like nationalists in their approach
to the economic problems of the continent."[11]

The heart of the European Recovery Program, as outlined in Secretary
of State George C. Marshall's Harvard speech, expressed the U.S. decision
to espouse European integration:

> It would be neither fitting nor efficacious
> for this Government to undertake to draw
> up unilaterally a program designed to place
> Europe on its feet economically. This is
> the business of the Europeans. The initia-
> tive, I think, must come from Europe.[12]

What Marshall did not add, of course, was that the United States intended
to use Western Europe as a buffer to Soviet expansion. The U.S. plan also

was a means to control Britain and the future economic development of Western Europe while rehabilitating and reunifying Germany. However, the Truman administration attempted to make the plan appear strictly humanitarian. As U.S. Undersecretary of State for Economic Affairs William Clayton observed, the plan for European economic recovery "should be a European plan and come—or at any rate appear to come—from Europe. But the United States must run the show."[13]

Since this American change of heart on European unity did not take place until early 1947, for the three preceding years Federalists found their escalating demands for a supranational European government increasingly ignored by the United States and Britain. (The Soviet Union strongly opposed the creation of any European federation as a capitalist threat to its security.) In May 1944, delegates from the Resistance groups of nine nations met in Switzerland where they called for the establishment of a temporary Allied "supreme authority" at the war's end. This provisional government would oversee the creation of a European Constitutional Assembly.[14]

For the Federalists, however, the key question remained the form that this future federal government would take. One detailed blueprint for a federal Europe did exist. A month before the Resistance leaders' Swiss conference, longtime pan-European Count Coudenhove-Kalergi unveiled his *Draft Constitution of the United States of Europe*. This comprehensive plan, published in New York in April 1944, was a blend of American political theory and European parliamentary tradition with a substantial addition of Coudenhove's unquenchable idealism. It provided for a Congress comprised of a house of representatives and a house of states. The members of the lower chamber were appointed by the national parliaments (not directly elected). The upper house delegates were selected "as each member state shall determine." The Congress could pass legislation with the joint approval of both houses and was authorized to create necessary federal agencies. Executive power rested in the hands of a seven-man Council which was elected for a four-year term by the Congress in special session. The Council could be removed by the latter. A titular president and vice-president (appointed by the Council from its membership) presided over meetings. The *Draft Constitution* also provided for a Supreme Court of fifteen judges elected by the Congress by a two-thirds vote from lists of candidates supplied by the Council. Amendment of the Constitution rested with the Congress, which could revise it with the approval of two-thirds of both houses.[15]

Coudenhove's proposal for a European federation was extremely significant, but not because it was a feasible plan or even a desirable one. Its importance lay in its emphasis on parliamentary supremacy. Although the lower house of Coudenhove's Congress was indirectly elected, it still was a "peoples' assembly," and this body, with the representatives of the states, controlled the legislative, executive, and judicial functions of the federation. Coudenhove's belief in a strong European Parliament was shared by the growing number of federalists who saw a legislature with far-reaching powers and elected by universal suffrage as the fundamental element of the new political system to be established at the end of the war.

The division of Europe into West and Soviet-dominated East, the increasing antagonism between the United States and the Soviet Union, and the restoration of the prewar nation-state system sorely disillusioned those who had visualized the dawn of a new era. The viability of the United Nations as a peacekeeping tool lost its early luster in the eyes of the Federalists as the General Assembly became a stage for Soviet-Western confrontation. The United States had accepted the necessity of regional security systems with the Act of Chapultepec and incorporated this concept into the UN Charter as Article 51. Physically, economically, politically, and spiritually, Europe remained devastated. The once-great powers which boasted far-flung world empires were, in the postwar world, mere specters of their former selves, pawns of the emerging superpowers— the Soviet Union and the United States.

All these elements added tremendous momentum to the growing drive toward a federal Europe. A number of groups and committees were formed that were dedicated to some form of European unification. On January 17, 1947, a British United Europe Committee was created under the leadership of former British Prime Minister Winston Churchill. On July 16, a similar committee was established in France under the venerable French statesman, Edouard Herriot.[16] Both committees cut across party lines. However, in a move that presaged the British Labour party's future opposition to European integration, Labourites held aloof from the crusade. The French committee included among its members former French Premier Paul Reynaud, leaders of the Socialist party and the *Mouvement Républicain Populaire,* and a handful of intellectuals. The two committees held a joint meeting on July 9 in Paris to plan their campaign.[17]

Although such pro-union associations as the British and French committees and the influential umbrella organization, the European Union of Federalists, championed the cause of a "United States of Europe," there existed no general agreement among the members within these various groups as to how this aim could be achieved. Many of these early *Europeans*—as the integrationists came to call themselves—agreed with Churchill that it was unwise to attempt to design any sort of constitution. As former British Foreign Secretary Anthony Eden observed, the British people preferred to muddle things out by "trial and error," and besides, Britain lacked a written constitution anyway.[18] On the other hand, Altiero Spinelli, one of Italy's foremost champions of unity and the head of the *Movimento Federalista Europea*, advocated total political integration through the formation of a European Parliament. It was Spinelli and his like-minded colleagues who best fit the term Federalist. The Federalists, as he noted, "ask that the political institutions of a democratic Europe be constructed first, taking certain powers . . . from the national executive, parliament and judiciary." According to Spinelli, these institutions would "derive their legitimacy from the consent directly expressed by European citizens."[19]

However, most advocates of a supranational Europe took a more conservative approach, fearing that the headlong rush to construct a new political system centered around a European legislature was far too radical a step. Rather, they preferred integration on a piecemeal basis—by "sector" (for example, the economic sector). The creation of Benelux was an example of this functional approach to European integration. As early as September 5, 1944, Belgium, the Netherlands, and Luxembourg had accepted the necessity of an economic union to rebuild and protect their respective economies in the postwar world. In April 1946, Benelux officially was established. According to those who were classified as Functionalists, the creation of such an association was the first step on the long road toward the creation of a federal Europe.[20] In March 1948, Britain and France joined the Benelux states in the Brussels Treaty. This pact set up a consultative council of foreign ministers, a military committee, and other institutions to coordinate defense matters. The early 1950s were to witness attempts along both functionalist and federalist lines to construct new European governmental institutions. The European Coal and Steel Community, with its powerless, non-elected Common Assembly, survived to develop into the European Economic Community.

The ambitious European Political Community, conceived hastily during the period when pro-union fervor reached its peak, died with the treaty to create a European Defense Community in the French National Assembly.

Europeans had to contend with much more than mere disagreement within their own ranks. The much-maligned nation-state system, far from being consigned to the scrap heap in the postwar era, was demonstrating remarkable vitality. Britain's extraordinary and successful struggle against Hitler served to inspire British patriotism to new heights. Despite the pro-union sentiment of many of her foremost statesmen, France clung defiantly to her resurrected national independence and to the remnants of her colonial empire. Throughout the following three decades, France was to undercut the limited but growing powers of the very federal institutions she would help to create. As far as the soon-to-be-born West German state was concerned, although future Chancellor Adenauer was a confirmed *European* for practical more than ideological considerations, the Social Democrats, who viewed potential West European union as incompatible with a reunited Germany, actively opposed the pro-European posture of the Christian Democrats. Italian and French Communists adhered to the Moscow line and rejected European integration as a threat to state sovereignty and a product of capitalism. It was this revitalized nationalism, particularly in France, which was to block any progress toward a "directly elected" European Parliament, that is, a supranational assembly elected by universal suffrage, until the late 1970s.

chapter 2

THE EXPERIMENTAL YEARS, 1949—1954

The more than seven hundred enthusiastic "Europeans" of sixteen nations who met in the Congress of Europe at The Hague May 7-11, 1948, would have been shocked if they had known that three decades would elapse before a directly elected European Parliament would become a reality. Churchill, Honorary President of the conference, presided over an assembly of illustrious advocates of European union which included such well-known figures as Adenauer, Spaak, de Gasperi, Georges Bidault, Leon Blum, Paul Reynaud, Robert Schuman, and Paul van Zeeland. (Several members of the British Labour party were present, although the party's National Executive attempted to discourage their attendance.) Despite the diverging views of Federalists, Functionalists, and Confederalists, the Congress adopted a number of ambitious resolutions. Arguing that a Europe based on a rigid nation-state system could not survive, the Congress called for a federal government founded on a European Consultative Assembly whose three hundred to four hundred members would be nominated by the parliaments of member nations.[1]

Four months later, the governments of France and Belgium submitted the recommendations of the Congress to the Permanent Council of the Brussels Treaty powers (France, Britain, and the Benelux states) for consideration. The Permanent Council in turn appointed a five-nation committee representing the member states for the study of European unity.

This committee, which met in Paris on November 26 under the chairmanship of that longtime supporter of a united Europe, Edouard Herriot,
debated both a Franco-Belgian proposal for a European Parliament and
a British counterproposal for a Council of Ministers. According to this
latter scheme, the foreign ministers of participating nations would meet
periodically to consider matters of a European nature. Defense and
economic policy would remain the province of the national governments.

The reaction of the Labour government foreshadowed the British
attitude toward attempts to further European integration in the 1950s.
Although Britain's world position was substantially diminished after
1945, successive British governments did not view their nation as a has-
been great power. Despite the extreme hardship of the last few years, the
British seemed unable to reconcile themselves to their new status. In
terms of goals, Britain's postwar policy differed little from her prewar
position. Whether a Labour or Conservative government was in power,
the foundations of this policy remained the same—the twin, related neces-
sities of maintaining (1) a worldwide, favorable trading environment and
(2) a balance of power that would enable Britain to retain this favorable
economic position. Thus, control of the seas was still a fundamental
aspect of British policy. Reliance on the commonwealth system, in light
of Britain's "export or die" situation, was a must. Likewise, the continued "special relationship" with the United States was imperative to
neutralize European competition. European union posed a threat, not a
boon, to Britain since it would undermine this fundamental policy. In
addition, on a psychological level, the submergence of Britain into a
European federation was unthinkable to a nation that considered its
historical experience to be unique. Britain, by tradition, was much closer
to the United States than to the European nations (particularly France)
with whom she had quarreled on and off for centuries.[2]

It was not surprising, then, that Europe's first attempt to set up a
viable international parliament was destined to end in failure. After the
continental members of the Brussels Pact threatened to create a European
assembly without Britain, the Attlee government reluctantly agreed to a
compromise.[3] The resulting "Statute of the Council of Europe" was
signed in May 1949 by the five Brussels nations and Denmark, Norway,
Iceland, Italy, and Sweden. The Council of Europe was a radically different entity from the customs union proposed by French Foreign Minister
Georges Bidault during the negotiations. The Bidault plan had envisioned

the creation of a European assembly to advise the nations on matters pertaining to economic integration. Indeed, a Consultative Assembly *was* part of the compromise agreement. But it quickly became apparent that real power rested solely with the other body of the Council of Europe—the Committee of Ministers. Although on paper the Council of Europe appeared to be an embryonic federal government, in reality it was a discussion group of national leaders.

Nonetheless, during the first months of its existence, the Consultative Assembly remained the keystone of the Federalists' aspirations. Its members charged gallantly onward in the supposed direction of European union, ignoring the warning signals of an impending roadblock. From its birth, the Assembly was a powerless institution. Although it offered a forum for airing pro-federation sentiment, the Assembly had no authority to convert proposals into laws, no constituency to whom it could appeal for support, and no executive to implement decisions. For a time, it could not even draw up its own agenda. The Consultative Assembly, in short, was aptly named. Although its members sat in alphabetical order rather than by national delegation, national divisions were all too evident. Furthermore, unlike the soon-to-be-established Common Assembly of the European Coal and Steel Community, the Consultative Assembly lacked any constitutional basis for expanding its powers or for substituting elected delegates for appointed ones.[4]

Undaunted, the 135 members of the Assembly met in the opening session in August 1949 to discuss "necessary changes in the political structure of Europe."[5] Accordingly, a Committee on General Affairs was established to investigate the path to eventual political union. Among the items that this committee ultimately considered were twenty-four various recommendations of momentous ramifications, including a proposal that the Assembly be allowed to determine its own agenda and that its jurisdiction be broadened to transform itself into "a European political authority with limited aims but real powers." On September 5, after hearing the committee's report, the Assembly voted to present a series of recommendations calling for an extension of its powers to the Committee of Ministers.[6]

There was little reason to believe that the Assembly would fail in its quest to alter the Council of Europe statute. The euphoria of the last few years still existed. The Council of Europe was only one of a number of experiments of a cooperative nature. (The creation of Benelux, the

OEEC, and the Brussels Pact have already been noted.) Just prior to the
opening meeting of the Council of Europe in April 1949, the United
States, Canada, and ten European states linked their defense policies in
the North Atlantic Treaty Organization.[7] The creation of NATO came
as a response to the Soviet blockade of Berlin. The hardening of the
division between East and West made it all the more imperative, as far
as American policymakers were concerned, to support all efforts to integrate Western Europe and especially to involve the newly created West
Germany in the continent's defense.

A second major factor appearing to insure the Consultative Assembly's
success was its illustrious membership. Churchill, Hugh Dalton, and
Harold Macmillan were among the British delegates. Herriot was the
Assembly's new president of honor and Belgian Foreign Minister Spaak
presided as president. Prominent French members included several past
and future premiers: Bidault, Guy Mollet, Reynaud, and André Philip.
A special "Maison de l'Europe," constructed in Strasbourg in the spring
of 1950, seemed to symbolize the beginning of the great federal experiment.

All this notwithstanding, it was becoming increasingly evident that
those members of the Consultative Assembly—mainly the French, Italian,
and Benelux delegates—who were dedicated to transforming it into a
true parliament, were not a strong enough majority to force the Committee of Ministers to accept the necessary amendments. Although these
Federalists were willing to compromise to a certain extent and retain a
measure of state sovereignty, most of the British, Irish, and Scandinavian
members of the Assembly preferred intergovernmental cooperation without any abandonment of national power.[8] A few months after French
Foreign Minister Robert Schuman unveiled a scheme for a supranational
institution to coordinate French and German coal and steel production,
Federalists in the Consultative Assembly made one last great effort to
transform the Council of Europe into a rudimentary European Parliament. A Labour M.P., R. W. G. Mackay, one of the three British members
of the Committee on General Affairs, offered a plan to amend the Council of Europe statute. The "Mackay Protocol" of August 1950 called
for the inclusion of the OEEC and the Brussels Treaty Organization
under the aegis of the Council of Europe. The latter would be transformed into a European government comprised of the Committee of
Ministers, an "Executive Council," and a two-house "Legislative Assem-

bly." This new Assembly would appoint members of the Executive Council and would, along with the Committee of Ministers, jointly pass legislation which would supersede domestic laws. However, Committee of Ministers' decisions would still have to be unanimous.[9]

The Mackay Protocol and other Assembly recommendations devised to alter the Council of Europe statute were routinely rebuffed by the statute's signatories. In a final futile gesture of defiance, the Assembly in December 1951 adopted a recommendation to draw up a new charter embodying a revised version of the Mackay Protocol—assuming correctly that Britain and the Scandinavian nations would veto the plan once again.[10] That same month, Paul-Henri Spaak resigned his post as president of the Assembly.

With the Federalists' hopes of creating a new European government momentarily frustrated, advocates of political union threw their support to Monnet's great functional experiment, the European Coal and Steel Community. Remarkably enough, the famous Schuman Declaration of May 9, 1950, made no mention of a European Parliament—or any assembly for that matter. The French Foreign Minister's announcement was actually in the form of a press communiqué. The plan was the brainchild of Jean Monnet, longtime supporter of international cooperation and the first director of the French Economic Planning Commission after the war. His extraordinary proposal to create a supranational "High Authority" to oversee French and German coal and steel production caught the industries involved, the French government, and the United States off guard.

After the initial surprise, American policymakers were delighted with the potential of the Schuman Declaration. The Council of Europe had not fulfilled their expectations. In a letter to the U.S. consul in Strasbourg, Secretary of State Acheson dismissed the Consultative Assembly as a vehicle for the federalization of Western Europe and noted the potential of the proposed Coal and Steel Community. As Acheson observed, although the United States would "obviously welcome the development of the Council of Europe into an organization which could effectively deal with the specifics of furthering European unity, we do not feel that on evidence to date it has shown itself as effective as the OEEC in dealing with concrete problems in the economic field. . . ." Acheson went on to indicate that it would not be beneficial for the United States to have two rival organizations active in the economic field and added that the Council of Europe was valuable merely as a "European forum" for public pro-union sentiment.[11]

The underlying premise of the Schuman Plan was the assumption that European unification was a necessary prelude to world peace and European economic and political resurgence.[12] The draft treaty for the set of institutions that came to be called the European Coal and Steel Community (ECSC) reflected this assumption and the political realities of the time. Under the influence of Monnet and West German statesman and professor Walter Hallstein, the treaty included not only the High Authority and Court of Justice mentioned in the Schuman Declaration, but a Council of National Ministers and a Common Assembly as well. These latter institutions, not by coincidence, bore a definite resemblance to the Council of Ministers and the Consultative Assembly of the ineffective Council of Europe. The determined treaty-framers optimistically included an embryonic legislature on the off chance it might mature into the much-sought-after European government. As outlined in the treaty, however, the Council of Ministers and the Common Assembly appeared to have little in common with a parliamentary system of government. The role of the Council of Ministers would be to scrutinize and harmonize the decisions of the High Authority with the policy of the member governments. The Assembly was to oversee the activities of the Authority, which in theory it could oust with a vote of censure.

The structure and functions of the Common Assembly were described in Articles 20-25 of the ECSC Treaty, which was signed in Paris on April 18, 1951, by the Benelux nations, France, West Germany, and Italy. Article 20 specified that the Assembly was to be comprised of the "representatives of the peoples of the States" who were members. Like the Consultative Assembly of the Council of Europe, the ECSC body consisted of delegates appointed by national parliaments on an annual basis. However—and very significantly—a member nation could choose to select its representatives by "direct universal suffrage" if it so desired and could hold these elections according to national procedures. The number of representatives allotted to each of the six signatories of the treaty corresponded to the state's size: 18 each for Germany, France, and Italy; 10 each for Belgium and the Netherlands, and 4 for Luxembourg. Article 22 provided for the holding of an annual session by the Assembly which would last no longer than the fiscal year. Allowance was made for scheduling extraordinary sessions if the Council of Ministers or High Authority so requested, or if the Assembly needed to comment on a question put to it by the Council. Members of the Council and High Authority could attend Assembly meetings, and the High Authority was responsible for answering oral or written questions put to it by the Assembly (Article 23).

Significantly, the Council of Ministers—the representatives of national governments—was under no obligation to the Assembly and not answerable to it. As far as Federalists were concerned, the Council's lack of accountability to the Assembly was a defect in the treaty—a crucial omission which was to be repeated in the Rome Treaties seven years later. However, it was as unlikely in 1951 as it was in 1957 that the treaty authors could have done otherwise and still have made the provisions palatable to the nations involved.

Furthermore, the Assembly's control over the High Authority was dubious indeed. Article 24 provided for a motion of censure. According to the provision, the Assembly would analyze the general report drawn up annually by the High Authority and either approve or reject it. A motion of censure passed by a two-thirds majority would force the High Authority to resign as a body, and the member states would select replacements. However, this power of dismissal meant little, as the Assembly would have no assurance that a new High Authority would prove any more responsive than the old. (Of course, this was assuming that disgruntled members could convince two-thirds of the Assembly to back them in an open vote.) Last, the Assembly did not have the power to amend the treaty. This task was left to the national governments. The Assembly, however, did have the authority to adopt its own rules of procedure (Article 25) and thus did not have to fight for this privilege as did the Consultative Assembly of the Council of Europe.[13]

As the ECSC Treaty painfully revealed, the Common Assembly hardly resembled a nascent European Parliament. The six nations embarking on this unique supranational experiment considered, perhaps quite logically, that if the Assembly was given too much latitude—the right to participate in the legislative process, for example—it might take the bit in its teeth and defy the sovereign states that created it. Likewise, despite the provision allowing the direct election of Assembly members, the national governments preferred to ignore the Federalists' calls for European elections lest a popularly based Assembly gain its independence from their control. Considering these fears, it is not clear why the six

ECSC states consented to the inclusion of an Assembly in the treaty at
all. As it was, the Common Assembly was simply democratic window
dressing for an international agreement among national governments.
It must be remembered, however, that in 1950 other concerns pre-
occupied Western Europe, and that it was not at all extraordinary that
the ECSC Treaty negotiators argued far more over the status of the Saar
than over the structure and functions of the potential nucleus of a
united Europe.[14]

The innocuous nature of the Paris Treaty did not insure it an easy
ratification in the national parliaments. Extreme conservatives and Communists alike fought the treaty from its inception. In the French National Assembly, the Gaullists and Communists opposed it, as did the
majority of the Social Democrats in West Germany, the Nenni Socialists
and the Communists in Italy, and the Communist parties of Holland,
Belgium, and Luxembourg.[15] Although a British rejection of ECSC membership was expected, it still caused consternation among the Federalists.
However, if the ratification process was somewhat rocky, at least it proceeded rapidly, taking a little more than a year from the signing of the
document by the negotiators to the final ratification by the last of the
six national parliaments in June 1952.[16]

On September 25, 1952, the European Coal and Steel Community
came into existence. The Common Assembly met in its first session at
Strasbourg University. Although the headquarters of the Assembly (and
later that of the European Parliament) was Luxembourg, due to the lack
of a suitable meeting place there, sessions were usually held in the audi-
torium constructed for the Council of Europe in Strasbourg. This extraordinary arrangement, meant to be only temporary, was to continue after
the Common Assembly evolved into the European Parliament in 1958,
necessitating a parade of papers, files, secretaries, and translators back
and forth from Luxembourg. As the bureaucratic paraphernalia increased
over the years, the costs grew enormously. Yet the Assembly leaders preferred not to construct a permanent meeting chamber since there was
general disagreement over which city should be the capital of a future
European government. Furthermore, it hardly seemed proper to debate
the selection of a site for a capital considering that the European Coal
and Steel Community was as yet merely an international organization.
The choice of an official language posed another problem. The dilemma
was solved by authorizing four official languages—Dutch, French, German,

and Italian—although French remained the language spoken by most Assembly members.

Notwithstanding the provision in the treaty allowing for the election of Assembly members by direct universal suffrage, quite naturally none of the six ECSC states chose this route. As a general rule, West German representatives were selected by the Bundestag (lower house only). In the Netherlands, members were designated by the presidents of both chambers after nomination by their respective political parties. In France, they were appointed from among the members of the French Assembly with a ratio of two to one in favor of the lower house. The Italian and Belgian parliaments selected their delegates in equal numbers from both chambers while Luxembourg's four members came from its single-chamber assembly. As a rule, the states attempted to make their delegations as representative of the political composition of their national parliaments as possible.[17]

Initially, the Common Assembly followed the example of the Consultative Assembly of the Council of Europe and seated its members alphabetically instead of by nationality. In fact, a great deal of attention was paid to the nationality factor in setting up the first Assembly. For example, the selection of the "Bureau" (the officers) of the Assembly was based to a major extent on this element. It is notable that in the election of Belgian Socialist Paul-Henri Spaak over German Christian Democrat Heinrich von Brentano as president of the new Assembly, a number of non-Socialist, French-speaking members voted for the former.[18] However, even as the Assembly convened in late 1952, members of Liberal, Christian Democratic, and Socialist affiliations began collaborating on the formation of European political groups. In June 1953, the Assembly voted to add a new article to its rules of procedure authorizing the creation of supranational political groups, that is, nascent European political parties. A minimum of nine representatives were necessary to constitute a group and members were limited to participation in one group. The Assembly also agreed to provide the groups with funds for general expenses and for the operation of a permanent secretariat for each at the Luxembourg headquarters. The alphabetical seating arrangement quickly gave way to seating by group affiliation. In June 1953, Christian Democrats numbered 38; Socialists, 23; and Liberals, 11. Four French Gaullists and one Dutch Liberal preferred to remain unaffiliated.[19]

As the Assembly took on more of the trappings of a genuine parliament,

many of its members who assumed that it would rapidly evolve into a
European legislature began to agitate for extension of the Assembly's
powers—especially for the direct election of its delegates. Within two
years, the Assembly had come far. It had set up an effective system of
four large and three small committees dealing with such matters as social
and political affairs, transportation, and administration. These committees
met regularly between sessions. Each had a chairman and a *rapporteur*
(who was often a more influential personage with greater expertise in
the area involved than the committee head). The *rapporteur* was responsible for presenting committee decisions to the general membership. In
addition, the Assembly went beyond the single session provided in the
treaty to examine the High Authority's annual report, meeting a minimum of four times a year—November, February, May, and October.[20]
The relations between the High Authority and the Assembly were generally
cooperative. The relationship with the Council of Ministers, if officially
cordial, was distant at best. The Council conveniently found it unneces-
sary to consult the Assembly and refrained, except on formal occasions,
from attending sessions.[21]

Not all Assembly members viewed their limited role within the Coal
and Steel Community with distaste. Just as had been the case in the Consultative Assembly of the Council of Europe, certain members of the
Common Assembly preferred a confederal Europe, or a "Union of European States," as Gaullist leader and future French premier Michel Debré
termed his conception of a future international government. The vast
gulf separating the divergent views of the Federalists and Confederalists
was starkly revealed in the abortive struggle to secure the ratification of
the European Defense Community Treaty and its companion plan for
a European Political Community.

With the outbreak of the Korean War in June 1950, the impetus toward
political and economic integration appeared to gain further momentum.
The precarious economic situation in Europe, which had prompted the
Schuman Declaration a few weeks earlier, was joined by an equally serious
dilemma—the question of German rearmament. To this latter problem
there appeared to be a unique solution—at least to the Federalists. If
coal and steel production could be shared among nations through supranational institutions, why not supranational coordination of armed forces
by means of a European Defense Community? The Truman administra-

tion, eager to involve West Germany in the Atlantic alliance, had toyed with the idea of expanding the original Schuman proposal to include the coordination of defense policy as well as steel and coal production. However, U.S. High Commissioner for Germany John J. McCloy counseled Acheson that "the introduction of [the] common defense problem into the Schuman Plan negotiations at this time might confuse and retard such negotiations without furthering the development of [a] common defense." In addition, McCloy noted that the architects of the future Paris Treaty were not "qualified or authorized" to discuss the matter. Furthermore, he observed that such an approach might alienate the German government and the German general public since West Germany's status in Europe was not yet clarified.[22]

The Korean conflict made a common West European defense policy all the more imperative as far as both the United States and its allies were concerned. France, Britain, and Belgium still retained large military forces in Asia and Africa. West Germany, on the other hand, possessed a great manpower potential. The alternatives were either the inclusion of German divisions in NATO—opposed by Britain and France—or the creation of a European army, a kind of Schuman Plan for the coordination of defense through a supranational agency.

As with the Schuman Plan, Jean Monnet supplied the needed proposal for a European Defense Community—although it was presented to the French National Assembly by Premier René Pleven on October 24, 1950.[23] This so-called Pleven Plan provided for the creation of a European army with national forces integrated at the battalion level. (Those states who joined the Defense Community would keep their own national armies.) A "European defense minister" appointed by the governments would direct the European army according to the policy of a Council of (national) Ministers. The plan also included a European Assembly, which, like the proposed assembly of the European Coal and Steel Community, would act in an advisory capacity. (Later, the proposal for a defense minister was changed to a nine-member commission similar to the ECSC High Authority; a Court of Justice was also added.)

The plan was a radical one, but the extreme insecurity of Western Europe in 1950 made some measure of federalism appear all the more desirable. The popularity of federalism, then at its zenith, explains why the French National Assembly approved the Pleven Plan despite Communist and Gaullist opposition. Accordingly, negotiators from France, Italy, West Germany, and the Benelux states met to draw up a treaty for the new Defense Community.

For dedicated Federalists, the prospect of a European army presented a golden opportunity to erect the new supranational state envisioned in the immediate postwar era. Proponents of the functionalist approach to European unity could not resist immediately jumping on the bandwagon. Most encouraging was the fact that Article 38 of the proposed treaty called upon the Common Assembly to act temporarily as the parliament of the new European Defense Community and to oversee the drawing up of a plan to establish a directly elected European Parliament.[24] The European Union of Federalists, in the forefront of the pro-integration forces, seized the opportunity offered by this plan. This group had drawn up a proposal back in 1949 for a federation based on a European Constituent Assembly. Paul-Henri Spaak, frustrated over the impasse in the Council of Europe, had resigned as president of the Consultative Assembly in December 1951 to become a spokesman for the Union. In May 1952, Spaak requested before the Consultative Assembly that the ECSC Common Assembly be authorized to draw up a blueprint for a European Political Community in which membership would be open to other nations as well as the six ECSC states. Although the Consultative Assembly defeated the proposal by five votes (47 to 42), the French Cabinet under Schuman's influence gave its strong support to the establishment of a European Parliament.

On September 10, 1952, both Schuman and his Italian counterpart, Foreign Minister Alcide de Gasperi, suggested to the ECSC Council of Ministers that the Common Assembly should draw up a treaty for a European Political Community. On September 11, Adenauer placed this extraordinary request before the one-day-old Assembly.[25] The irony of the situation was that the EDC Treaty—signed the previous May 9—remained to be ratified. Federalists were in so great a hurry to design a federal political system that they undertook the task even before they had been authorized to do so. Such boundless optimism was excusable considering that enthusiasm over European union was reaching its peak in 1952. The modest progress made toward international cooperation since 1945 obscured the political realities of the time.

On September 15, 1952, the Common Assembly officially transformed itself into the Ad Hoc Assembly for the express purpose of constructing a European Political Community.[26] This new entity in turn appointed a special Constitutional Committee of twenty-six members to draft the treaty. On January 7-10, this committee submitted a general report for debate. The completed plan was presented to the Ad Hoc Assembly on March 6, 1953.[27] Although the proposed European Political Community was decidedly radical in some respects, it reflected an overall spirit of compromise on the part of the Federalists. It was quite evident, however, that the assembly of the EPC was meant to resemble a genuine parliament far more than its ECSC counterpart. The proposed assembly would have two chambers, a lower house—the "Peoples' Chamber"—of 268 members directly elected on a European-wide basis by a flexible proportional voting system, and an 87-member Senate selected by the national parliaments in the manner of the Common Assembly. The Senate, rather than the Peoples' Chamber, would choose by majority vote the Community's executive (that is, the president of the European Executive Council), thus insuring that the national governments had a measure of control over the Community's leadership. This president would select the rest of the Executive Council. To further safeguard the interests of member states, the Executive Council would be responsible to the Senate, which reserved the right to force the resignations of the president and Council and to select new officers in the event of disagreement over Community policy.

Significantly, the Peoples' Chamber had much less control over the executive. A vote of three-fifths of all members was necessary to pass a motion of censure requiring the selection of a new Council. (This was somewhat of an improvement over the two-thirds majority of the Common Assembly needed to oust the High Authority.) In the realm of legislation, the power of the two houses was restricted. The Executive Council could not implement laws until one year had elapsed after the ratification of the treaty. Within the following five years, all executive bills would require the unanimous approval of a Council of National Ministers. After this trial period, the Parliament could enact legislation initiated by the executive (*after the Council of Ministers approved the measures*) by a simple majority of the Peoples' Chamber and a two-thirds majority of the Senate. However, a member state still had the means to kill an enacted law by claiming it jeopardized national interests.

The EPC as conceived by the Ad Hoc Assembly reflected the influence of American constitutional experts and the aspirations of various pro-union European groups. It was anticipated that the new Community would regulate the finances and commerce of the member states as well as defense policy so as to achieve a West European Common Market. Under the terms of the draft treaty, the ECSC institutions, with the exception of the High Authority (which would operate under the control of the Executive Council) would be incorporated into the new "super-Community."[28]

Despite the restrictions placed on the Parliament of the proposed European government, the creation of the EPC had far-reaching implications—a fact that was not lost on the nations involved. In contrast, determined *Europeans* sensed that the time to establish a Western European federation finally had arrived, and they threw their support behind the European Defense Community and its companion Political Community. During the June 1953 Joint Meeting of the Consultative Assembly of the Council of Europe and the ECSC Assembly, High Authority President Monnet noted that the foremost goal of the two assemblies was not merely to create a limited supranational entity of a functional nature such as the Coal and Steel Community but to create a "new organization, to which the countries of Europe will surrender a part of their sovereignty. . . ." According to Monnet, this modified federal government would

> keep in mind what is best for Europe as a whole
> and will take decisions under the democratic
> control of a Political Community and a Euro-
> pean Parliament elected by universal suffrage,
> solely in the interests of the Community. Only
> such organizations are likely to show greater
> wisdom.[29]

The enthusiasm of the *Europeans* was in sharp contrast to the pessimism verging on antipathy shared by the opponents of the EDC-EPC. Although the Ad Hoc Assembly unanimously endorsed the Political Community (50 to 0), thirty-seven members abstained or were absent in the final vote. Of the five members who officially abstained, three were French Socialists, one of whom was party leader Guy Mollet, a staunch supporter of European union.[30] Fear of the exclusion of Britain from the new Community and possible German domination to the detriment of French interests formed the basis of this opposition. German Social Democrats in the Assembly also refused to vote since an endorsement of the EPC implied approval of the Defense Community.

The Assembly's Gaullists simply absented themselves from the voting.

The Gaullist concept of a confederal Europe had long been at odds with the Federalists' idea of a supranational government. Michel Debré, destined like Mollet to serve as French premier, was the chief spokesman in the Assembly for the confederal approach to union in the formative years of the ECSC. Early in the Ad Hoc Assembly's deliberations, Debré presented his own alternative plan—a "Preliminary Draft of a Pact for a Union of European States."[31] This scheme, which laid the foundation for the Gaullist "Europe des états" proposals of the early 1960s, provided for a Political Council comprised of "the heads of governments of Member States." This Political Council would coordinate defense, social, and economic policies. Decisions would be made by a majority vote and would be binding on member nations—unless a national parliament opposed a Council directive, in which case a Legal Council composed of delegates from each state would render an "unappealable decision" by majority vote. Supervision of the Political Council and the adoption of the Council's budget would be in the hands of a Parliamentary Assembly of the States made up of members of the national parliaments appointed by each body or elected by popular vote according to domestic electoral laws.[32]

The Union of European States was anathema to fervent Federalists since, unlike the proposed EPC, it retained power in the hands of the national governments. Debré defended his draft treaty, arguing that the nation was "the safeguard of its peoples' liberty," and was historically "the essential feature of Europe." French membership in the European Political Community, he claimed, was a dangerous, irrational undertaking:

> The path we have taken leads to nowhere. . . .
> Whether we like it or not, the fact is that
> Europe is not a single nation and does not con-
> stitute a single sovereignty. To set up a govern-
> ment based on a non-existent nation (a united
> Europe) and to expect this authority to rule
> over governments securely based upon their re-
> spective nations is to court disaster.

Furthermore, he noted that Federalists were refusing to accept the fact that the ECSC was by far still an imperfect organization:

> To cling obstinately to the principles underly-
> ing the Coal and Steel Community as if they

> were inviolable and to extend them into the
> realms of politics and defense is not the sure
> way to success. . . .[33]

Finally, Debré argued that the obvious limitations placed on the European Parliament of the proposed EPC reflected the reservations of the national governments.

Although he claimed that his Union of European States was a much simpler form of political system than the Federalists' plan, "much more vague" was actually a far better way to describe Debré's concept of a European government. The Political Council outlined in his preliminary draft treaty was little more than a series of monthly summit meetings which a national leader could avoid attending by sending a stand-in official (there was a provision in the plan allowing for such a substitution). No provision existed for enforcing a state's membership in the Council. The Parliamentary Assembly, as described, had only a tenuous hold over the Political Council through the dubious ability to reject the Council's budget. It possessed neither legislative powers nor authority to force the governments to heed its demands.

Debré's proposal was ignored by the Federalists, who viewed the ratification of the EDC Treaty and subsequent acceptance of the Political Community as a definite possibility. They were equally oblivious to the diminishing enthusiasm for the proposal among the political leadership of the six ECSC states. Although the foreign ministers of the Six dutifully discussed the EPC at a number of meetings throughout the fall of 1953, it was evident that the states were having second thoughts about the scope, functions, and even the need for a Political Community.[34] To complicate the issue, the fate of the EPC was irrevocably tied to the ratification of the Defense Community Treaty. This factor was indeed an ominous one, since from May 1952, when the EDC Treaty was signed by the six nations, to March 1953, when the Common Assembly approved the plan for the EPC, the former remained unratified. Although in the smaller states involved—Belgium, the Netherlands, and Luxembourg— ratification was a fairly easy process, the German Social Democrats posed a formidable obstacle for the Adenauer government.

By April 1954 only Italy and France had not ratified the Treaty. In Italy the situation was complex. The Communists and Nenni Socialists, rejecting supranationalism as capitalistic and a threat to state sovereignty, allied with a portion of the extreme right wing in opposition. The Italian government, wishing to gain as much as possible from the situation, sounded out the possibility of territorial concessions in return for ratification. However, prospects still remained good for Italian approval, since Prime Minister de Gasperi was an avowed *European.* The key to Italian ratification ultimately came to rest on French acceptance of the treaty, and the latter appeared elusive at best.[35]

In the two years since the spring of 1952, when the Defense Community was conceived, the world political situation had changed significantly. The Korean conflict was resolved, Stalin was dead, and a détente with the Soviet Union seemed possible. The British were unwilling to participate in the venture. Apprehension over a resurgent Germany and fear of increased American involvement in Western European economic and defense affairs replaced the danger of Soviet expansion as primary foreign policy considerations. Nationalists viewed the EDC, with its far-reaching political arrangement, as a threat to state sovereignty. General de Gaulle roundly condemned the treaty. It was obvious from the beginning that French ratification would be difficult to secure. Governmental instability in France compounded the problem. The cabinet headed by Antoine Pinay, in which Schuman remained as foreign minister, was supplanted by that of René Mayer with Georges Bidault as foreign minister. Bidault, although pledged to the concept behind the EDC, made it clear that concessions would have to be made to appease the opposition within the French Assembly.[36] Accordingly, the Mayer government proposed a series of revisions to the treaty which enhanced the French position at the expense of the other future EDC members, allowing France the discretion of withdrawing from the Community at will. Later, the settlement of the Saar issue was made a prerequisite for French ratification.[37]

In the meantime, both Britain and the United States were pressuring France for approval of the treaty. Paul-Henri Spaak met with Secretary of State John Foster Dulles in Paris on April 24, 1954, to discuss the French government's reluctance to submit the EDC Treaty for ratification. Dulles indicated that the United States would terminate its "policy of military aid to Europe" in the event of a French rejection of the Defense Community.[38] At the end of June, Eisenhower, Dulles, British Prime Minister Churchill, and Foreign Secretary Eden met in Washington and issued a joint statement which pointed out that four of the six states had ratified the EDC and that "further delay" in the ratification process would "damage the solidarity of the Atlantic alliance."[39] (While refusing to commit Britain to a role in the proposed Defense Community, Churchill supported the EDC because, as Eden put it, "This is what the Americans are doing and it is the course Eisenhower wants us to take."[40]

The unwillingness of the French government to accept an unamended EDC Treaty met with an equal amount of intransigence on the part of West Germany and the Benelux nations. By June 18, 1954, when Radical leader Pierre Mendès-France took over the leadership of a Gaullist-Radical coalition government, yet another factor jeopardized the ratification of the EDC. The new government was embroiled in a controversy over French withdrawal from Indochina, and the French public, roused by the debacle at Dien Bien Phu the previous month, did not look favorably upon a proposal which would subordinate France to a supranational institution partially controlled by a former enemy. Mendès-France, in a meeting with the leaders of the other five ECSC nations at Brussels in mid-August, offered additional revisions to the treaty but these, too, proved unacceptable. By this time, however, Mendès-France was determined to wash his hands of the matter. Although the time was inopportune and his cabinet was divided on the EDC, he submitted the treaty to the French Assembly on August 30, 1954, without either an endorsement or rejection. An unholy alliance of Communists, Gaullists, and disenchanted Socialists and Radicals voted by a margin of 319 to 264 to postpone the debate on the Defense Community indefinitely.[41] The Euoropean Political Community, its fate tied to the EDC, became a dead issue.

The abortive treaty was less than two months in the grave when a convenient alternative British-sponsored plan was adopted by a nine-nation conference (the United States, Britain, Canada, and the six ECSC states) which met in London in late September. According to Eden's proposal, the Brussels Treaty of 1948 which coordinated British, French, and Benelux defense would be expanded to include West Germany and Italy. This new military alliance, called the Western European Union (WEU), was a sorry substitute for the EDC-EPC. The WEU provided for a pseudo-Parliament called the WEU Assembly and a council comprised of foreign ministers of member states. The former was allowed to do little more than determine its own agenda and "proceed on any matter arising out of the Brussels Treaty" (that is, the Assembly would debate the Council's annual report). The Assembly was composed of the same delegates who sat in the powerless Consultative Assembly of the Council of Europe, and its role was strictly advisory in nature. There was little of a federal nature about an agreement which constituted merely an old-fashioned international defense pact with supranational trappings.[42]

The EDC was dead but the Ad Hoc Assembly had anticipated its demise and incorporated an article into the draft treaty allowing the European Political Community to come into existence without the EDC. (The defense provisions of the EPC Treaty would be scrapped.) However, the popularity of federalism had peaked in 1952 as the Cold War reached its nadir. The functionalist approach—the approach of the Schuman Plan and the European Coal and Steel Community—remained the only path open for those who still clung to their belief that Europe's future lay in the creation of a directly elected European Parliament.

chapter 3

THE EUROPEAN PARLIAMENT TAKES SHAPE

Once the impending death of the
European Defense Community appeared inescapable, Federalists wasted
little time trying another direct route to political unification. Certain for-
ward-looking members of the Common Assembly had been trying since
its creation to expand the Assembly's powers as a prelude to developing
it into a European Parliament. Avid *Europeans* had not been particularly pleased with the Paris Treaty as far as the proposed ECSC Assembly
was concerned. During the winter of 1951-52 when the six national parliaments were debating the treaty prior to ratification, Federalists had
found little to praise in an assembly that was a mere advisory body.[1] But
once the Common Assembly was established, most of its seventy-eight
members immediately began to make plans to transform it into a real
federal legislature. The committee charged with devising the Assembly's
rules of procedure formulated them in such a manner as to give the Assembly the appearance of a legislative body. In addition, seven standing committees were created to oversee the development of the ECSC in such
areas as political affairs and foreign relations, a common market, invest-
ments, finance and production, labor policy, transportation, accounting
and finance, and legal questions.[2]

A year later in the fall of 1953, the Common Assembly began to call
for a political *relance* focusing on further development of the Coal and
Steel Community institutions. Reflecting on the flaws inherent in the

proposed EDC, Pierre-Henri Teitgen, leader of the French *Mouvement Républicain Populaire,* observed that supporters of integration had a tendency to propose the creation of new "communities," each with its own "little parliament." According to Teitgen, this approach to European unification was folly, especially since the nucleus of a supranational government already existed in the guise of the Coal and Steel Community with its Common Assembly. The obvious solution, he argued, was to construct "*absolutely* a single authority."[3]

In May 1954—four months before the French refusal to ratify the EDC Treaty—Fernand Dehousse called for expansion of the Common Assembly's powers to give it control over the High Authority and advocated the institution of direct election of the Assembly's membership.[4] After the failure of the projected Defense Community, frustrated Federalists embraced the ECSC as the only means left to achieve the political integration of Western Europe. High Authority Vice-President Albert Coppé noted in an address to the National Press Club in Washington, D.C., on April 20, 1955, that political integration was not dead despite the rejection of the EDC. "Economic integration," he claimed, would be the "steppingstone to the political goal."[5] Within the Assembly there were many members who believed that this rudimentary pseudo-parliament was meant to evolve into a genuine federal legislature. On December 2, 1954, the Assembly adopted a resolution based on the Teitgen Report. The report called for the Assembly to examine how it could extend "political control" over the High Authority if the Assembly's present privileges, as enumerated in the Paris Treaty, proved ineffectual. The following May a special working committee was established to investigate ways to expand the Assembly's powers.[6]

Federalists within the Common Assembly were immeasurably aided by Jean Monnet.[7] Monnet was in close contact with like-minded national leaders, chiefly in the Benelux states, who also had further but more limited plans for the Coal and Steel Community. In February 1953, Dutch Foreign Minister Johan Willem Beyen had suggested to the ECSC Council of Ministers that the six states should broaden economic integration beyond coal and steel.[8] With the defeat of the EDC Treaty, Beyen reiterated this request, this time before the Netherlands Council of the European Movement in April 1955. The Dutch minister joined with his Belgian counterpart, Paul-Henri Spaak, and with Joseph Bech, premier and foreign minister of Luxembourg, to call for a meeting of the Council of Ministers in order to examine the proposal.[9]

The Benelux Memorandum, as Beyen's plan came to be called, reflected the growing sentiment among the more moderate Europeans for a gradual "sector by sector" approach, first to economic and later to political integration. As expressed in the initial paragraph of the memorandum,

> [t] he Governments of Belgium, Luxembourg,
> and the Netherlands believe that the time has
> come to make a fresh advance toward European
> integration. They are of the opinion that this
> must be achieved first of all in the economic
> field.[10]

The plan called for a common market—a "European Economic Community"—with integration of transportation, electricity, and nuclear energy and control in the hands of a "common authority." The memorandum made no mention whatsoever of a federal parliament. This was not a groundless omission. The impetus toward the immediate creation of a European Parliament had been dealt a temporary setback by the unhappy end of the Defense Community and the European Political Community.

Federalists within the Common Assembly, however, had a different vision of this new European Economic Community. During its May 1955 session, the Assembly called for the strengthening of the Coal and Steel Community's institutions. All three political groups—Liberals, Socialists, and Christian Democrats—adopted a resolution urging the six foreign ministers to request proposals from the ECSC on how to expand its "competence and its powers." More importantly, the resolution proposed that the Community institutions aid the national governments in drafting a treaty for a broader supranational system.[11]

However, governments chose to downplay political integration for practical or policy reasons. Economic integration, in contrast, had been far from discredited by early June 1955 when the foreign ministers of the six ECSC nations met in Messina, Sicily, to discuss the Benelux proposal and related German and Italian recommendations calling for increased economic and social cooperation. The Coal and Steel Community had met with considerable success after a disappointing first two years. In 1955, it was embarking on a period of impressive economic growth. German and French steel and iron output had been steadily increasing. The institutional machinery of the Community had not transformed the organization into a technocracy as opponents of the Schuman Plan had

predicted.[12] Furthermore, the political climate in mid-1955 was more
favorable to the development of European institutions. The anti-EDC
government of Mendès-France had fallen in February 1955. The government headed by Edgar Faure which replaced it included *Europeans*,
among whom the most dynamic was Robert Schuman as minister of
justice.[13]

At Messina on June 1, Beyen, Bech, and Spaak found their colleagues—
French Foreign Minister Pinay, Italy's Gaetano Martino, and German
Permanent Undersecretary Walter Hallstein—amenable to further economic
integration. The resolution which they adopted to this effect bore a remarkable resemblance to the Benelux Memorandum. In fact, with a few
additions, much of the text was the same, indicating general satisfaction
with the sector-by-sector approach to European union.[14] The ministers
also gave their approval to a Benelux proposal to set up a special Committee of Governmental Representatives under the chairmanship of a
"political personality." This body, called the Spaak Committee after its
illustrious head, met over a nine-month period from July 1955 to March
1956 at the Chateau de Val Duchesse near Brussels. Although a British
"observer" (a Board of Trade official) was present both at Messina and
during meetings of the Spaak Committee for the first few months, by
November the Eden government had rejected even the most limited of
associations with the deliberations due to the supranational character
of the evolving treaties.[15]

The Spaak Report was adopted by the six foreign ministers at Venice
in late May 1956. The proposed European Economic Community (EEC)
and the European Atomic Energy Committee (Euratom) had institutional
arrangements not unexpectedly patterned on those of the Coal and Steel
Community. Like the latter, the two new communities were to have
executive bodies (called "commissions" rather than high authorities),
and each was to have a council of ministers. A single assembly and court
of justice would serve all three communities (EEC, Euratom, and ECSC).

The decision to create a single assembly was a controversial one. Although the logical alternative was to utilize the Common Assembly as
the new assembly of the Common Market and Euratom, apprehension
still existed among supporters of the communities that the federal aspirations of the Common Assembly might jeopardize ratification of the
treaties. On the other hand, the creation of yet another European assembly—a fourth (the other three were the Consultative Assembly, the

Western European Union body, and the Common Assembly)—was opposed by many Europeans who recognized that such a move would only result in additional confusion. Moreover, members of the existing assemblies feared that the work load involved in participating in several such bodies, when added to their duties as representatives to their national parliaments, would prove to be intolerable.[16] Furthermore, a fourth assembly could well work at cross-purposes with the other three. On January 19, 1957, Fernand Dehousse, president of the Consultative Assembly of the Council of Europe, led a group of fellow members in registering disapproval of a fourth assembly before the Intergovernmental Committee (which had been transformed into a treaty-making body). Their view was seconded by the parliaments of Belgium, West Germany, and Luxembourg.[17] On February 2, officials of the three assemblies joined to request that either the Common Assembly become the watchdog of the proposed new communities, or that a new assembly be established which would not only absorb the ECSC body but which would also include some members of the Consultative Assembly.[18]

Chiefly as a result of this pressure, the draft treaties were revised to provide for the creation of an assembly along these lines. This new entity would subsume the functions and powers of the Common Assembly, serving the ECSC, EEC, and Euratom.[19]

During the intervening months between the Messina Conference and the signing of the treaties creating the Common Market and Euratom on March 27 in Rome, certain political developments proved favorable to the future success of the negotiations. Socialist Guy Mollet, who had become French Premier in February 1956, had established closer ties with the Adenauer government. A notable development was the return of the Saar to West Germany at the beginning of 1957. The Soviet invasion of Hungary in October 1956 revived Cold War fears in Europe, while United States and United Nations opposition to the joint French-British invasion of Egypt that same month demonstrated all too clearly the impotence of the once-great European powers. By the time the negotiations which resulted in the Rome Treaties came to a close on February 20, 1957, the strictly economic character of the proposed Common Market had evolved into a customs union with decidedly political institutions.[20] The official name of the Common Market—the European Economic Community—reflected the desire of the experiment's supporters to camouflage the political ramifications. As far as economic union was concerned, the treaty set up a common market and a common external tariff which would be achieved over a twelve- to fifteen-year period in three stages. The treaty also provided for joint administration of other sectors such as agriculture, transportation, labor, and the like.

It was the constitutional arrangement of the European Economic Community that reflected the old hopes of the supporters of political union. The EEC Treaty contained 248 articles. The first sentence of the preamble underscored the political thrust of the new Community. The six nations were "determined to establish the foundations of an even closer union among European peoples."[21] In attempting to lay the groundwork for a future European government, the architects of the treaty went as far as they could go in designing institutions that had the potential to develop into a federal system. However, this blueprint for a supranational state was highly imperfect, to say the least. A critical analysis of the treaty's institutional provisions quickly revealed the structural weaknesses and the potential problem areas. Modeled on the ECSC Treaty, the Rome document's provisions reflected the faith of the *Europeans* that such an arrangement, if its jurisdiction and powers were later expanded, could develop into a federal government. Unfortunately, the EEC Commission and Assembly (later called the European Parliament) ended up with somewhat less authority than their ECSC counterparts.[22]

The beneficiary of this subtle shift in emphasis was the Council of Ministers. Comprised of one minister from each of the six states, the Council wielded the real power under the terms of the Rome Treaty, rejecting or approving proposals put forth by the Commission by a complex system of either a unanimous, simple majority or "qualified" majority vote.[23] It was the Council which was the "final decision-making body."[24] The Commission, like the High Authority of the Coal and Steel Community, served as the executive, overseeing the implementation of policies and the administration of the Community—according to the wishes of the Council of Ministers (that is, the governments of the six states). Although the states selected the Commission members, they were expected to function independently of national influences during their four-year renewable terms. Under the provisions of the treaty (Article 189) the Commission, as well as the Council, was authorized to issue (1) "regulations" applying directly to member nations, (2) "directives" binding on a state but allowing it the flexibility of selecting its own means of enforcement, (3) "decisions" not only binding on nations, corporations, and the like, but enforceable in national courts, and (4) "recommendations and opinions" which simply outlined EEC views.[25] The legislative process involved continual interaction among the Commission and the Council. The latter investigated Commission proposals and might refer (*must* refer, in the case of West Germany) them to the national parliaments. Only then would the Commission send a copy of the proposed measure to the third and least important organ of the European Economic Community, the Assembly.[26]

And what of the Assembly, that focal point of the *Europeans'* aspirations? On paper, the Assembly appeared to be a step in the direction of a federal Europe—at least a step beyond the ECSC Common Assembly. The future European Parliament was outlined in Articles 137-144 of the treaty. According to Article 137, the Assembly was to be composed of representatives of the member states and it would "exercise the powers of deliberation and of control which are conferred upon it by this Treaty."[27] Assembly members initially were to be selected by the national parliaments as each saw fit. As for the number of delegates allotted each nation, Germany, France, and Italy would have 36 each, Belgium and the Netherlands 14 each, and Luxembourg 6 representatives (Article 138). Just as in the Paris Treaty, provision was made in the EEC document for the eventual direct election of Assembly members:

> The Assembly shall draw up proposals for election by direct universal suffrage in accordance with a uniform procedure in all member states. *The Council acting by means of a unanimous vote shall determine the provisions which it will recommend to Member States for adoption in accordance with their respective constitutional rules.* [Article 138, paragraph 3, emphasis mine.][28]

The great significance of the second sentence of this provision lay in the fact that the time and method chosen to make direct elections a reality was left solely to the governments and national parliaments of the six Common Market states. Furthermore, their approval of any scheme for such elections would have to be unanimous. Looking back, it obviously would have been too extreme a move for the treaty authors to place the power to determine when and in what manner a European election should be held in the hands of the new Assembly. In order to secure what appeared to be a difficult ratification of the treaty, its creators attempted to downplay its political implications as much as possible. But perhaps a less cut-and-dried sentence could have been substituted for the provision which expressly gave the states the power to block the development of a potentially serious threat to their national sovereignty.

As was to be revealed in the early 1960s, the whole key to the evolution of a political union founded on a European Parliament lay in the institution of universal suffrage for the election of its membership. So long as the EEC Assembly remained indirectly elected, comprised of representatives chosen by diverse methods from among national parliamentarians far more concerned with domestic issues, the Assembly could not claim to represent a European electorate. It followed that without this popular mandate, the Assembly could hardly demand an expansion of its role in the decision-making process. Furthermore, since this process, as has been demonstrated, was dominated by the Council of Ministers, it was equally unlikely that the Council would willingly commit political suicide by authorizing direct elections. Article 138,3 was to cause unimaginable frustration and dissension among *Europeans* in the first decade of the Community's existence. While opponents of political integration, along with many practical Federalists, felt that an extension of the future Parliament's authority was an essential prelude to holding direct elections, just as many advocates of integration called for universal suffrage as a prelude to further development. This "chicken or egg" argument, as *Europeans* termed their dilemma, was to have no solution for nearly two decades.

The exasperation of the *Europeans* was understandable, for the new Assembly's "powers of deliberation and control," as outlined in the treaty, left it by far the weakest of the four Community institutions.[29] Its powers were similar to those of the Common Assembly. The EEC body was authorized to hold an annual session, beginning the third Tuesday in October, to discuss the general report drawn up by the Commission. The Assembly could hold special sessions at the request of its membership or at the request of the Council or Commission (Article 139). As with its predecessor, it could submit oral and written questions to the Commission, which was under obligation to reply. No such questioning authority, however, applied to the Council. According to Article 140, the Council specified in its own rules of procedure "the conditions" governing any Council appearance before the Assembly. The Commission, too, had the option of attending Assembly meetings. The EEC body, then, like the Common Assembly, was strictly advisory in nature. Other than the right to elect its president and officers and draw up its own rules of procedure, the Assembly merely made its feelings known on matters concerning the Common Market, Euratom, and the ECSC through the adoption of resolutions made, in most instances, by an absolute majority vote.

The structure and functions of the future European Parliament fell far short of the expectations of most of the members of the Common Assembly. While the Spaak Committee labored to produce the draft treaties, the Assembly continued to call for greater powers. During the extraordinary session of November 22-25, 1955, Assembly President Giuseppe Pella had claimed that since the Assembly was "the only European Parliament with deliberative powers" it should evolve into "a political body in the true sense of the word." French Christian Democrat Alain Poher presented the ambitious report of the special Working Party on European integration. The report proposed that the Assembly strengthen its control over the ECSC by "establishing direct contact" with the Council of Ministers and that it collaborate with the national parliaments.[30] The report singled out one of the Assembly's chief weaknesses: lack of control over the Council. To somewhat rectify this imbalance, it proposed that the Council present an annual report of its activities to the Assembly, that the ministers participate in Assembly sessions, and that the two bodies meet jointly at least once a year.[31] Furthermore, the Council should respond to written questions and conduct its business with less secrecy. Finally, the report recommended that the national governments should consult the Assembly before selecting the president and vice presidents of the High Authority. In regard to the national parliaments, the report specified that each should hold an annual debate on ECSC affairs in order to enable Common Assembly members to promote integration in a national setting.[32]

The majority of the members of the Common Assembly were encouraged by the Spaak Committee's proposals that the new, enlarged assembly should have genuine budgetary powers, the authority to vote on certain commercial and agricultural measures, and the power to demand policy explanations of the communities' executives and Councils of Ministers. The Common Assembly kept in close contact with the Spaak Committee through the special Working Party on integration. Yet, the Spaak Committee's recommendations did not go far enough for many members of the Assembly. They noted that the new assembly would still have no control over the ministers. In regard to the communities' purse strings, the assembly would only approve or reject budgets as a whole. Federalists wanted the power to examine financial measures on an item-by-item basis and propose amendments. They also wished to have the authority to confirm the nomination of the members of the executives.[33]

As it turned out, the Common Assembly's criticism of the Spaak proposals was irrelevant, for the majority of the recommendations went unheeded by the six states. The Federalists were forced to content themselves with a larger version of the Common Assembly. It should be noted that a small minority of the Assembly was displeased with the entire rationale behind the Rome Treaties. During the May 11, 1957, session, Michel Debré and a fellow Gaullist charged that the Spaak Committee's proposals were but another attempt to create a European Political Community. There was heated exchange between Spaak, who was on hand to explain the proposals, and Debré, with the latter attacking the committee's recommendations as "a fairy-tale promising the golden age."[34]

Having little to boast about, advocates of a strengthened Assembly made much of its potential, particularly the provision authorizing direct elections and Article 144, which gave the Assembly the much coveted right to oust a recalcitrant Commission through a motion of censure. Members of the ECSC Common Assembly, as previously noted, had been quite self-congratulatory about this dubious power, feeling that the accountability of the Commission to the Assembly was evidence of the latter's clout. This erroneous assumption was encouraged by a Socialist attempt to secure the necessary support for a motion of censure in the waning months of the Common Assembly's existence. The Socialists, from the beginning the most active among the European political groups, had castigated the High Authority for its lack of enthusiasm for further economic and political integration. Since the High Authority had the support of the Christian Democrats and Liberals, its fate was never really in question. However, observers of the Common Assembly at the time (and especially overeager Federalists) interpreted the Socialists' vocal opposition to signify that the Assembly had come to the brink of a motion of censure.[35]

Even if the Socialists had managed to round up the necessary two-thirds majority, they would have gained a Pyrrhic victory. The motion of censure, like the doctrine of massive nuclear retaliation, was in effect a useless weapon because it would in all likelihood destroy both combatants.

An Assembly which exercised its right to force an unresponsive executive's resignation ran the risk of undermining the vitality, even the foundations, of a future supranational European government before it had become well established. In addition, a motion of censure could resurrect and intensify the fears of the six states which so recently had come to accept gradual progress toward political union. Federalists had no desire to see the national governments clamp down on an upstart Assembly in its all-important formative years. Keeping this in mind, it is understandable that during the lifespan of the Common Assembly and its successor, the European Parliament, both bodies never resorted to the adoption of a motion of censure.

In the matter of control of the three communities' purse strings, the new Assembly could investigate the budget (which temporarily was to be financed through state contributions), but it could not control the allocation of funds. The EEC Commission submitted a draft budget to the Council, which joined with the former to thrash out the terms of the final measure. Only then was the Assembly allowed to suggest revisions which the Council was not bound to uphold. In the realm of finance, as with the general legislative process, the Assembly was victimized by the murky language of the treaty.[36] It could at most make recommendations. Despite the Assembly's claims that it influenced the formulation and approval of Community policy, it had no power of decision making. After receiving proposed measures from the Commission, the Assembly referred them to the appropriate committees. After hearing committee reports and holding debates on the proposals, it merely adopted recommendations for consideration by the Council.[37]

Irregardless of the inherent weaknesses in the EEC Treaty's institutional arrangement, the creation of the Common Market and also Euratom was nonetheless the highest point thus far in the evolution of European political and economic union. The enthusiasm surrounding this latest supranational experiment obscured the future problems. For many Federalists, the new Assembly was destined to be the catalyst which would speed up the course of federalization. To them, it now was simply a matter of designing an acceptable plan for direct elections and then, with this popular mandate, pushing for revision of the Rome Treaty to give the Assembly control over the budget and the general legislative process.[38]

The treaties establishing the EEC and Euratom were signed on March 27, 1957, and went into effect on January 1, 1958. Although ratification was by no means an easy matter, by mid-December, the parliaments of the six states had given their approval.[39] On January 6-7, the foreign ministers of the participating nations met in Paris and officially appointed the members of the new commissions, selecting Walter Hallstein to head the nine-man EEC body. The Assembly met for the first time on March 19, 1958, in the Council of Europe chamber in Strasbourg. Like the Common Assembly, the future European Parliament could not claim a particular site as its home. During a later session, the question of a suitable meeting site came under discussion. Possible cities were rated according to preference, with Strasbourg coming out on top followed by Brussels, Nice, Milan, and Luxembourg, in that order. However, due to the delicate nature of such a decision, the Assembly refrained from officially designating Strasbourg (a rather out-of-the-way place for commuting members) as its permanent location.[40] Although it continued to use Strasbourg as a regular meeting place, the Assembly could and did meet elsewhere.

Despite the lack of a permanent home, the Assembly looked and operated like a full-fledged parliament when it opened for its first session. With a membership nearly twice the size of that of the Common Assembly (142 as opposed to 78 members for the latter), its ranks swelled by the visiting commissioners of the EEC and Euratom, the ECSC High Authority, and members of the various Councils of Ministers, the Assembly appeared to be the answer to the Federalists' long-cherished hopes. Europe seemed on the verge of political and economic union. But then, a decade before at the opening session of the Council of Europe assembly, a similar optimism and self-confidence had prevailed.[41]

Accordingly, the Assembly christened itself the *Assemblée parlementaire européene*–European Parliamentary Assembly–(in Italian, *Assemblea parlamentare europea*). In German and Dutch, however, the assembly was called the *Europäisches Parlement* and *Europees Parlement*, respectively. It was this latter designation (European Parliament) which came to best reflect the ambitions of its membership, and four years later on March 30, 1962, the French and Italian governments dropped any reference to "assembly," adopting the names *Parlement Européen* and *Parlamento Europeo*.[42] Successive British governments stubbornly clung to the original title. The basis for this interesting distinction rested not so much on the chauvinistic attitude that there existed only *one* parliament, which, of course, was British; it was rather the supranational nature of the new name that lay at the root of the British reluctance to use it.

In addition to the name change, members of the European Parliament seated themselves by political group affiliation as they had done in the old Common Assembly.[43] The Christian Democrats boasted the largest membership (sixty-seven) and numbered among their ranks such illustrious *Europeans* and national leaders as Pierre Wigny, party president; Alain Poher; Pierre-Henri Teitgen; and Robert Schuman. The Socialists, the second largest party and the most active, made up for their decidedly smaller size (thirty-eight members) with their energy. Prominent Socialists included Pierre-Olivier Lapie, party president; Fernand Dehousse, a party vice-president; Helmut Schmidt; and Hent Vredeling. The Liberals were an interesting assortment of personages of various political interests. René Pleven presided as president over a thirty-five-member group which included Gaetano Martino, Walter Scheel, and Antoine Pinay. Only two members refused to affiliate with a European political group—Gaullists Michel Debré and Yves Estève—an action that foreshadowed the later creation of a fourth group, the Gaullist European Democratic Union.[44]

Such was the self-confidence of the European Parliament at its first meeting that it rejected the recommendation of the Council of Ministers that an Italian be elected as the body's first president in order to balance the nationalities, choosing instead by acclamation that longtime champion of federalism, Robert Schuman.[45] The parallels between the European Parliament and the Common Assembly in terms of organization and rules of procedure were, not unexpectedly, strikingly similar. Many members of the latter who were now members of the former body used the Common Assembly as their model, making the transition remarkably smooth. At its initial session, the Parliament set up thirteen committees to oversee various areas such as agriculture, transportation, economic and commercial cooperation, health and safety, the budget, and scientific and technical research. Significantly, the committee heading the list of thirteen was the twenty-four-man Committee on Political Affairs and Institutional Questions.[46] Members of this all-important committee included several of those who had been the most outspoken advocates and, in one particular case, opponent, of expansion of the Common Assembly's powers: Dehousse, Teitgen, Pinay, Wigny, Gaetano Martino, and Debré. A subcommittee to study the issue of direct elections was set up under the chairmanship of Fernand Dehousse.[47]

The Rome Treaty had authorized the Parliament to draw up its own rules of procedure. As was the case with the outward trappings of the

Parliament, the rules of procedure reflected the desires of its members to give it as much of an appearance of a genuine legislature as possible.[48] Article 1 of the regulations specified that the Parliament would hold an annual session in October and would meet in extraordinary session at the request of its president, of one of the Councils or Commissions, of the High Authority, or of a majority of the membership. Articles 3-10 set forth procedure governing the verification of members' credentials, the length of term and method of member replacement, and the composition and election of the Parliament's "Bureau" (its officers), and outlined the duties and authority of the president. Articles 11-33 dealt with parliamentary procedure, the order of business, publication of documents, official languages (German, French, Italian, and Dutch), committee reports, debate over the budget, the submission of questions to the Commissions, Councils, and High Authority, amendments, constitution of a quorum, and method of voting. Rules regulating motion of censure were outlined in Article 22. Such a motion and its justification would have to be submitted in writing, distributed in the four official languages and communicated to the executive in question. The Parliament's president would announce that a motion of censure had been tabled immediately upon its receipt if the Parliament was in session or, if it was not, at the beginning of the next session. The debate on the motion could open no earlier than twenty-four hours after this time. At least three days would have to elapse after the president's announcement before the holding of an open vote. If the two-thirds majority necessary for adoption of the motion was not secured, the motion was dropped.[49]

The remaining fifteen articles dealt with miscellaneous aspects. Article 34 placed the minimum number necessary to constitute a political group at seventeen. Article 43 provided for the designation of a secretary-general by the bureau along with supporting staff to run the administrative affairs of the Parliament. Provision was made to continue the interaction between the Council of Europe and the Parliament that was initiated in the early days of the Common Assembly. Finally, Article 48 specified that a majority of the Parliament was necessary to modify the rules of procedure.[50]

On paper, then, the European Parliament looked like a genuine legislature—although it possessed no lawmaking ability whatsoever. For Federalists in the first months of 1958, the obvious way to end this embarrassing dichotomy was to devise a system for direct elections as quickly as possible. The composition of the political committee of the Parliament by and large reflected this simplistic assumption. Dehousse and Teitgen were old champions of European elections. (Debré, as revealed by his earlier confederal plan for a union of nations, represented the anti-supranational forces who were destined to triumph over the Federalists in the 1960s.) The refusal of the British to participate in the communities did little to diminish the aspirations of the Parliament's supporters. They had become reconciled to the loss. During the treaty negotiations, despite continual pressure from the United States and pleas from *Europeans,* the British government had remained aloof from the Common Market and Euratom just as it had refused to join the ECSC. Although Prime Minister Harold Macmillan earlier had been a strong advocate of European unification, he preferred the idea of a Free Trade Area whose members could retain tariffs on imports from nations outside the arrangement. At most he viewed a desirable political union as confederal in nature—something along the lines of a strengthened Council of Europe and Western European Union.[51] Originally, the British had hoped that the Common Market states would join the Free Trade Area. However, Federalists became convinced that the British scheme would jeopardize the EEC and vetoed any cooperation.[52] By late 1958, it was becoming evident that European integration could proceed without British participation.

The Macmillan government had no choice but to establish a smaller European Free Trade Association in November 1959. The seven-nation EFTA (Britain, Sweden, Norway, Denmark, Switzerland, Austria, and Portugal) was not a true union in the sense that there existed no free flow of labor and capital or coordination of industry, transportation, and agriculture as there would be in a common market. In establishing EFTA, Britain attempted to get the best of both worlds while avoiding having to choose between her Commonwealth and the European Economic Community.

As it turned out, the major obstacle to the Federalists' hope of achieving direct elections was not Britain but France, that is, Charles de Gaulle. On June 1, 1958, de Gaulle emerged from retirement to form a new government after riots in Algeria and mutiny within the French armed forces paralyzed the two-week-old government of Pierre Pflimlin, former mayor of Strasbourg. De Gaulle's assumption of power in France quickly dampened the enthusiasm of the *Europeans.* The General had opposed the ECSC, the Common Market, and Euratom. That Debré was his prime minister boded ill for any further development of supranational institutions. Debré's opposition to the federal Europe envisioned by Schuman, Monnet, and Spaak was well documented. Fortunately for the Federalists, although the actual machinery of the Common Market was not scheduled to be put into motion until January 1959, the institutional foundations of the communities already had been laid in the early months of 1958. De Gaulle, in effect, was presented with a fait accompli. Supporters of integration could also take heart—at least for the moment—that in his memoirs the General claimed he had advocated during World War II the creation of "a strategic and economic federation" of Western Europe.[53] But de Gaulle's goal of a nationalistic France returned to a preeminent position in Europe and free from dependence on the United States differed radically from the *Europeans'* dream of federation. The French president's move to develop a warm relationship with West German Chancellor Adenauer foreshadowed his plan for a "Europe of States," a form of cooperative association of government leaders.

Still optimistic and unaware of the implications of the advent of the Fifth French Republic, the more active members of the European Parliament continued to make preparations for the transformation of the Parliament into a directly elected body with greatly expanded powers. Little did they know that their first plan for direct elections in the early 1960s would meet the same fate at the hands of the redoubtable General as Britain's first attempt to enter the European Economic Community.

chapter 4

DIRECT ELECTIONS:
FIRST TRY

At the end of the European Parliament's first year, its prospects for rapid development into a genuine federal legislature appeared excellent. True, its members were aware of the Parliament's shortcomings, but they viewed these limitations as temporary obstacles. Early analysts of the European Economic Community, however, were less charitable in their assessments. As Eric Stein noted in his 1959 study of the newly created Parliament:

> There is little outward splendor about the Strasbourg Assembly. It sits in a building borrowed from the Council of Europe; it is served by ushers borrowed from the parliaments of the six member states still wearing their national uniforms; it even had to christen itself, having been born with the bland name of "Assembly." Its administrative services, located in Luxembourg, migrate to Strasbourg at session time. Its standing committees are peripatetic—sitting in Strasbourg, Luxembourg, or Brussels. Its legal powers are limited.[1]

Nevertheless, as soon as procedural matters had been dispensed with, the Parliament immediately turned its attention to Article 138,3 of the EEC Treaty. On October 22, 1958, the Political Committee appointed

a nine-member subcommittee under the chairmanship of Fernand
Dehousse.[2] This "Working Party" was entrusted with the difficult task
of devising a plan for direct elections that would be acceptable to the
national governments while appeasing the most impetuous Federalists.[3]
The scope of the project soon necessitated the expansion of the Working
Party to thirteen members. Care was taken that the group reflected both
national and political group strength within the Parliament as a whole.
Of the thirteen, six were Christian Democrats, four were Liberals, and
three were Socialists (including Dehousse). As for nationality, the Work-
ing Party was comprised of three Germans, three Italians, and three
Frenchmen with two members from the Netherlands and one each from
Belgium and Luxembourg.[4]

In all, the Working Party met for a total of thirty days spread out over
a fifteen-month period. Although these conferences took place chiefly
in Strasbourg and Brussels, meetings were also held in each of the national
capitals in order to facilitate discussions with government leaders. The
list of influential political figures, scholars, and heads of various associations consulted by the Working Party was a veritable "Who's Who" of
Western Europe. National leaders interviewed included West German
Chancellor Adenauer, French Foreign Minister Maurice Couve de
Murville, Italian Foreign Minister Giuseppe Pella, and Jacques Chaban-
Delmas, president of the French National Assembly. In addition, the
subcommittee worked closely with the EEC and Euratom Commissions
and the ECSC High Authority, and even sought out the views of the
EEC's non-European territories—the Ivory Coast Republic, the Malagasy
Republic, and the Federation of Mali—on the question of their representa-
tion in a directly elected Parliament.[5]

Meeting in Paris on December 16-18, 1959, the Working Party hammered out a compromise draft convention. The final text was adopted at
Strasbourg on January 12, 1960. Along with five explanatory reports
provided by Dehousse, French Socialist Maurice Faure, Dutch Christian
Democrat W. J. Schuijt, German Socialist Ludwig Metzger, and Italian
Christian Democrat Enrico Carboni, the draft convention was presented
in February to the full Political Committee for scrutiny prior to submission to the Parliament. Although the committee unanimously approved
the accompanying reports after a few slight revisions, the draft convention
itself, with a few small changes, did not win wholehearted support. The
final vote was 20 to 2 with three abstentions—Carboni and fellow Italian

Christian Democrat A. Piccioni and German Christian Democrat Maria Probst. The two dissenting votes of Metzger and his German Socialist colleague, party president Willi Birkelbach, presaged the upcoming debate in the full Parliament.[6] The opposition to the convention was by no means a rejection of the principle of direct elections. On the contrary, certain of the dissidents such as Probst felt that the convention allowed the national governments too much control over the method of election and that it should specify a uniform electoral procedure. In the case of Metzger and Birkenbach, their opposition was based on the premise that the Parliament's powers must be expanded through revision of the EEC Treaty before any European elections could be held. This belief was one that was shared by many members of the Parliament, who, as former delegates to the ECSC Common Assembly, had experienced the frustration of dealing with the Council of Ministers. Although the Rome Treaty had transformed the common Assembly into a larger institution of wider scope, the fundamental weaknesses remained. Already, after just a few months' existence, the Parliament found itself forced to witness new evidence of its continuing impotence. In the realm of foreign affairs, the Council had found it expedient to delegate authority to a fast-growing "extra-treaty" institutional system of national administrators which included a powerful Committee of Permanent Representatives. This was particularly painful to the Parliament, which aspired to a dominant role in foreign policy, especially in regard to the ratification of treaties.[7]

The budget was another sore spot. According to the EEC Treaty, the Community institutions participated in the budget process by submitting estimates of expenses to the Commission, which in turn drew up a draft budget for consideration by the Council—which had to consult the affected institution in the event of any revision. However, because of the confusion surrounding the creation of the communities in 1958, the 1959 budget process was delayed. The fault lay with the Council, which had been slow in communicating its expenses to the Commission. Rather than collaborate with the Commission, the Council bypassed it entirely, referring the budget to a committee of national experts who substantially trimmed the estimates. The Parliament strenuously criticized this unorthodox procedure but to no avail.[8]

The desire of many of the Parliament's members to expand its powers, then, was quite understandable. There was a distinct possibility that if direct elections were held prior to such strengthening, the democratically based body might continue to be a parliament in name only—thus thoroughly discrediting supranationalism as a means of achieving political integration. Considering that so many looked askance upon the Working Party's draft convention, why was it so hastily adopted by the full Political Committee and by such a large margin? The answer lay in the leadership's determined belief that the convention was as near to perfect as it could possibly be under the circumstances. In essence, it was a compromise between national interests and *European* aspirations.

An examination of the draft convention revealed several unexpected features. The size of the Parliament had been increased dramatically. Membership of the directly elected body was set at 426 as opposed to the 142 specified by the Rome Treaty. The three largest states, France, West Germany, and Italy, would have 108 representatives each; Belgium and the Netherlands, 42 each; and Luxembourg, 18. A unique twist was added to the concept of direct elections in the form of a "transitional period" (Article 3). Under this provision, only two-thirds of the delegates initially would be chosen by a European electorate. The remaining one-third would continue to be appointed by the national legislatures from among their own ranks. This transitional period would become effective when the first direct elections were held, with the decision as to the period's termination left in the hands of the European Parliament (provided the date selected was not before the end of the third stage of the development of the Common Market nor later than the end of the legislative period during which that stage came to a close).[9] The length of term for directly elected members was set at five years. However, the tenure in office for non-directly elected members remained dependent on domestic politics. If a change of government in one of the states cut short a member's term, he would continue to serve in the Parliament until it approved his successor.

The question of conflicting mandates was a crucial one. Many of the current members of the Parliament held national offices; a blanket restriction on holding any other political or bureaucratic position other than that of representative to the European Parliament necessarily would exclude many of the Parliament's most valuable members. The convention circumvented this touchy dilemma by authorizing the Parliament to decide which mandates were acceptable at the end of the transitional period. However, the convention did specify a number of offices which a representative could not hold. A Parliament member could not hold a national office nor be an official of any of the other Community institutions.

In regard to the electoral procedure itself, the convention set the minimum voting age at between twenty-one and twenty-five years (later amended to twenty-one).[10] Voter and candidate eligibility would be determined according to national law. Any citizen of a Community nation would be allowed to run for election in another Common Market state. The minimum age for candidates was established at not under twenty-five nor above thirty years of age (later amended to twenty-five). National regulations governing the participation of political parties in domestic elections would be applicable to European elections.[11] One of the major concerns of supporters of direct elections was *how* they were held. To be at all effective, the elections would have to take place simultaneously (or as close to this ideal situation as possible) in all six states and not under any circumstances in conjunction with national elections. These requirements were incorporated into the convention along with a provision allowing the states to hold the elections one day later or one day earlier or to spread them over three days if tradition or geographical conditions made a specific date unfeasible.

Once the first elections had been held, subsequent European elections would take place no later than one month before the end of each "legislative period." The first sitting of the new Parliament would commence on the first Tuesday a month after the elections. (Officially, the old Parliament would continue in existence until that time.) Different procedures regulated the filling of vacant seats. In the event a Parliament member who was directly elected resigned (for example, to accept a national ministry), his seat would remain vacant until the next election, thus eliminating the next-to-impossible task of holding a European by-election. However, seats held by indirectly elected members during the transitional stage would be filled in the event of vacancies by the national parliaments. Finally, candidates or party lists that won at least 10 percent of their constituency's vote would be reimbursed for a portion of their election expenses.

The obvious problems involved in implementing the draft convention were not lost upon the Working Party. The final provisions of the convention provided for the creation of an "interim advisory committee" held by the Councils of the EEC, Euratom, and the ECSC. This committee, comprised of one-half national delegates and one-half delegates of the European Parliament, would pave the way for the first direct elections. Committee decisions would require a two-thirds majority vote. The date for the first European elections was set for the first Sunday six months after the convention was ratified by the national parliaments. With the intention of making the three Councils' acceptance of the convention as painless and speedy as possible, the Working Party attached a provision calling upon the Parliament's president, in collaboration with the chairman of the Political Committee, to appoint a special delegation to serve as a liaison between the Parliament and the Councils. A motion for a resolution was also included in the convention stipulating the need for adequate "preparation of public opinion" to insure that direct elections, unlike earlier European projects, would not end up a failure.[12]

One of the most disturbing aspects of the draft convention, from the *European* point of view, was the retention of *in*direct elections for one-third of the Parliament's membership. Yet, as the convention's supporters argued, the Parliament had to reach some accommodation with the national governments on direct elections or else the Councils would withhold their approval and the plan would prove as useless as the European Political Community. Dehousse defended the idea of a transitional period as an "essential feature" of the plan. While admitting that a transition period was not mentioned in the treaties, he noted that its inclusion in the convention offered the Working Party a means "to deal with problems to which there appeared no immediate solution." One such problem was the requirement in Article 138 that direct elections be held in accordance with a "uniform procedure" in all six states. As Dehousse explained:

> The Working Party did not feel obliged to adhere slavishly to the letter of the Treaties . . . it saw no reason why arguments based on a literal reading of the texts should, by definition, weigh more strongly than political considerations.[13]

The use of a transition stage allowed the Parliament to postpone for several years the thorny problem of coordinating various national electoral laws. According to Maurice Faure in his report on the composition of the directly elected Parliament, the Working Party's desire to retain a large number of nationally appointed representatives determined to some extent the substantial expansion in the Parliament's size. As he remarked, it was necessary to "preserve firm links with the national parliaments . . .":

> European integration is only beginning. Major decisions are being taken, and will continue to be by the national Governments set up and controlled by the Parliaments. It is in the latter . . . that the process of political integration will take place.[14]

Faure added that the Working Party had never felt it "desirable or even conceivable that direct elections should result in an assembly composed entirely of fresh faces, none of which had been seen in a national Parliament." Furthermore, it was quite possible that "the part of the European Parliament nominated by indirect suffrage could serve as the nucleus for an Upper Chamber and, therefore, the start of a bicameral system."[15]

The other factor determining the substantial increase in the Parliament's membership was the extensive size of the electorate. In supporting the 426-member figure specified in the draft convention, Faure argued that, considering the "sheer magnitude" of such an election involving six nations and 165 million potential voters, the present 142-member Parliament was "inadequate." He noted that the Working Party preferred to keep the membership proportions that were outlined in the EEC Treaty "since it reflected a political balance that had been accepted by the signatory States." The convention authors finally decided simply to triple the number of current members.[16]

Another controversial aspect of the plan was the exclusion of members of the national governments and of Community executives from membership. Especially in the latter instance, the Political Committee found itself sharply divided. (Members of the EEC and Euratom Commissions and the ECSC High Authority naturally were in favor of joint membership.) The Political Committee finally agreed on the exclusion of Community executives from holding a parliamentary mandate by a close vote of 11 to 10 with three abstentions. The question of incompatibility in the case of national ministers was less of a problem. Although certain members of the Working Party felt that the Parliament's prestige and influence would be considerably enhanced if government leaders were numbered among its members, most felt that since these same leaders sat on the Councils of Ministers, this might prove less beneficial than it appeared.

The convention's failure to specify a uniform electoral procedure was also a major sticking point. Devising such a system, as W. J. Schuijt explained, was extraordinarily difficult. A proportional representation system would tend toward the proliferation of a great many political parties while a majority system would tend to encourage the domination of a handful of large political parties.[17] The Working Party had investigated three proposals in this regard. One plan, submitted by Maria Probst, recommended a procedure that combined both electoral systems in which every voter would cast two votes, one for a party list and the other for a particular candidate. This "mixed system" was rejected as being too complicated for the person who was used to a simpler system. The second proposal, suggested by an Italian expert and similar to the Probst plan, also was rejected on the same basis. The third system—"single transferable vote"—proposed by a Dutch electoral law specialist, involved a complex, weighted voting procedure which was deemed far too complex for an electorate unfamiliar with European elections. Although the majority of the Working Party preferred proportional representation, incorporating such a requirement into the draft convention increased the risk that some of the six nations might reject direct elections entirely rather than accept a foreign voting procedure. On the other hand, as Schuijt noted, "The Working Party could consider the holding of direct elections in accordance with an electoral system to be worked out by the various states. The unavoidable difficulty would then be that different voting procedures would be used in making up the European Parliament."[18] The Working Party and the Political Committee ultimately chose this second alternative, successfully bypassing the sensitive issue for the moment.

The draft convention was presented to the Parliament on May 10, 1960, and after three days of at times heated debate, it was adopted with minor amendments at the end of the May 17 session. The debates closely paralleled the discussion between the Political Committee and the Working Party. From the beginning, the convention's supporters were determined to avoid the expected large number of amendments. In his address opening the debate, Political Committee Chairman Emilio Battista warned his colleagues to refrain from attempting too much alteration. "The Committee made a few changes in the convention and there is no doubt that these filled gaps improved it. Indeed, the principle underlying the draft convention is that too sudden change should be avoided." Dehousse put it more succinctly in his introduction to the convention:

> We have, time and again, been obliged to choose
> between the desirable and the possible which
> means—life being what it is—that we have often
> been obliged to sacrifice the desirable to the
> possible. Does this mean that we have here be-
> come "Mensheviks"? Allow me to say in reply
> ... that we do not think so. We simply wanted
> to be realistic and to give the political Europe
> every possible chance.[19]

Notwithstanding Dehousse's pleas for unity, substantial dissatisfaction
surfaced during the debate. The problem areas were the same as before:
the transition period, the size of the directly elected Parliament, the exclusion of national leaders and Community executives from holding a parliamentary mandate, and the convention's failure to outline a uniform
electoral procedure. Far more disquieting, however, was the insistence of
a number of members, led by Metzger, that expansion of the Parliament's
powers should precede direct elections. Again, it was a question of "which
comes first, the chicken or the egg?" As Metzger convincingly deduced,
"If the elections are conducted on the basis of the Treaty, we shall be
asking the peoples of Europe to elect a parliament which in fact will not
be a parliament at all":

> We are faced with a dilemma. Either we spin a tale
> to the voters, telling them what they are being
> asked to elect is a really grand affair, and that
> they will then see meeting in Strasbourg . . . a
> parliament that will carry out grandiose European
> tasks. If we say this . . . we shall be lying to the
> electorate. Later, disillusion will inevitably follow.[20]

The strong opposition of Metzger and his fellow German Socialists met an
equal amount of intransigence from the proponents of direct elections,
who skillfully piloted the draft convention around what could have been
deadly obstacles. The view of the Parliament's leadership prevailed. As
Dehousse and Battista convincingly argued, the Parliament stood to gain
nothing by waiting for the governments to revise the treaties to give it
more authority. Demands by the Parliament, Dehousse maintained, only
would "torpedo both direct elections and this increase in powers." Battista
best summed up the argument. To shelve the convention and campaign for

greater powers not mentioned in the treaty, he noted, was illogical. "On the other hand, we can already do something the Treaty permits: we can submit the draft convention on direct elections."[21] Although the convention underwent a great deal of criticism and suffered a barrage of proposed amendments, it emerged unscathed. Fortunately, the plan was backed by the Liberals, who shared the leadership's view that revision of the convention would jeopardize its approval by the states.[22] However, the Socialists and the Christian Democrats were divided and were responsible for most of the forty-one amendments submitted to the Political Committee. Although the Socialists had met two days before the opening of the debate and adopted a resolution supporting the concept of direct elections, they extended no such approval to the convention, as was shown by the German Social Democrat's decision to abstain in the final vote on its adoption.[23] During the May 17 session, most of the forty-one amendments were rejected, and the convention was adopted with a few innocuous revisions by a 70 to 0 margin with an estimated 12 to 15 abstentions.[24] A substantial number of members were present. Along with the convention, the Parliament adopted a resolution supporting collaboration between the Parliament and the Councils on electoral procedure and on the problem of aligning direct and indirect elections during the transition period. Resolutions calling for preparation of public opinion and another instructing the Political Committee to draw up proposals for increasing the Parliament's powers were also adopted.[25]

Perhaps it was a premonition or simply intuition on the part of Schuijt which prompted him to insist that the first paragraph of the resolution on the preparation of public opinion be deleted on the grounds that it placed direct elections in a negative light. The offending phrase read as follows: "The European Parliament . . . convinced that the failure of certain European projects has been partly due to inadequate preparation of public opinion. . . ."[26] As Schuijt pointedly reminded his colleagues, it augured ill to begin so important a resolution by raising the specter of the dead European Political Community. Such concern was well founded, for there was growing evidence that the Parliament's ambitious blueprint for European elections, so laboriously constructed, was doomed to join the EPC in legislative limbo. Four days before the Parliament formally submitted the draft convention to the Councils, French Premier Michel Debré, that old opponent of supranationalism, voiced the Gaullist view of direct elections before the French National Assembly:

> The Government has not yet considered this
> project. . . . Nevertheless, after the first discus-
> sion, the first exchange of ideas, I can state the
> following conclusion: the essential thing in our
> view, as General de Gaulle had said, confirming
> the attitude that he has always held, is the politi-
> cal association of states . . . through governmental
> cooperation. . . . At the present moment, before
> this effort has been made, I do not see what direct
> elections by universal suffrage of a political assem-
> bly dealing with technical bodies or with higher
> civil servants can accomplish.[27]

Undeniably, the European Parliament could not have chosen a more
inopportune moment to produce a completed plan for direct elections.
De Gaulle and Debré were in the initial stages of reviving their old idea
of a European confederation into a form very similar to Debré's 1952
proposal for a Union of European States.[28] The French government
had begun to lay the foundation for the union soon after de Gaulle came
to power by encouraging close collaboration with West Germany. By the
fall of 1959, the French were proposing that the Common Market nations
meet periodically to discuss various political matters and that the six
states set up a permanent secretariat and four commissions dealing with
political, economic, defense, and cultural matters in Paris.[29] It was fast
becoming obvious to the other EEC members and to the *Europeans* that
de Gaulle had no use for the communities other than as convenient tools
with which he could politically and economically dominate Western
Europe. Still, France's five partners agreed to meet four times a year to
discuss foreign policy issues.

Needless to say, the Parliament's presentation of the draft convention
to the Councils on June 20, 1960, did not have the intended effect. On
the contrary, the possibility of further progress toward political integration through holding European elections only served to spur de Gaulle
to speed up his plan for a French-dominated association of heads of state.
Another impetus behind the French determination to move quickly was
fear of a possible British bid for admission to the European communities.
The European Free Trade Association, Britain's belated answer to the
Common Market, thus far had met with little success. The Macmillan
government was "rethinking" its position on the Common Market. Since

British involvement would counteract French influence within the EEC, de Gaulle was forced to act as fast as possible if he wished to present Britain with a fait accompli.

Not unexpectedly, the other five EEC nations were wary of the plan. Adenauer in particular was worried over a possible weakening of NATO and his ties with the United States—not to mention fear of a French-controlled confederation headquartered in Paris. In a meeting in July at Rambouillet, de Gaulle persuaded him to see the merits of such a scheme. However, the General was not so successful with the Belgians and the Dutch, who viewed the French plan as a threat to the European communities.[30] The Dutch preferred to have Britain join the Common Market to counter France. However, the General was unconcerned about the smaller EEC nations, whom he dismissed as inconsequential. (This turned out to be an erroneous assumption.)

Looking back at the Gaullist vision of a "united" Europe, it is difficult to comprehend why Belgium, Luxembourg, the Netherlands, and most of the Federalists were willing to accept the premise behind a "Europe of the States." De Gaulle, Debré, and French Foreign Minister Couve de Murville had voiced their disapproval of the Schuman approach on numerous occasions. The explanation lay in the *Europeans'* fear that the French plan offered the only reasonable chance of achieving some measure of political union. It was hoped that de Gaulle would be willing to incorporate the existing supranational institutions into his own conceptual framework, utilizing a directly elected European Parliament as the popular institution of the Union of States. Seen in this light, the Federalists' acquiescence to the French plan was not misguided capitulation based on political expediency but a conditional endorsement—the conditions being the holding of direct elections, expansion of the Parliament's powers, merger of the three communities' executives, and acceleration of economic integration along with British inclusion in the Common Market.

Expectant *Europeans,* however, received little assurance from the French government that strengthening the communities was part of de Gaulle's plan. In a press conference on September 5, 1960, the General developed a theme that was to become a dominant strain in his later statements. According to de Gaulle, only the states could be the "pillars" on which Europe could be built. The Community institutions, while possessing "technical value," lacked the authority to make political decisions. "To imagine that something can be built that would be effective for action and that would be approved by the peoples outside and above the States—this is a dream."[31] Following de Gaulle's statement, Alain Peyrefitte, a conservative French deputy and a Gaullist member of the European Parliament, analyzed the role of the Parliament as envisioned by de Gaulle in a series of articles in *Le Monde* (September 14-17). According to Peyrefitte, an *in*directly elected Parliament in the early stages of a confederation would be more "democratic and fair" than one chosen by direct suffrage since the general public would have little understanding of the candidates' programs or knowledge of the candidates themselves.[32]

Notwithstanding the antipathy of the French government to direct elections and supranationalism, the Parliament energetically pushed toward the elusive goal of European union. In its October session, it debated the impact of the French plan on the Rome Treaty institutions and reaffirmed the principle of federalism. In the November session, the Parliament showed its irrepressible optimism by adopting yet another resolution on the need to prepare the public for European elections. A second resolution was approved on the desirability of the merger of the communities' executives. Perhaps the best indication of the Parliament's intentions was its adoption of a resolution calling for a European legation and a flag.[33]

As the Federalists blindly rushed headlong down their chosen road to political union, de Gaulle marched resolutely in the opposite direction. At the first quarterly summit meeting in Paris on February 10-11, 1961, the six states issued a communiqué announcing the creation of an intergovernmental committee to study the twin problems of national cooperation and development of the communities. In its March session, the Parliament responded to this proposal with a majority of its members amenable to the "building of Europe 'on two pillars'—progressive integration by means of the Treaties and intergovernmental cooperation in other fields."[34] On June 28, after hearing a report by Dehousse, the Parliament adopted a resolution affirming its support for continued meetings such as the Paris summit but on the condition that (1) the communities' executives be allowed to participate in any discussions dealing with matters within their competence, (2) the meetings did not undercut the authority of the communities, (3) the governments "effect" the draft convention on direct elections, (4) the executives were merged, and (5) a European University was established.[35] When the six nations met for a second summit meeting in Bad Godesberg outside Bonn on July 18, 1961, they issued a declaration which incorporated the strengthening of the European communities into the proposed Union of States. According to the communiqué, the six nations "decided":

> [to] give expression to the will for political unity
> already contained in the treaties instituting the
> European Communities. . . . To hold regular
> meetings for exchanging opinions harmonizing
> policies and reaching joint positions so as to
> promote the political union of Europe, thus
> strengthening the Atlantic Alliance. . . . To have
> a study made of the various questions raised in
> the resolution adopted by the European Parlia-
> mentary Assembly on 28 June, 1961, on political
> cooperation between members of the European
> Communities.[36]

In addition, a study committee under the chairmanship of French deputy Christian Fouchet was instructed to draft a treaty for the creation of a Union of States.

For *Europeans* in the late summer of 1961, the situation definitely looked promising. Not only did there appear to be general agreement on the principles underlying political union, but on July 31, British Prime Minister Harold Macmillan announced that Britain would apply for entry into the communities. Ireland and Denmark shortly announced similar intentions, and negotiations in Brussels to this effect began the following October. However, the Union of States was destined to fail from the beginning, for de Gaulle was not about to compromise on the issue of further development of supranational institutions. The first draft treaty prepared by the Fouchet Committee bore a remarkable similarity in many respects to Debré's 1952 "Pact for a Union of European States." The version of November 1961 provided for the creation of three institutions: a Council of heads of state, a European Political Commission comprised of senior foreign affairs officials, and a European Parliamentary Assembly. This assembly could hold debates on "matters concerning the aims of the Union." It could advise the Council, make recommendations, and pose questions. In sum, the proposed assembly was as powerless as the existing European Parliament. The only difference was that the Parliament at least had a legal basis to increase its authority through the Rome and Paris Treaties.

Needless to say, the Parliament did not welcome the Fouchet Committee's first effort. On December 21, René Pleven presented the Political Committee's conception of an acceptable plan. The Pleven Report emphasized the need for an independent secretary-general who would be responsible to the Parliament through a vote of no confidence. This executive would implement the decisions of the Council and would have the authority to select his staff and to take the initiative on his own. As for the Parliament, first, it would be directly elected; second, it would be entrusted with ratification of international treaties; and third, it would have the power to break a deadlock in the Council arising from a lack of unanimity. Furthermore, after the merger of the communities' commissions, the single executive would be represented at Council meetings.[37]

Due to its poor reception, the French government decided to shelve the first Fouchet Plan on January 16, 1962. Two days later, the committee produced a second draft treaty. This effort was even less acceptable. As then EEC Commission President Walter Hallstein noted, "The purpose was clear: to reverse the evolution of the Community."[38] The second draft treaty included a fourth institution—committees of ministers (one dealing with foreign affairs and the other with education). In this new version, the Political Commission of national leaders would "prepare the deliberations of the Council and would supervise the execution of its decisions" as well as "carry out the other tasks which the Council entrusts to it." The Political Commission would also control the budget. The powers of the Parliament remained the same. Ominously, the draft treaty included economic matters under the Council's jurisdiction.[39]

The French president's aim to strip the EEC Commission of any semblance of control over the Common Market was plainly obvious. The second Fouchet Plan came on the heels of the conclusion of lengthy and traumatic negotiations over the creation of a common agricultural policy—in de Gaulle's eyes crucial for France. The negotiations involved the fixing of prices for French agricultural products at a higher level than world prices but on a lower level than German prices. The common external tariff would be augmented by levies on farm imports and German prices would sink to the French level. The end of internal barriers would allow French agricultural surpluses to flow into West Germany. Despite German and Dutch opposition, the six nations finally agreed upon a common agricultural policy after grueling negotiations that ended in the early morning hours of January 14. (During the negotiations the clock was

officially stopped at midnight, December 31.) In all, there were 137 hours
of discussion, with 214 hours in subcommittee, 582,000 pages of documents, and three heart attacks.[40] The prospect of British entry into the
Common Market made it imperative that de Gaulle achieve a policy favorable to France. He had succeeded, but the whole episode had reinforced
the General's already ingrained distaste for the European Economic Community "system"—hence, the second Fouchet Plan's inclusion of economic
matters under national control.

Not to be intimidated by France, the other five states submitted their
own version of a draft treaty for a "European Union" as opposed to a
Union of *States.* The counterproposal differed from the French plan in
that it included a Court of Justice and omitted the Political Commission.
Although the powers of the proposed European Parliamentary Assembly
were still limited to consultation, it did provide for the eventual holding
of direct elections. Far from ignoring supranationalism, the draft treaty
meshed confederal development with the evolution of a federal Europe,
providing for an eventual general revision of the Rome Treaty "to integrate the Common Market, the European Union and the European Communities . . . in an organic institutional framework, respecting the frame-
works provided by the Treaties of Paris and Rome." In addition, the draft
treaty pointedly specified that this revision should be directed at expanding the independence and powers of the existing European institutions,
that is, the holding of direct elections and the expansion of the Parliament's role in the legislative process, the creation of an independent executive, the extension of the jurisdiction of the Court of Justice, and the use
of the majority vote rather than unanimity for Council decisions.[41]

The gap between the position of France and her EEC partners was
too wide to bridge. One last attempt was made to reach a consensus. On
March 15, both sides issued a joint text presenting the French plan and
the counterproposal by the five states. On March 20, the foreign ministers
met in Luxembourg but failed to work out a compromise. By now, Dutch
Foreign Minister Joseph Luns and Spaak, the new Belgian foreign minister,
were convinced that a "Gaullist Europe" would mean the end of the supranational experiment.[42] Undeterred, de Gaulle attempted to revive the
Union of States by convincing first Adenauer and then Italian Premier
Amintore Fanfani of its necessity. When the foreign ministers met again
in Paris on April 17, the Benelux states were presented with what appeared
to be a fait accompli. Spaak and Luns again balked.

Spaak's intransigence seemed contradictory to many leading *Europeans* who were reconciled to some form of the Gaullist scheme. Even the Action Committee for a United Europe had felt that the French plan offered a more feasible means of achieving political integration than the Schuman approach. The European Parliament saw the issue as far from dead. During its May session, it unanimously approved a resolution calling for the resumption of negotiations by the foreign ministers. The Parliament even adopted a plan of its own for political union on May 9. Authored by Dehousse and Dutch Christian Democrat Jean Duvieusart, it incorporated many of the conditions previously laid down by the Parliament in its debates on the Fouchet drafts.[43] Spaak, however, defended his position before the Consultative Assembly of the Council of Europe on May 15, claiming that the French plan would create an organization which was too vague and ineffective to lead to a federal Europe.

In a press conference on that same day, de Gaulle was forced bitterly to admit defeat:

> The objection (of the Benelux states) is presented
> to us with the words, "Let us merge the six
> States into a supranational entity; this way things
> will be quite simple and practical." But such an
> entity cannot be found without there being in
> Europe today a federator with sufficient power,
> authority and skill. That is why one falls back on
> a type of hybrid, in which the six States would
> undertake to comply with what will be decided
> upon by a certain majority. At the same time,
> although there are already six national parlia-
> ments, plus the Consultative Assembly of the
> Council of Europe . . . we must, it seems, elect
> yet another parliament, a so-called European
> one—which would lay down the law for the six
> States.[44]

Clearly, de Gaulle's antipathy toward the European communities was exacerbated by the rejection of his long-cherished vision of a French-dominated confederation. It was pique as much as foreign policy considerations which led to the French president's determined pursuit of a Franco-German treaty of cooperation (signed January 22, 1963) and to his pugnacious rejection of British participation in the European communities that same month.[45]

There was no question of there being any hope for the European Parliament's proposal for direct elections.[46] The draft convention, conceived in the wave of optimism accompanying the creation of the communities, had remained with the Councils of Ministers for over two years, obscured by the furor over the Union of States. Even the most fervent advocates of direct elections were coming to the conclusion that expansion of the Parliament's powers would have to come first. Unfortunately, this alternative route to the creation of a genuine European legislature was to prove as impassable as the path originally chosen.

chapter 5

THE PRECOCIOUS PARLIAMENT AND THE CRISIS OF 1965

At the beginning of 1963, the
forward progress of European integration once again ground to a halt.
Yet, the cyclical pattern of development that was becoming associated
with the European Community—energetic optimism followed by crisis
culminating in disillusionment and frustration—was about to repeat itself.[1]
The two-year span from April 1963 to mid-1965 was to witness the
Federalists recover from the twin disappointments of the de Gaulle veto
and the collapse of talks on political union to enthusiastically lobby for
the strengthening of the powers of the European Parliament and the EEC
Commission. This overzealous pursuit of greater federal authority precipitated yet another crisis—a crisis which came close to undermining the
carefully constructed foundations of supranationalism.

Early 1963 found the Parliament plunged in a state of gloom. Although
its members steadfastly called for a revival of negotiations among the six
states on political union and routinely complained about the Council's
neglect of the draft convention for direct elections, these protests lacked
their customary vitality and urgency. The Parliament made one last, forth-
right effort to confront the Council on the draft convention through the
submission of a written question bluntly demanding that the ministers
specify when they intended to act on the matter. In its reply, the EEC
Council merely issued a restatement of an earlier communiqué:

> The problem of election of members of the
> Parliament by direct universal suffrage has been
> discussed by the Councils on several occasions.
> Under the terms of Article 108 of the Euratom
> Treaty, 21 of the ECSC Treaty and 138 of the
> EEC Treaty, however, the Councils must decide
> unanimously on provisions they recommend
> member states to adopt. As this condition has
> not so far been fulfilled, the Councils are not in
> a position to say when they will be able to decide
> on the provision in question.[2]

In the few months following the de Gaulle veto, the Parliament clearly
was fumbling about to recapture some sort of direction. There was a
general feeling that closer collaboration between the Parliament and its
national counterparts might enhance its image.[3] An attempt was made
to investigate this possibility. In January, the Parliament sponsored a
special conference in Rome. Parliament President Gaetano Martino hosted
the presidents of the national assemblies and their secretaries-general. The
basic objective of the meeting was to coordinate the activities of the
Parliament and the national bodies. However, the meeting proved less
than successful. Even Martino's most rudimentary request that the Parliament's schedule of debates and the timetables of the assemblies be "har-
monized" to curtail absenteeism in the former was rejected. The conference ended after the national delegates passed a resolution which in part
condescendingly stated that the European Parliament should not set up
its timetable until it had consulted with the national parliaments.[4]

By late March, the majority of the Parliament supported a new political
relance. On March 27, the need for a "fresh impetus" toward European
unification was the subject of lengthy debate. Metzger and Battista, formerly at odds over whether direct elections should precede an expansion
of the Parliament's powers, joined with Dutch Liberal F. G. van Dijk,
Italian Socialist Luciano Granzotto Basso, and other members to call for
the strengthening of the European Community. The unhappy fate of the
draft convention was discussed. Although it was generally agreed that
direct elections were crucial to the development of the Parliament, it was
recognized that the probability of the states agreeing to hold European
elections in the near future was remote. Dehousse observed that no stric-
tures existed in either the Paris or Rome Treaties against a nation uni-

laterally deciding to directly elect its delegates to the Parliament.[5] Some members expressed the fear that the recent Franco-German Treaty would undercut the evolution of the Community. After reaffirming the necessity of a "United States of Europe" based on a "supranational and democratic" system, the Parliament adopted a resolution sponsored by all three political parties supporting British membership in the Community and underscoring the need to fulfill the provisions of the treaties. In what was to become a common occurrence in the following years, the Gaullists refused to join the Liberal group in tabling the resolution.[6]

Gradually, the Parliament's prospects were becoming brighter. That same month, EEC Commission President Hallstein noted that the Commission felt the Parliament's limited role in the legislative process should be rectified and that direct elections should be held. In a speech at Columbia University on March 4, he singled out the Parliament as "the most essential point of constitutional progress" and noted that the Community was the only true path to a united Europe.[7]

A much-encouraged European Parliament met in Strasbourg June 24-28 to hear Hallstein introduce the EEC's Sixth General Report and to discuss the best means of increasing the Parliament's powers. On June 27, German Christian Democrat Hans Furler outlined the recommendations of the Political Committee. In this ambitious report, the Committee proposed the extension of the Parliament's powers in five major areas: the selection of the Community executive, the legislative process, treaty ratification, the budget, and nomination of members of the Court of Justice. The report included a strongly worded resolution:

> The European Parliament, convinced that any
> real progress made by the Community must be
> accompanied by a strengthening of its institu-
> tional structures, considers that the transfer of
> legislative powers from the national to the
> Community sphere must go hand in hand with
> a corresponding strengthening of parliamentary
> powers at the Community level; regards it as
> essential to widen the powers of the European
> Parliament so as to strengthen the Community's
> democratic structure and the Community spirit.[8]

The resolution urged that the Parliament achieve specific substantial powers as soon as possible. In regard to the Community executive, a new

Commission president would be required to make a "policy statement" to the Parliament which would be subject to debate. The Parliament also would "play an effective part in the appointing of the executive."

In the area of legislation, the Commission would be required to consult with pertinent parliamentary committees on all proposed regulations before they were submitted to the Council of Ministers for approval. The Commission also would be bound to respond to any amendments put forward by the Parliament and to keep the members informed of its discussions with the Council. Furthermore, the Council would be required to accept further suggestions from the Parliament if it chose to reject a particular proposal and to provide an explanation as to why the Parliament's opinion was ignored. Points 7 and 8 of the resolution were particularly far-reaching:

> 7. Where a second opinion has been adopted by the Parliament by a two-thirds majority of the votes cast, the Council of Ministers shall be able to disregard such an opinion only by a unanimous decision;
>
> 8. The Council of Ministers shall consult the Parliament on all matters of importance, *even where the Treaty does not provide for such consultation* . . . that its consultative powers be replaced by a *right of approval* on all fundamental issues and in principle on *any* legislative decision [emphasis mine].

In regard to foreign affairs, the resolution proposed that the Parliament be kept informed of all external Community developments, that its opinions be honored, and that it ratify "all international agreements entered into by the Community." On budget matters, the resolution stated that the executive should include a detailed policy statement with its draft budget. In addition, the preliminary draft budget should be submitted simultaneously to both the Parliament and to the Council. Finally, control over the budget would revert to the Parliament as soon as the Common Market was producing its own revenue. A final provision stipulated that the Parliament would nominate members of the Court of Justice from a list of candidates submitted by the states. The resolution ended with yet another supplication to the Council for action on the draft convention for direct elections.[9]

After hearing the Furler Report and the accompanying resolution, Hallstein offered the Commission's view. While he strongly cautioned the Parliament not to make demands which would necessitate a revision of the treaties, he nonetheless felt that the Parliament's legislative and budgetary powers could be gradually increased by the Council. As the Parliament's ensuing debate revealed, spokesmen for the three political groups had mixed reactions. German Socialist Käte Strobel noted that "a very powerful Council of Ministers and a dynamic Commission" needed a strong, directly elected Parliament to insure that the public's interests were not sacrificed. The Liberals argued that direct elections were more important than endowing the Parliament with greater authority, although such increased powers were desirable. In addition, the Community had to guard against creating an imbalance by giving the Parliament too much authority over the executive. The Liberal party as a whole called for the Furler Report to be referred back to the Political Committee for further revision.[10] Joseph Illerhaus, spokesman for the Christian Democrats, agreed that parliamentary approval of the selection of the Commission president and members of the Court of Justice was a premature demand. While he deplored what he termed the Council's "light treatment" of the Parliament's recommendations, he also agreed that only a directly elected body could make the Furler proposals a reality.[11]

Although most of the members clearly preferred that direct elections precede expansion of powers, they were realistic enough by this time to know that the states would not act on the draft convention. Thus, despite dissension over the resolution, it was adopted at the close of the debate.

The Parliament's strenuous campaign to expand its authority, however, fell on deaf ears. Notwithstanding its repeated calls for action, during the next two years the political development of the European Community stagnated.[12] It was not so much a question of lack of determination to carry out the Furler proposals as it was a definite lack of the proper atmosphere. Federalists had not yet recovered fully from the impact of the de Gaulle veto of British membership in the Community. Relations between France and West Germany were rapidly deteriorating. Erhard, who had replaced Adenauer in the fall of 1963, did not share his predecessor's willingness to cooperate with the French president. On the question of the future development of the EEC, Erhard supported increasing the role of the Parliament and, in general, broadening the scope of the Community.[13] Erhard's Atlanticism alienated de Gaulle. A related factor was the contro-

versy over the MLF (multilateral force).[14] Yet another factor adding to
the unfavorable climate was the continued impasse on political union
(that is, intergovernmental cooperation). Although de Gaulle had not
abandoned his dream of a French-dominated European confederation,
he had thus far refused to resume negotiations. Federalists tended to
dissipate their energy by channeling it in two different directions—toward
strengthening the Community on the one hand and toward the resumption of summit talks on political union on the other.

By the end of 1963, there was a general consensus among supporters
of European unification of all persuasions that some means to restart the
stalled progress of political integration must be found. As Erhard noted
in a speech to the Bundestag on January 9, 1964, "It is obvious that a
feeling of uneasiness is surrounding the idea of European political integration. But we must not allow Europe to be weighed down by lassitude. I
have no doubt about the urgency of making a new start."[15] Erhard failed
to expand on his theme of a new start—although he indicated that intergovernmental collaboration was a possible answer to the dilemma. What
was clear was that he had many misgivings about the Paris and Rome
Treaties as the appropriate path to political union:

> The French President is well aware that we
> Germans do not consider the present Europe
> of the Six the ultimate in wisdom: . . . I have
> always said that the automatic clauses of the
> Treaties of Rome, economic integration alone,
> will not make Europe. . . . All our effort and
> inherent political will will be necessary to
> unite Europe politically as well as technocratically.
> This opinion is in no way a criticism of the institu-
> tions created so far: ECSC, EEC or Euratom. The
> merging of these institutions is another problem.
> It may be useful, but we must not expect a Euro-
> pean political miracle.

Furthermore, Erhard argued, how could national sovereignty be relinquished
to a supranational entity such as the EEC Commission which was not qualified to "assume this responsibility constitutionally, politically and according
to the concepts of parliamentary democracy? The question of the structure
and form of the European Parliament and its competences will remain un-
answered this time, but it raises a very serious problem."[16]

Five days after Erhard's address, Paul-Henri Spaak attempted to express his now-revised concept of how political integration should proceed in a speech before the Consultative Assembly of the Council of Europe. Although he still emphasized that the Community was a "stage on the way to political union," he admitted that the old élan was gone. "I must admit that I am not content, or that I am no longer content, to accept this sort of historic fatalism and to say that things are bound to happen. . . ." While he still believed in the inevitability of a United States of Europe, he realized, "that this ideal is quite unattainable at the present time. It remains to be seen whether some compromise is possible between those who want the Europe hoped for by the pioneers of the European idea— de Gasperi, Jean Monnet, Robert Schuman, Adenauer—and those who believe that much slacker links would suffice to make a framework for Europe." He implied that a modified Fouchet Plan was the Federalists' only hope. *Europeans,* he conceded, "were probably wrong" to think that they could create a federal Europe by simply drawing up a constitution for ratification by the states. "It seems to me it might be a useful compromise to give up, at least for the time being, all thought of a supranational structure, or organizing really strong and effective institutions. . . ."[17]

Such exaltations to compromise, to slow down the development of the supranational experiment, especially coming from one of the foremost founding fathers of European federalism, served to discourage further efforts for a political *relance.* On January 31, de Gaulle added his voice to the rising dirge. "The European Community," he stated, "could not survive . . . without political cooperation." But France's proposals for political union (that is, the Fouchet Plan) had been rejected by her five partners, who claimed that British participation, the Atlantic alliance, and further federal development were necessary preconditions. "Yet it is clear," de Gaulle truculently observed, "that not one of the peoples of Europe would allow its destiny to be handed over to an assembly composed mainly of foreigners." The French president concluded his statement with the observation that the Five's objections to the Fouchet Plan had lost their "virulence" and that France would be willing to consider a resumption of discussions on political union.[18]

As the impetus toward further political integration languished, de Gaulle's "assembly of foreigners" resumed its discussions on the necessary strategy to increase its authority. The situation was looking somewhat more promising. On March 23-25, the EEC Council of Ministers had met to discuss several of the Parliament's long-cherished goals: the merger of the Rome and Paris Treaties, fusion of the three communities' executives and Councils, and the strengthening of the European Parliament.[19] The Council had agreed to combine the two Commissions and the ECSC High Authority by January 1, 1965. A new treaty merging the three communities was scheduled to take effect on January 1, 1967. The name and size of the new single executive was left unresolved as was the manner of voting of the single Council of Ministers.[20]

On May 12, the Parliament met to debate a report presented by French Socialist Francis Vals on budgetary powers. Many of the members criticized the report for not offering stronger measures to correct the Parliament's embarrassingly limited financial powers and some of the speakers felt that the Parliament should not be forced repeatedly to request Council action on the same issues. An increase in the Parliament's budgetary powers seemed logical in light of the Council's decision to merge the communities. At the end of the session, the Parliament adopted a resolution stressing the need to strengthen its financial authority and to broaden its democratic base so that it could adequately oversee the allocation of the potential revenue generated by the merged Community. According to the resolution, the Parliament would examine the preliminary draft budget. After the Council approved the draft by a "qualified majority" (a five-sixths vote), it would send the draft to the Parliament along with a detailed policy statement. If the Parliament approved the draft budget within six weeks of its submission, it would go into effect. However, if two-thirds of the Parliament amended the draft, it would be sent back to the Council, which would vote on the amended version by either a unanimous vote (in the case of expenditures financed with the Community's "own resources") or by a qualified majority vote in other cases.[21]

The Parliament's drive for control of the merged Community's revenues was encouraged by a series of favorable developments. The Commission had responded positively to the idea. On June 23, the Commission seconded the Parliament's call for the simultaneous strengthening of both federal institutions. In a communication from the Commission to the EEC Council of Ministers on October 2, the former voiced its hope that in the current "malaise" gripping the Community lay the start of a new stimulus toward European unification. The Commission also stated that in regard to the future of supranationalism "the overriding problem here is that of strengthening the role of the European Parliament." It noted that despite repeated requests the Council had failed to fulfill Article 138 of the EEC Treaty even though a suitable plan for direct elections existed in the form of the 1960 draft convention.[22]

On October 21, German Socialist Strobel introduced a fifteen-point question to the Commission on behalf of her party. In her address, Strobel claimed that unless the Parliament was directly elected, an institutional imbalance would be created by an overpowerful Commission and an increasingly dominant Council. The fifteen questions unequivocally put the Commission on the spot.[23] Hallstein's point-by-point replies to at times very specific inquiries were, on the whole, very encouraging. Hallstein placed the Commission on record as "fully and completely" supporting the Parliament in its attempts to expand its legal authority and its competence. He noted that the Commission was "in the same quandary" as the Parliament when it came to dealing with the Council and that forcing radical changes on the national governments at a time when merger of the treaties hung in the balance would prove to be a "dangerous tactic":

> The method adopted should, on the contrary, be
> constantly to strengthen the forces carrying us
> forward towards our political objectives by going
> ahead energetically with making a reality of the
> Communities, by creating more and incontrovertible
> arguments in support of these objectives and thus
> in the long run forcing them through. Otherwise
> there is a risk that both the completion of the
> European Economic Community and the attain-
> ment of the political objectives may be prevented.[24]

As events within the next ten months were to reveal, Hallstein failed to heed his own advice. In his seemingly well-timed but ill-advised attempt to "force" proposals aimed at broadening the authority of the Commission and the Parliament at the expense of the states, he underestimated the tenacity of the French president and precipitated a crisis of extraordinary dimensions.

In the meantime, however, it appeared that the long-anticipated political *relance* was at last at hand. By the end of 1964, interest in political union had revived. On September 9, Spaak had suggested in a speech before the

WEU General Affairs Committee that the states resume discussions based on a revised version of the Fouchet Plan. On November 4 and 28, respectively, West Germany and Italy offered their versions of political union. Both proposals outlined a substantially increased role for the European Parliament within the Community. The German plan provided for a gradual increase in the Parliament's powers in the areas of legislation, finance, and foreign affairs. The Italian proposal specifically called for direct elections and parliamentary control of the Community's resources.[25]

The Italian government had supported direct elections from the initial submission of the 1960 draft convention to the Council of Ministers. During the February 1964 session of the Council, Italian Foreign Minister Giuseppe Saragat remarked that he felt the elections should be held in full or in part on January 1, 1966, since this date marked the beginning of the third and final stage of the Common Market. Such a procedure would make "full-scale" direct elections a reality by January 1, 1970.[26] Saragat noted that he had made a proposal to the Italian government to this effect.

Not unexpectedly, the beginning of 1965 was characterized by a growing euphoria on the part of supporters of the Community. One account of the Parliament's irrepressible optimism during its January session, written by an impressed journalist, must have made depressing reading but a few months later. According to Edward T. O'Toole, correspondent for *The Reporter,* in Strasbourg there was "a feeling that 1965 may be the time of awakening for the legislative branch of Europe's supranational community":

> Not since the European Parliament held its first meeting in 1952 has there been such journalistic interest in an opening session as there was at Europe House here last month. . . . It seems certain that the parliament's representative dimensions at least will be dramatically broadened during the months ahead.[27]

Certainly O'Toole's prophecy was well founded. At a meeting at Rambouillet on January 20, de Gaulle and Erhard reportedly agreed to proceed with discussions on political union. (The New British Labour government expressed a desire to take part in the talks but was refused.)[28]

The European Parliament heartily endorsed the eventual resumption of the negotiations and passed yet another resolution to this effect in its

January session.[29] In addition to the revival of political union, the imminent merger of the two commissions and the High Authority appeared to signify that the new single executive would automatically experience a great increase in authority. Furthermore, in December the six states had agreed to create a common agricultural system for the Community by July 1, 1967, along with the establishment of a common tariff to protect Community farmers from cheap foreign imports and the creation of common external duties on imported industrial goods. Economic experts could only speculate how much revenue would be raised by this external tariff. Estimates ranged from half a billion dollars initially to several billion dollars in the future.[30]

Even more extraordinary was the Council's decision to authorize the Commission to draw up proposals on how the common agricultural fund would be financed. The European Parliament (with the exception of the Gaullists) fully expected the Commission to give it some measure of control over "the Community's own resources" as befitted any genuine legislative body. The Dutch parliament had already gone on record as supporting extension of the federal assembly's financial powers. Hallstein and Sicco Mansholt, Commission vice-president, earlier had concurred in this regard—although they were aware that such an action would inevitably lead to a clash with de Gaulle.

Despite his earlier caution, Hallstein was as caught up in the enthusiasm of the moment as was the majority of the members of the Parliament. It appeared that now was the optimum time to act. The six governments had first reached accord on a common agricultural system on January 14, 1962, after a marathon negotiating session. At that time, they had agreed on the organization of various markets and had outlined the gradual assumption of farm expenditures by the Community. Until June 30, 1965, the member states would provide Community funds. However, from then until January 1970 Community financing would come from agricultural levies. When the so-called Mansholt Plan (a common price for grains on July 1, 1967, and Community appropriation of levies) was adopted in December 1964, the states had agreed to come up with the necessary regulations to cover the 1965 to 1970 end of the transition period *before June 30, 1965.*[31] It was then that the governments asked the Commission to come up with an appropriate plan. France was particularly eager to reach an agreement before the deadline. The importance of the creation of a common farm policy to de Gaulle has already been noted. What Hallstein sought was to greatly expand the authority of the

Commission and the Parliament through linking the agricultural proposals
with measures which would have placed the two federal institutions in
control of potentially huge community revenues.[32]

The Commission's complex proposals for financing the common agricultural policy were in three parts. The first section was uncontroversial.
It proposed that joint financing should proceed gradually in progressive
fashion with the fund covering a greater percentage of expenditures
until after July 1, 1967, when the fund would cover all expenditures.[33]
The second of the Commission's proposals, while radical, was still legal
under the provisions of the Rome Treaty. In simple terms, it gave the
Commission control of the fund, which was expected to reach a billion
dollars by 1970. In addition, it scheduled the completion of the industrial
customs union for July 1, 1967, along with the beginning of the common
agricultural market, creating a single Community market two and a half
years before the end of the transition period. Based on the establishment
of a single market and Article 201 of the EEC Treaty authorizing the
Community to control its "own resources," the Commission proposed
to gradually take over customs duties in mid-1967 and to place the revenues in the fund.[34]

This was controversial indeed. But even more so was the third part of
the Commission plan—the European Parliament would share budgetary
control with the Commission. As Hallstein and Mansholt saw it, the granting of budgetary powers to the Parliament was a necessary, logical step.
While the Community was financed by national contributions, the Parliament's involvement in the budget process was superfluous. As the funds
were allocated by the national assemblies, the Community budget was
subject to popular control. However, once the Community had its own
source of revenue, only the European Parliament could provide the necessary oversight. As the Commission argued, if the Parliament were shut
out of the budget process, a hundred million people would relinquish
control over an undemocratic technocracy. Naturally, it followed that
the Parliament would have to be directly elected if the people were to be
truly represented.

The Commission proposed to expand the Parliament's budgetary
powers through revising Articles 201 and 203 of the Rome Treaty. According to Article 201, as previously noted, the Commission could make
proposals to substitute "other resources available to the Community itself" for national contributions. Under the *revised* Article 201, however,

as soon as the Parliament was directly elected, the Commission's future proposals for replacing national financing with Community-generated funds would be adopted by the Council by a qualified majority vote if the Parliament backed these proposals by a two-thirds majority. If not, the Council would approve the measures by a unanimous vote.[35]

The unrevised Article 203 outlined the EEC budget process: the Commission drew up a draft budget from estimates of expenditures provided by the Community institutions (including reasons why the Commission chose to alter these estimates); the Council considered the draft budget, and, if it wished to make changes, consulted the Commission and any affected institutions. The Council then approved the draft by a qualified majority vote and sent it to the Parliament. If, within one month, the Parliament made no amendments, the budget was adopted. If there were amendments, the draft was sent back to the Council to repeat the previous process, after which the ministers voted again on the draft budget using a qualified majority vote. Whether or not the Council chose to incorporate the recommendations of the Parliament was up to the Council.

Most significantly, in the third section of its plan, the Commission proposed to alter Article 203 to give the Parliament the power to make actual amendments—not mere recommendations—by a majority vote. Under the revised article, the amended budget would be resubmitted to the Council *and* the Commission. If, within fifteen days, the Commission instructed the Council that it accepted the Parliament's modifications, the Council could overrule the changes only by a five-sixths majority vote. On the other hand, if the Commission revised the amendments, the ministers could approve the Commission version by a simple majority (four out of six states). Obviously, under such a procedure, the Council—although still in ultimate control of the purse strings—was relegated to a spectator's role in the budget process. The Parliament's authority was greatly enhanced since there was little chance of one state (France, for example) mustering five of six votes needed to reject an amended budget.[36]

Needless to say, such an ambitious plan would not be warmly welcomed by the Gaullists. Considering the French president's repeated attacks against supranationalism, it was hardly likely that he would view the extensive strengthening of European federal institutions with anything other than the utmost horror. Keeping this in mind, it is hard to fathom what motivated Hallstein to unveil the plan before the "assembly of foreigners" that de Gaulle so much detested. Perhaps Hallstein anticipated the French reaction and tried to head off possible rejection through favorable press coverage of his address to the Parliament. Or, perhaps, like his fellow *Europeans,* he was caught up in the euphoria of the moment.

Whatever the case, on March 24, Hallstein described the Commission's proposals to an approving (Gaullists excepted) Parliament.[37] The Commission had been meeting in Strasbourg in order to put the finishing touches on the plan prior to its submission to the Council of Ministers on April 1. Although Hallstein admitted that he was aware that custom normally called for the Commission to place all proposals before the Council first, he pointed to other instances when this rule was not followed.[38] In addition, he justified his action as a logical one, since most of the budget plan was by then public knowledge. Furthermore, he argued that the Parliament should be the first to know rather than be left to piece together the plan from press reports.[39] The Parliament responded warmly to the address. At one point, Hallstein indulged in a bit of rhetoric reminiscent of another assembly's struggle for control of the purse strings two centuries ago. *"Le vieil adage qui est à la base de toutes les traditions parlementaires ènonce en effet*: no taxation without representation."[40]

The French government reacted to Hallstein's faux pas with unexpected fury. Although de Gaulle made it quite clear that he felt the Commission's proposals were unnecessarily far-reaching, he allowed the plan to go through the customary channels. After its submission to the Council, discussions were scheduled for the ministers' May and June meetings. The proposals were formally placed before the Parliament during its May session. The members' enthusiasm had not diminished in spite of the French reaction. Rather, the Parliament was more eager than ever. The intransigence of the French opposition was not yet apparent. On April 8 in Brussels, the six states signed a treaty establishing a single Council and Commission for the three communities in preparation for the later merger of the Rome and Paris Treaties.[41] A few weeks earlier, the Italian government had invited the six foreign ministers to meet in Venice in May to discuss plans for a resumption of summit talks on political union. Although the French government had rejected the invitation, the door was left open for a meeting later in the year if an acceptable common farm policy was produced before the June 30 deadline.[42] Even more encouraging was the introduction of direct elections bills in both the Italian and German parliaments. On February 8, several Italian senators including Granzotto Basso had introduced a measure providing for the election of Italian delegates to the European Parliament by universal suffrage. The following day, an estimated one hundred Christian Democrats put forward a bill before the Chamber to amend the Italian constitution to make direct elections possible. A similar bill was introduced by the Socialists in the Bundestag on May 20.[43]

The Parliament's debate on the Commission's proposals proved to be one of the high points in an evolution not notable for exciting or rapid development. Hallstein and Mansholt were present to explain and defend the plan. As was to be expected, the report of Francis Vals, chairman of the Budget and Administration Committee, praised the proposals while chastising the Commission for not going as far as supporting the Parliament's acquisition of "full budgetary powers" by 1972 (the date when all Community revenues would be self-generated). Vals stressed that the holding of direct elections by 1972 at the latest was imperative if the Parliament intended to fulfill its duties as overseer of the Community's finances. The Socialists and Christian Democrats gave their blessing to the proposals. The former in particular called for the Parliament to assume the real legislative powers characteristic of national assemblies and several amendments were proposed to this effect.

Gaetano Martino noted on behalf of the Liberals that the Commission's ambitious attempt to revitalize the stagnating drive for political integration came at an opportune time since the French government seemed in no hurry to resume talks on European union. Hallstein, reflecting on the Parliament's future role, once again sounded a note of caution:

> This does not mean that we can at once take the final step toward full federation, where the budgetary powers of the European Parliament are concerned. We realize that, in this field as in others, progress must be gradual. . . . The proposals we have put forward to strengthen the position of the Parliament only constitute the first step, and that other steps can be taken as opportunity offers. In this first stage, the solutions we have proposed seem to us absolutely imperative, absolutely unavoidable.[44]

Nonetheless, the resolution on the plan ultimately adopted by the Parliament included an amended version that went much further than the Commission's proposals. Specifically, the amendments required the

Commission to attach an explanatory memorandum if it altered the draft budget. In addition, the Council could, by a qualified majority, amend the draft budget within twenty days, but it would have to inform the Parliament and the Commission of any changes and the reasons for these changes. The Parliament could, however, reject the Council's alterations within twenty days by a two-thirds majority.[45] René Plevan summed up the sentiments of most of the members:

> The moral support that our vote will give
> tomorrow to President Hallstein and his Com-
> mission when they appear before the Council
> is very great, but the value of these proposals is
> much greater still—and it will be greatly to his
> credit to have presented them; they have on
> their side the logic and dynamism of a very great
> cause.[46]

The French government could not have agreed less with the Parliament's assessment. As far as de Gaulle was concerned, the only pressing matter which needed to be solved was the question of how the common agricultural policy would be financed after July 1, 1965. This problem had an obvious solution. The states could continue to supply the necessary funds. The second and third parts of the Commission's package were irrelevant and should not be considered at all. When the Council of Ministers met to discuss the plan in mid-May shortly after the Parliament's debate, it was soon evident that the French view—as had been the case with the Fouchet Plan—differed considerably from that of the other five states, who were more or less willing to allow the Community to have its own resources and to strengthen the Parliament's control over the budget.[47]

The headstrong behavior of the Parliament and Hallstein's and Mansholt's appeal to the Assembly for support only further infuriated de Gaulle. In the following weeks, the unabashed ambition of some of its members added insult to injury. On June 3, in an address to the German Bar Conference in Augsburg, Parliament Vice-President Hans Furler claimed that "the Council of Ministers should in the future be required to consult the European Parliament about all regulations"— whether enumerated in the treaty or not. He went so far as to argue that the Council "should of its own free will enter into a gentleman's agreement to cede some of its powers 'thereby binding itself' to the Parliament."[48] In mid-June, as the Council prepared to meet to thrash out a compromise before the end-of-the-month deadline, the Parliament continued adding new demands to its list of goals during its June session— demands which included a "re-drafting of the Constitution of the European Community."[49] In the month spanning the May procedural talks and the actual negotiations scheduled for the June Council meeting, the proposals underwent detailed scrutiny by the Committee of Permanent Representatives and other national experts. They were also the topic of discussion during de Gaulle's visit to Bonn June 11 and 12.[50] Despite the obvious difference of opinion, there still appeared to be room for compromise when the ministers met in mid-June. Certainly, there was no reason to anticipate the crisis of June 30. The clock had been "stopped" before in previous lengthy negotiating sessions.[51] However, by the end of the month after intensive negotiations, it was clear that France was willing to continue to financially support the Community until January 1, 1970—thus postponing the creation of the Community's own resources— in order to avoid acquiescing to the second and third parts of the Commission's plan.[52]

When the Council met for its last session on June 30, Couve de Murville hinted that failure to reach an accord on financial regulation would have dire results. His refusal to discuss any subject other than the financing of the common agricultural fund met equally firm opposition from his colleagues. German Foreign Minister Gehard Schroeder's theatrical announcement of a just-adopted Bundestag resolution supporting a strengthened European Parliament only reinforced the French government's determination to hold firm.[53] Just before two o'clock on the morning of July 1, Couve de Murville abruptly ended the meeting. In a statement released later in the day, the French government deplored the breakdown of the talks and threatened that "the government has decided, as far as it is concerned . . . to accept the legal, economic, and political consequences of the situation which has just been created."[54] The statement noted that the July 12 Council meeting was canceled. De Gaulle had decided to boycott the Community's activities. The future of supranationalism and the fulfillment of the Federalists' dreams hung in the balance.

chapter 6

IN SEARCH OF THE ELUSIVE POLITICAL <u>RELANCE</u>

Although Federalists tried to play down the unprecedented French decision to boycott the Community, it was obvious that the crisis effectively halted further political integration. Not only did de Gaulle nip the much-heralded political *relance* in the bud, but he succeeded in wiping out the gains of two years' work as far as the *Europeans* were concerned. Even more foreboding was the possibility that France would pull out of the EEC altogether, negating two decades of European federal development.[1]

What was the root cause of the June 30, 1965, debacle? Community analysts disagreed in their assessments of blame. According to F. Roy Willis, the crisis was only a part of a "carefully thought-out campaign" geared to impress de Gaulle's "world policy" on his European partners. Other elements of the General's grand design included the exclusion of Britain from the Community, the blocking of further supranational development, withdrawal from NATO and the creation of a French "force de frappe," refusal to aid United Nations peace-keeping efforts, restoration of the gold standard, and rapprochement with Communist states.[2] Miriam Camps argued that the European Community's challenge to French leadership on the continent was at the heart of the crisis. Hallstein's unveiling of the Commission's plan to the European Parliament in March 1965 was the catalyst that hastened a crisis which would have occurred in the near future irregardless.[3] According to John Newhouse,

the French action was, on one level, a "visceral reaction" by de Gaulle
to the Federalists' attempts to limit French sovereignty. On a deeper
level, it was a product of the struggle between Federalists and Confederalists to determine what path European integration should take—the
European Economic Community or the Europe of the states.[4]

Newhouse's assessment is the most valid. The unexpected intensity
of the French reaction to the failure of the Six to hammer out the necessary financing regulations by the June 30 deadline revealed de Gaulle's
inability to reconcile his old vision of a French-dominated European confederation with the realities of the mid-1960s. Supranationalism in the
guise of the European Community was progressing inexorably. For
France, membership in the Common Market *had* become irreversible.
The French president was forced to watch this federal "monster" grow
in power and prestige at the expense of the country he had saved from
ruin in 1958. At the same time he witnessed his own scheme for a Union
of States ignominiously fail—blocked by France's five partners unless he
agreed to strengthen and safeguard the supranational institutions he so
detested. Caught in a no-win situation, de Gaulle's overreaction to the
Commission's financing package was understandable.

Supporters of the European Community were stunned by the French
"empty chair" policy. The EEC Commission's first reaction was to treat
the French action as a minor incident. Speaking before the Christian
Democratic Union/Christian Socialist Union Economic Congress in
Düsseldorf on July 8, Hallstein strongly cautioned against "dramatizing"
the situation. He defended the Commission's financing proposals, particularly those concerning the European Parliament, as "very moderate."
While admitting that the Council did not "explicitly" ask the Commission
in its resolution of December 15, 1964, "to enhance the part played by
the European Parliament in connection with budgetary questions . . . it
did so implicitly."[5]

However, by September Hallstein was publicly voicing the fears of the
Federalists. On September 24 in an address to the European Parliament
he conceded that "despite every disinclination to dramatize matters, I
think the word 'crisis' is the proper one to describe this situation." Although he maintained that the confidence and vitality of the Community
remained unshaken, and although the Parliament unanimously passed a
resolution supporting the Commission's actions, it was apparent that the
prospects for parliamentary control of the Community's "own resources"
had vanished.[6]

De Gaulle showed no sign of ending the French walkout. On the contrary, he did not confine his slashing attack to the Commission and its presumptive plan, but he challenged the rationale behind European federal institutions. At a press conference on September 9, he claimed that the crisis would have come sooner or later, since the Rome Treaties—concluded before France made her "comeback" in 1958—made France a "pawn to a predominantly foreign technocracy. . . ."

> Now, we know—heaven knows that we know!—
> that there is a different concept of a Europe
> federation in which, according to the dreams
> of those who conceived it, the countries would
> lose their national personalities and which,
> furthermore, for want of a federator . . . would
> be ruled by some technocratic, stateless and
> irresponsible Areopagus. We know also that
> France is opposing this project, which contra-
> dicts all reality, with a plan for organized
> cooperation among the States, evolving, doubt-
> less, toward a confederation.[7]

In an atmosphere made tense by growing frustration and apprehension, the Parliament met on October 20 to debate the continued French absence from the Council of Ministers. Ostensibly, the topic of discussion was the EEC Commission's Eighth Annual Report. However, Hallstein used the occasion to launch his counterattack. Charging that the crisis had been "provoked" by France, he claimed that the Rome Treaty provided "all the means necessary whereby a state feeling its interests damaged may obtain redress."[8] The extremely heated debate resulted in the suspension of the session at one point and caused the Gaullist European Democratic Union to walk out of the meeting on two occasions. This tactic was a disruptive but not a disabling one, since the EDU comprised one-tenth of the total membership of the Parliament and customarily abstained from voting on resolutions supporting further federalization.

The Gaullists were hard-pressed by the other three groups. At one point, Dutch Socialist Paul Kapteyn compared de Gaulle's proposed confederation to Metternich's concept of Europe at the end of the Napoleonic Wars—with the exception that the Austrian foreign minister was at least willing to accept the other European great powers as Austria's equals. (This assertion among other charges of a similar nature led to one of the two Gaullist walkouts.) French Christian Democrat René Charpentier charged that protectionism and nationalism would impede the Community's development. He singled out de Gaulle's use of the term *foreigners* to describe the non-French members of the EEC Commission in the president's September 9 press conference. The EDU spokesman, Jean de Lipkowski, presented the Gaullist side of the argument. He was particularly incensed at his fellow Frenchman Charpentier, whose address he found "shocking and exaggerated." He denied rumors that France would attempt to revise the EEC Treaty and ended his rebuttal by criticizing the Parliament's endorsement of the Commission's financing proposals.[9]

Ironically, while de Lipkowski was addressing the Parliament, its teleprinter was transcribing a speech then being delivered by French Foreign Minister Couve de Murville before the French National Assembly. With news of the address (which purportedly called for "a complete revision of the Treaties") spreading rapidly throughout the assembly hall, President René Pleven adjourned the session until nine o'clock that evening.[10] Couve de Murville's assessment of the state of the Community proved not to be as menacing as it sounded to the distraught members of the European Parliament. The speech was more of a reiteration of the Gaullist position on supranationalism than a statement of intent. The foreign minister emphasized that an overall revision was necessary to safeguard French interests, that Community membership was voluntary, and that the Commission had overstepped its authority by attaching political proposals to its financing plan. Furthermore, he noted that if the Six had set up a confederal system along the lines of the Fouchet Plan, the entire unhappy situation would have been avoided. As far as a solution to the present impasse was concerned, he claimed that only the national governments could reach a compromise to end France's empty-chair policy.[11]

When the European Parliament resumed its debate in the evening session, Hallstein joined many members in voicing their irritation. Italian Christian Democrat Armando Sabatini charged that France was deliberately isolating itself in a changing world. His colleague, Mario Scelba, claimed that the common farm fund had become an excuse for France to publicize its dislike for federal institutions. Speaking for the Liberal group, Pleven cited France as responsible for the crisis. (After a flurry of exchanges between de Lipkowski and his critics, the Gaullists once again left the chamber.) At the end of the debate, the Parliament passed a resolution which reaffirmed its support of the Rome and Paris Treaties while deploring the crisis and the failure of the states to strengthen the Parliament's budgetary and legislative powers and to aid in its "democratic evolution." The resolution also expressed the desire that "the European idea" would be given a "fresh impetus."[12]

The hopes of the Parliament were in vain. As in the case of the crisis of January 1963, the progress toward political integration languished for years afterwards.[13] Because the crisis of 1965 was far more severe than its predecessor, the time needed for recovery was longer. In all probability, without de Gaulle's resignation in late April of 1969, it would have taken considerably longer for another political *relance* to get under way. As it was, the outcome of the June 30 crisis—while not as destructive as Federalists had feared—nonetheless stymied any further efforts by the Parliament to convince the states to expand its authority or to consider the problem of direct elections.

The willingness of France's five EEC partners collectively to oppose the French boycott ultimately led to an uneasy compromise. Behind the leadership of West Germany, the Five invited France to join in a special Council of Ministers meeting in Brussels to analyze the existing status of the Community.[14] The concerted pressure of the Five together with the upcoming French presidential election and the unpopularity of the empty-chair policy with French farmers prompted de Gaulle to consider accepting the invitation.[15] However, up until the date set for the Council's January meeting in Luxembourg, the General left his Common Market partners in the dark as to the nature of French demands.[16]

Although the Community as a whole emerged from the crisis relatively unscathed, the European Parliament fared badly. The Luxembourg Agreements of January 29, 1966, fulfilled French requirements to a point without endangering supranationalism. On the question of majority vote, the compromise stipulated that when "very important issues" were at stake, the Council "must" attempt to continue discussions until a unanimous decision had been reached.[17] On the issue of strengthening the Commission, the agreements specified that the Commission should work more closely with the Council. In addition, the Commission was not to divulge "proposals and other official acts" prior to their communication to the Council and to the national governments. Furthermore, the Council *and* the Commission would "define methods" to control the Community's own resources and both institutions would deal jointly with Community-related foreign affairs.[18] Finally, the agreements outlined a timetable for the resumption of negotiations on farm financing regulation, membership of the single Commission, and the selection of a new Commission president.[19]

And what of the European Parliament? As Dutch Foreign Minister Luns admitted, "One of the main victims, if not the only victim of the crisis which broke out in Europe on June 30 was beyond doubt the European Parliament and its powers."[20] (Contrary to Luns's assessment, the Parliament was not the only casualty. At de Gaulle's insistence, it was agreed that Commission President Walter Hallstein would be replaced by Belgian Jean Rey as head of the single Commission.)[21] The view of the Dutch government toward any further attempts to strengthen the Parliament was shared by the Federal Republic, Italy, Belgium, and Luxembourg—that is, the best policy was to stand pat and protect what limited authority the Parliament possessed.[22] During the fall of 1965, the Five had quickly abandoned the Parliament, feeling that, logically speaking, rescuing the Community was a difficult enough task without additional complications.

For those Federalists dedicated to enhancing the status of the Parliament, it was a matter of finding yet another route to their goal. The 1960 draft convention for direct elections, technically still under consideration by the foreign ministers, had remained a dead issue since early 1963. The West German and Italian bills providing for the unilateral direct election of members of the European Parliament had gone nowhere.[23] The German measure, introduced in the Bundestag by the Social Democrats (SPD) on June 10, 1964, had been rejected after considerable discussion on May 20, 1965. The Christian Democratic Union/Christian Socialist Union (CDU/CSU) and the Free Democrats voted against the bill after hearing a negative report by Hans Furler on behalf of the Foreign Affairs Committee. The committee objected on the grounds that European elections would lose their significance if they were not held by all six states. Thus, unilateral elections would be counterproductive to the development of the Parliament. In addition, the legality of holding such elections was questionable, since the Rome and Paris Treaties clearly specified that the Councils had to agree on a uniform procedure for European elections in all six states. As far as the Italian bill was concerned, in 1965 the Italian Chamber debated a draft constitutional amendment designed to expand the chamber by twenty-four members and the Senate by twelve. These new delegates would comprise the Italian delegation to the European Parliament. This measure, like the previous Italian direct elections bills, made little headway.

If the most convenient route to a democratic Parliament was blocked, the indirect path via increased budgetary powers was equally impassable. The Commission's proposals to strengthen the Parliament's power over the purse strings had been quietly buried in the wake of the June 30 fiasco. Until January 1970, when the transition stage ended, the question of control over the Community's "own resources" was irrelevant. One path that the Parliament had not seriously tried thus far was strengthening its *legislative* powers. It had commonly been assumed that the holding of direct elections would have to precede expanded authority in this area. However, after the Luxembourg compromise, some effort was made to investigate this possibility. European Parliament member Henk Vredeling recommended before the Second Chamber of the Dutch States-General that the EEC body should center its attention on increasing its legislative authority. Dutch Secretary of State August De Block concurred and added that this move might prove of greater value than useless agitation for budgetary powers that were not forthcoming.[24]

However, for the Federalists, the momentum had been lost. At the seventh meeting of the Community institutions (the three Councils, the executives, and the Parliament) held immediately after the Luxembourg compromise, the Parliament could only voice its approval that the crisis had been resolved. Italian Christian Democrat Edoardo Martino, Gaetano Martino, and Käte Strobel presented the old arguments on behalf of the Parliament but the often-heard demands failed to rouse even the staunchest Federalists among the Council members. As Paul-Henri Spaak claimed, if the "process of disintegration" started on June 30 had continued for even a few weeks longer, it might have resulted in irreparable damage to the Community.[25]

For Europeans devoted to further development of supranational institutions, the following four years were the most depressing of nearly two decades of political integration. Unlike the stagnation of the earlier 1963 to 1965 period, the inertia of the mid-1960s was caused by a pervasive fear that any positive change involving the European Community, no matter how innocuous, might precipitate another crisis. The debates of the European Parliament on political matters during these years lacked their customary vigor. Lip service was continuously given to the old goals of direct elections and expanded budgetary powers and the EEC Council was routinely condemned for its procrastination. But the idealism was gone.[26]

This frustration was understandable, for despite an ever-increasing parliamentary bureaucracy, much output of resolutions, press statements and questions to the Councils or Commissions, and a copious amount of debate—the Parliament had progressed no further than the old Common Assembly in its pursuit of greater prestige and authority.[27] The Rome and Paris Treaties contained provisions for the Parliament's election by "direct universal suffrage," but in the first ten years of its existence, nothing had been accomplished. The Parliament still lacked a permanent home. For one week out of each month, its Secretariat set up shop in Strasbourg at the slowly deteriorating Maison d'Europe, lining the halls with crates and files of office equipment and documents brought from the Luxembourg headquarters.[28] Many of the parliamentary committees met in Brussels, necessitating a constant migration of members between Strasbourg and Brussels on the one hand and between their home capital and either Strasbourg or Brussels on the other. The expense involved in such peregrinations was enormous, not to mention the wear and tear on the unfortunate M.P. who had to divide his time and allegiance between his home constituency and his duties as a representative to the national legislature and his tasks in Strasbourg and Brussels. European elections would, of course, take care of this latter problem, since the members of a directly elected European Parliament could devote their entire time and energy to it and a European constituency. The proponents of direct elections often pointed to this fact.

What is remarkable is that the Parliament refused to give up the seemingly hopeless struggle to amount to more than a mere debating forum. Notwithstanding the tremendous work load, endless commuting, and lack of tangible gains, its members continued agitating for a strengthened Parliament. But the six governments, despite occasional pro-Community pronouncements, seemed quite willing to let affairs drift.[29] De Gaulle and Spaak had raised the subject of political union (a modified Fouchet Plan) once again. The French president had remarked at a press conference on February 21, 1966, that since the Luxembourg Agreements had allowed "the economic organization of the Six" to resume "its normal course . . . it is more advisable than ever to put political meetings of this kind onto a practical footing."[30]

However, de Gaulle's withdrawal from NATO postponed any constructive activity in this direction until the end of 1966, when the Erhard government was replaced by the Kiesinger-Brandt Grand Coalition. In December, Italian Foreign Minister Amintore Fanfani consulted the other five EEC states on the possibility of holding a Rome summit meeting in the spring of 1967.[31] Although the ostensible reason for the summit was the celebration of the tenth anniversary of the Rome Treaties, it was assumed that political union and the future of the European Community would be discussed.

The one bright spot other than the scheduled summit in the spring and the progress toward the anticipated completion of the customs union on July 1, 1968, was British Prime Minister Harold Wilson's long-awaited official declaration before Commons on May 2, 1967, that Britain would make a second bid for membership in the European Community.[32] Although Wilson had every intention of going into the Common Market at "one hell of a pace," as he colorfully phrased it, de Gaulle had other ideas.[33] He did not allow any time for the advocates of an enlarged Community to get a pro-British campaign off the ground before he made his reservations known. At a May 16 press conference, he claimed that British participation in the Community would "amount to necessitating the building of an entirely new edifice, scrapping nearly all of that which has just been built." The Common Market would be subsumed in a "free trade area of Western Europe" which in turn would be merged into an "Atlantic area" that would destroy Europe's unique personality.[34] Although de Gaulle emphasized that he was not vetoing British entry but merely analyzing whether it could succeed without jeopardizing the Community, the statement was a clear warning that his views had not changed in three years.

Notwithstanding the General's thinly veiled opposition to enlargement of the Community, Federalists considered British entry a distinct possibility in the spring of 1967. The European Parliament planned its strategy for the summit meeting with cautious optimism. In its May session, the Parliament decided to avoid making any of its customary demands for increased powers and direct elections at the summit in favor of concentrating on promoting the merger of the three communities.[35] This was despite activity in the Italian Senate on behalf of the Parliament. On April 11, seventy Italian senators had introduced a motion calling for a revival of European integration. Among other demands, the motion urged the Italian government to support and promote direct election of the European Parliament.[36]

The summit and the ceremony commemorating the Community's tenth anniversary took place on May 29, 1967, in the Salone degli Orazi e Curiazi of the Capitol Palace in Rome. Although the site selected was the room where the Rome Treaties were signed on March 25, 1957, and much was said about the progress of the past ten years, the underlying atmosphere was one of pessimism. Following the ceremony on May 29 and 30, the summit meeting was held.[37] But the meeting accomplished little of note. The six governments issued a bland communiqué that spoke of the "spirit of cooperation" that now existed and that the merger of the EEC, Euratom, and the ECSC would take effect July 1, 1967.[38]

As the normally positive *European Community* glumly noted, a "vague dissatisfaction and a deep concern about the future permeates the European Parliament. . . ."[39] During its June 19-23 session, the Parliament heard outgoing Commission President Hallstein counsel "patience," "prudence," and caution against "impetuosity" in his farewell speech:

> We all know that the climate in which we are
> working today has lost the springtime freshness
> of the fifties and the golden sixties when every-
> thing was new and everyone was carried away by
> a great new burst of energy. A little dust has
> settled on what has already been achieved and
> here and there we find weariness, lassitude and
> a certain numbness of heart and mind.[40]

The Parliament's debate on the summit and its communiqué contained a mixture of grumbling and hope. Certain members (Edoardo Martino, Furler, and Dehousse) expressed dismay over the exclusion of the Community representatives from the meeting and the unspectacular nature of the governments' joint statement. As Dehousse remarked, the summit had its "shadows and silences." Hallstein had not been invited to speak at the ceremony and the communiqué made reference to neither the EEC Commission nor the European Parliament. Yet, members of the Parliament were on the whole in agreement that the Rome meeting signaled a change of attitude on the part of France. Martino noted that the summit marked a return to the more favorable climate of the spring of 1962 when the year ahead seemed full of promise. The Parliament ended its discussion by officially stamping its seal of approval on the results of the summit with a rather meek resolution expressing satisfaction over the outcome.[41]

The Federalists' short-lived hopes that the spring of 1967 heralded the beginning of a new impetus toward European political integration were dashed once again by the inimitable French president. In his press conference of November 27, de Gaulle hammered the last nail in the coffin as far as British participation in the Community was concerned. His arguments were similar to those he outlined in his May press conference: British entry would entail such a "mutation" of the Common Market that it would cease to exist.[42] The French attitude toward enlargement and strengthening of the Community had not changed since the advent of the Fifth Republic. Two weeks before this final de Gaulle veto, French Foreign Minister Couve de Murville had remarked on a French television program that a directly elected European Parliament reminded him of "certain phases of the French Fourth Republic when there was a Parliament without a government." He also argued that the construction of the Community over the past decade had not clashed with French interests. "I would even say that the construction of Europe has been largely promoted, and probably made possible, by French policy in Europe."[43]

Such sentiments were enough to drive any dedicated Federalist into a frenzy. Adding to the depressing climate was the Kiesinger-Brandt government's increasing emphasis on seeking ties with Eastern Europe at the expense of promoting political integration. West German Foreign Minister Willy Brandt had priorities other than further federal development despite the fact that the SPD had supported direct election of the European Parliament and the strengthening of it and the Commission.[44] In pursuing his long-range goal of rapprochement with the Federal Republic's Communist neighbors, he naturally found further federalization of Western Europe a distinct hindrance since it would tend to perpetuate the division of the continent.

The unhappy state of affairs elicited a spate of dolorous articles and books on the fate of the Community. The descriptive terms commonly used in these pessimistic accounts included *stagnation, malaise, disillusionment,* and *sterility.* In his lively portrait of Western Europe in the late 1960s—*The New Europeans*—journalist Anthony Sampson painted a dour picture of the "Eurocrats" and their bleak "capital" of Brussels. Patriotism, Sampson wryly observed, while a taboo subject ten years previously, had suddenly come back into fashion due to "the thaw, the fading memories of war, and the sheer dullness of the new Europe. . . ."[45] One distinguished Dutch journalist went so far as to claim that European unification was "congenitally impossible." According to his thesis, man was born with an "identification urge" which impelled him to "lose" his identity to the nation. The urge being spent, man had no desire to become part of some larger, supranational entity.[46] Federalist Altiero Spinelli spoke of the Community as "still dominated by a fervor for projects and actions, but the flow of accomplishments threatens to dry up alarmingly." As Spinelli aptly pointed out, part of the problem lay with the Federalists themselves who had succumbed with a minimum of protest to the same "malaise" as the national governments.[47]

Perhaps the most negative assessment of the European Parliament was written by a German journalist for the *Frankfurter Allgemeine Zeitung*:

> Nothing has changed in the European Parliament.
> Groups of school children armed with pamphlets
> explaining how the Community works listen to
> the debates. A member of Parliament from
> southern Germany looks after a group of women
> from his constituency. Three Alsatian waitresses
> serve black coffee in the restaurant. At the main
> post office "Europa" postage stamps find a
> steady demand. The Telex spits out mountains
> of paper on the subjects under debate: Harmoniz-
> ing technical standards for crystal glass, the situa-
> tion in Czechoslovakia, proposals for a common
> fisheries policy, potatoes, inland waterways tech-
> nology, association with the African states. . . .
>
> Is the work of unification now wilting? Is it even
> wrecked? . . . Depressed as never before, members
> of Parliament describe the situation in military
> terms: "We are surrounded. We mustn't let the
> troops find out. Somehow, we'll get out."[48]

Certainly paranoia as much as pessimism gripped Federalists. Whereas until the mid-1960s, supporters of the Community had stressed its irreversibility and the need for a new impetus to get political integration going again, by the latter part of the decade, they were obsessed with simply preserving the gains of the past twenty years. For the Parliament, it was a matter of enduring "three or four years of drought" while conserving what water it possessed.[49]

Through 1968 to the spring of 1969, the national legislatures of West Germany, Italy, and the Benelux states escalated their criticism while the governments maintained an attitude of forced optimism. In the Federal

Republic, a large majority of the Bundestag was pressuring the Kiesinger-Brandt government to renew its efforts to strengthen the European Community. By April 10, 1968, 313 members representing all political parties had sent the government postcards backing the request of ten Bundestag delegates that the Common Market be completed by the end of 1969. Two of the ten were leading members of the European Parliament—Illerhaus and Metzger. During the June 25 session, an estimated half the members of the Bundestag called upon the government to sponsor a meeting of the EEC Council and representatives of the four nations who wished to join the Community—Britain, Denmark, Norway, and Ireland—even if France refused to attend.[50] On March 19, 1969, the Free Democrats assailed the government's European policy for allowing France to impede enlargement and further development of the Community. The Christian Democrats again raised the question of strengthening the European Parliament and the Commission.[51]

The Dutch parliament voiced a similar attitude. During the June 11, 1968, session of the First Chamber, the Dutch government was criticized for not following a more aggressive pro-Community foreign policy.[52] In the Italian Chamber of Deputies, sixty-nine Christian Democrats tabled a motion on October 7, 1968, calling on the Italian government to use its influence to convince the other five states to approve a plan for the direct election of members of the European Parliament.[53] The Belgian Chamber of Representatives and the Senate continuously pressed the Belgian government to achieve some tangible results. On February 27 and again from March 4-6, 1969, the Liberal party deplored the failure of the Six to transform the European Parliament into the institution envisioned by the authors of the Rome and Paris Treaties. The Socialists observed that the campaign for a "political Europe" had been going on for twenty years with little to show for it.[54]

Even within the French National Assembly, proponents of direct elections pressured the Six to act. In the spring of 1968, Pleven and other members of the *Progrès et Démocratie moderne* group introduced a bill which designated May 9, 1969, as the date on which French direct elections would be held. This measure also required that the government "make known the arrangements for these elections, as decided by the Council of Ministers of the Communities, before October 1, 1968." The bill further specified that if the Council members failed to agree, the National Assembly would appoint a committee to devise an electoral procedure for French direct elections.[55] The *Féderation de la gauche démocratique et socialiste* (Vals, Spénale, and Faure, among others) introduced an identical measure before the National Assembly. Both bills were referred to the Foreign Affairs Committee.

Despite the activities of the national parliaments, the political climate of the late 1960s was not conducive to further European unification. The international situation was unstable. A bipolar world had given way to a multipolar one in which Japan, China, and the Third World were significant actors. The United States was embroiled in the Vietnam War and beset by opposition to the conflict from within and without. Economic relations between East and West Europe continued to bring both sides toward détente.

Federalists liked to blame the "resurgence" of nationalism as the chief cause of the Community's dilemma, and they pointed to de Gaulle as the embodiment of this discredited and divisive force. But nationalism was not as significant a factor as it appeared. The strong pro-Community sentiment within the national parliaments reflected the general public's acceptance of supranationalism and its commitment to further development of federal institutions.

De Gaulle's continued opposition to a federal Europe was only part of the problem. By the late 1960s, the General had lost his aura of invincibility. In the presidential election of December 1965, he had been forced into a runoff election with Socialist candidate François Mitterrand. A year later, his replacement of Finance Minister Valery Giscard d'Estaing had precipitated a feud between the Gaullists and their allies, the Independent Republicans. In the 1967 elections for a new National Assembly, the Gaullists lost forty seats to retain only a slim majority. The French president's withdrawal from NATO in March 1966 was unpopular with the French and his attempts at détente with the Soviet Union were discredited by the invasion of Czechoslovakia in August 1968. His pro-Arab policies and outspoken anti-Semitism after the Israeli-Arab 1967 war further alienated a large number of French people. The student riots of May 1968 and a severe monetary crisis at the year's end foretold the approaching end of the de Gaulle era.[56]

If de Gaulle was an obstacle to political unification, the other five Community members for their part made little effort to encourage further federalization. Despite continual reassurances, the governments lacked the will and the unity of purpose to inspire another political *relance.*

The Benelux states did make some attempt to prod their partners to action. In January 1968, the three nations had issued a memorandum on the political unification impasse which stated that they had "decided to step up their political cooperation" while respecting and promoting the "development and extension" of the European Community. Although the Benelux states had no intention whatsoever of setting up yet another European institution, they hoped that West Germany, Italy, France, and other nations who wished to join would collaborate on matters not covered by the Rome and Paris Treaties.[57] Although Italy evinced interest in the Benelux Plan, West German Foreign Minister Willy Brandt preferred "cultivating Franco-German relations to avoid a crisis in the EEC."[58] The following November, Dutch Foreign Minister Luns invited the Six to meet at the invitation of the Dutch government in a major conference to discuss European unification. However, at that time the request sparked little interest.[59]

The debates of the European Parliament during the period from 1967 to March 1969 revealed a dispirited membership. Delegates reiterated the usual demands for direct elections and for increased powers. They routinely chastised the Council of Ministers for failing to fulfill its obligations under the treaties. But just as often they deplored the "stagnation" and "malaise" blocking the realization of their aims. In its March 1968 session, the Parliament celebrated its tenth anniversary. While Parliament President Alain Poher pointed to the few positive achievements of the past decade, he remarked not too convincingly that it was quite conceivable that the Parliament's growing rapport with the Council would allow the Parliament to "turn its attention once again to the scheme for elections . . . by direct universal suffrage."[60]

The Parliament found a staunch ally in Jean Rey, the new president of the single Commission. Rey proved to be as pro-Community as his predecessor, although inclined to be more low key. In his address to the Parliament on May 15, 1968, he noted that the upcoming July 1 completion of the customs union and the merger of the executives of the three communities had infused "fresh vigor into certain essential sectors of Community activity." Citing the second French veto of British entry into the EEC, he added that Federalists could not allow themselves to become "paralyzed" but should set "an example of wisdom and strength."[61]

However, the Gaullist antipathy toward federalism continued undiminished. During the July 3 session, at one point the proceedings were dominated by a heated exchange between Commission Vice-President Mansholt and Gaullist spokesman Michel Habib-Deloncle, who charged the former with meddling in the domestic affairs of France. Mansholt had reputedly claimed that the outcome of the recent French election was "a serious setback to political progress in Europe." He defended his position on the basis that, as the French government was not favorably disposed toward a strengthened, directly elected European Parliament, a strong Commission, or majority voting in the Council, it followed that the sweeping Gaullist victory in the June 23 election would impede political integration.[62]

For supporters of supranationalism, 1969 marked the beginning of the long-awaited political *relance*. De Gaulle's stunning resignation on April 28 only further invigorated a renewed interest in political unification that had begun earlier in the year. At its opening session of 1969, the European Parliament went on the offensive for the first time since the halcyon days of the spring of 1965. When the Parliament met on March 10, 1969, in Strasbourg, Communist members were present for the first time.[63] Mario Scelba, its newly elected president, delivered a strident address which proclaimed the Parliament's determination to develop into a true federal legislature:

> Under a democratic regime there is no authority unless it derives from the expression of the popular consensus. That is why we shall continue to demand with insistence that the rules of the Treaties be implemented by electing the European Parliament by direct universal suffrage. ... Together with election by universal suffrage, we shall continue to press also for powers of its own to be conferred on the European Parliament, the powers of a popular representative assembly, which today, with scant respect of the rules of democracy, are entrusted to other bodies.[64]

Scelba's speech was far more positive than the presidential statements of the preceding years. An extraordinary incident in the chamber before his election undoubtedly added a good deal of zest to this address. Federalists in the Parliament were outwardly delighted although shocked by the unexpected interruption of the proceedings by a number of youthful advocates of direct elections who rained leaflets down upon the members from the public gallery. The estimated fifty German and French students chanted antinational slogans and shouted "a federal Europe!" These self-styled "European Federalists" received a round of applause from some of the less restrained members and several of the groups of visitors in the gallery—much to the horror of the Gaullist delegation, who defiantly marched out of the assembly hall. They refused to return until plainclothes police had restored order. When the EDU members were once again seated, Italian left-wing independent Ferruccio Parri, who, as the Parliament's oldest member had been overseeing the presidential election, voiced his support of the students' ideas (although he objected to their mode of expressing them). This comment was greeted with more applause from the Socialists and further loud protests from the Gaullists. The latter condemned the actions of the "pseudo-students" and demanded an investigation into the disturbance to insure that it was not repeated.[65]

The following day, the Parliament tackled the business at hand—direct elections. After nearly nine years of demands for the states to take action, the more daring among the members advocated forcing the Council of Ministers to come to an agreement on holding European elections. As with the draft convention of May 1960, Dehousse served as *rapporteur,* in this case for the Legal Affairs Committee. The supporters of direct elections had decided to resort to the treaties for a legal basis to back up their demands.[66] Dehousse noted in his report that on May 14, 1968, he and a number of other members including Scelba, Arved Deringer, Laurent Merchiers, André Armengaud, André Rossi, and Theodorus Westerterp had tabled a motion on direct elections. This motion pointed out that Article 138,3 of the EEC Treaty authorized direct elections and that the Parliament had submitted the draft convention to the Councils on May 17, 1960, but the ministers had failed to discuss the plan. The second part of the motion required the president of the Parliament to "urge" the Council to investigate the draft convention and to "draw the ministers' attention to the first and second paragraphs of Article 175 of the treaty which read as follows":

> Should the Council or the Commission in violation
> of this Treaty fail to act the member states and
> the other institutions of the Community may
> refer the matter to the Court of Justice. . . .
>
> No proceedings . . . shall be heard unless the insti-
> tution concerned has been called to act. If within

> two months of being so called upon, the institu-
> tion concerned has not made its attitude clear,
> the said proceedings may be brought within a
> further period of two months. . . .[67]

According to Dehousse, the Council had reneged on its responsibility to analyze the draft convention and to communicate its decision to the Parliament. The important question was whether or not a *time limit* existed within which the Council had to meet its obligations. The treaty authors, he argued, envisioned a "gradual transfer of national preroga-tives" to the Parliament. Keeping this in mind, the link between the EEC having its own resources and a directly elected Parliament was obvious. Tracing the unhappy fate of the draft convention after its submission to the ministers, Dehousse dwelt on the frustration of the three following years during which the Council became less and less disposed to take direct elections seriously. He added that the revised resolution which the Legal Affairs Committee proposed in place of the May 14, 1968, motion was based on Article 175. This resolution cited the Council's neglect of the draft convention for the past six years and called on the ministers to act "without delay." Finally, Dehousse pointed out that—contrary to the views of a few members who still felt that the draft convention was adequate—the majority of those who authored the plan felt it needed to be revised.[68]

The following debate revealed a general consensus supporting the re-port of the Legal Affairs Committee. The Gaullists, quite naturally, were the exception. René Ribière, spokesman for the European Democratic Union, charged that the election of the Parliament by universal suffrage would not lead to further political integration unless it was "coupled with the whole series of measures of creating a real European constitu-tion":

> The present Treaty is now out of date and must
> be renewed in light of the experience of the last
> twelve years. A treaty providing for a real Euro-
> pean constitution with an executive also elected
> by universal suffrage, must be negotiated.[69]

Furthermore, Ribière argued, a federal European government must have a two-chamber system with the upper house representing the states and the lower house directly elected on the basis of one man, one vote. A Gaullist amendment to the resolution supporting this last demand was rejected by the Parliament. (This extraordinary demand for a "real European constitution" was designed to give the Gaullists the appearance of staunch advocates of a federal Europe governed by a strong executive while undercutting supporters of a directly elected European Parliament.)

The Socialists, Liberals, and Christian Democrats differed in their degree of support for the resolution. The Socialists were particularly pleased that, as Italian Socialist Alessandro Bermani put it, direct elections had "returned to the forefront of the Parliament's preoccupations." He noted that it was even more important that the issue "should not again be allowed to run aground."[70] Several speakers were disturbed at the legal implications of the proposed resolution. Italian Liberal Nicola Romeo questioned the ability of the Parliament to resort to the Court of Justice since the treaty specified that the Council's decision on direct elections must be made by a unanimous vote. Dutch Christian Democrat Westerterp rejected the Gaullist view of European elections but maintained that the Council probably could circumvent a confrontation with the Parliament by simply rejecting the draft convention—thus avoiding any involvement by the Court of Justice in the controversy. Westerterp returned to the old idea of each state holding its own elections.[71]

Nonetheless, the Parliament unanimously adopted the resolution.[72] Although flawed, it was a statement of intent on the part of those who were determined to rekindle enthusiasm for political integration. Little did they know that in a mere six weeks, an event of extraordinary proportions would stir the Six from four years of lethargy to embark on the much-desired political *relance.* That momentous event was the resignation of the European Community's bête noire—Charles de Gaulle.

chapter 7

THE CYCLE STARTS ANEW

Until his sudden resignation, Charles de Gaulle remained an insurmountable obstacle blocking any further supranational development. The General's vision of Europe had remained unchanged over the decade. Despite the setback to his confederal scheme in the early 1960s and the Federalists' continuing calls for a strengthened Community, he still embraced the idea of a union of states. On March 4, 1969, former Prime Minister Michel Debré, now foreign minister, reiterated the old Gaullist position on Europe. Responding to journalists on the "Meet the Press" television program, he observed that "relations between Eastern and Western Europe" were "improving" despite the invasion of Czechoslovakia. The French rejection of further federal development thus was justified: "What we are striving for is closer bonds between the nations of Europe so that they may achieve greater independence in relation to the other major powers of the world."[1]

Debré's statement helped to lay the groundwork for de Gaulle's meeting with German Chancellor Kiesinger toward the middle of that same month. Noting that the European Economic Community "could be doing better" and that détente was progressing, de Gaulle maintained that European cooperation (along the lines of the Fouchet Plan) was even more imperative than before. As he had argued so often, he insisted that this all-encompassing cooperation—in economic, political, and social matters—must be based on the state, not supranational institutions.

Whereas any European nations who wished to do so might join such a confederation, allowing these states to join the European Community would "be tantamount to abolishing it."[2]

Although de Gaulle's successor, Georges Pompidou, shared the General's concept of Europe, he was far less intransigent and much more the politician. Publicly, he was willing to take a moderate stance.[3] During his election campaign (May 15 to June 15), Pompidou talked of maintaining ties with the United States while continuing to pursue closer relations with the East European states and the Soviet Union. In regard to European integration, he carefully straddled the fence. While espousing the need for "the creation of common political machinery," he cautioned against putting up "the roof . . . before the walls. . . ." Yet he called for a summit conference of the heads of the six Community states to "see how all this can be set going once more." He also claimed that he was ready to reopen negotiations for British participation in the Community.[4]

This change of heart on enlargement of the Community was not really a concession to the Federalists. British entry would no longer inconvenience France after 1970. The common agricultural policy was in operation. Britain would make an excellent market for French farm surpluses. In addition, Britain was willing to accept the EEC Treaty and gave indication of accepting the Gaullist vision of a confederal Europe.[5]

Pompidou's position on European unification and British entry owed much to the avowed federalism of his chief opponent for the presidency. Moderate Alain Poher, longtime member and former president of the European Parliament, campaigned on a strong pro-integration platform which included enlargement of the Community and the holding of a summit conference to spearhead another political *relance.* Poher also called for a European defense community (this was opposed by Pompidou) and for the direct election of the members of the European Parliament.[6]

Although Poher was not considered a serious threat to Pompidou's election, he nevertheless garnered 41.78 percent to the latter's 58.21 percent of the vote on the second ballot.[7] This was impressive considering the disunity of Pompidou's opposition. With a substantial part of French public opinion disposed toward further European unification, the new French president was pressured to make good his campaign promises. Furthermore, he was far from deaf to the charges of the Federalists and the other Community states that France stood in the way of political integration. Accordingly, at the July 22 meeting of the Council of Min-

isters, France called for a summit conference at the end of the year at
The Hague for the purpose of assessing past integration efforts and launch-
ing a new political *relance*.[8] Thus, in a matter of months, France appeared
to be the driving force behind a renewed effort for further economic and
political integration whereas previously she had been the major obstacle.
Federalists hailed this new state of affairs as the beginning of a new
era. Those who were members of the European Parliament pressed on
with even greater vigor in their attempt to force the Council of Ministers
to consider direct elections. On May 7, shortly after de Gaulle resigned,
Parliament President Scelba presented the Council with the Parliament's
March resolution concerning the ministers' failure to approve a plan for
European elections. Scelba also reminded the ministers of the treaty provisions respecting the Court of Justice.[9] In addition, he repeated the Parliament's demands for budgetary powers, for representation of the Council
at parliamentary sessions, and for explanations as to why the Council dis-
regarded the Parliament's recommendations.

Supporters of direct elections were considerably encouraged by actions
taken by the Luxembourg, Italian, and Belgian parliaments. On April 24,
the Luxembourg Chamber of Deputies passed a motion which called
upon the government to table a bill as soon as possible outlining procedures for the direct election of Luxembourg delegates to the European
Parliament.[10] On June 11, a "Peoples Bill" on the direct election of
Italian representatives was introduced in the Chamber of Deputies and in
the Senate. The bill provided for the elections to be based on proportional
representation and a single constituency. Only members of the Italian
parliament would be eligible as candidates, and half of those elected
would come from the Senate and half from the lower house. The elections would not coincide with national elections.[11] (The bill was referred
to the Internal Affairs Committee and the Foreign Affairs Committee.)
The Belgian bill, introduced by two Christian Democrats on June 27,
resembled the Italian measure.[12]

Apart from the parliamentary activities of the Six, another encouraging
development was the pro-federal declarations of the British government
and also of *The Times,* which published two favorable editorials on supranationalism on May 7 and 21. In the former instance, on April 28, the
British and Italian governments had issued a joint declaration on European
integration which stated that "Europe must be firmly based on democratic institutions" and that "the European Communities should be sus-

tained by an elected parliament, as provided for in the Treaty of Rome."[13] In regard to *The Times,* the first piece—"A European Election"—called upon the British government to propose the election of members of the European Parliament by universal suffrage. Direct elections were seen as necessary if the Parliament were to be "taken seriously." The second piece—"A Time for Unity"—observed that the "mechanics of setting up an elected European Parliament with power to bring the Eurocrats to account and control the Community's funds would inevitably be immensely complicated":

> It is, however, a task that cannot wait for the slow evolution of the Economic Community, especially as left to itself the Commission may well become less and less happy about being submitted to parliamentary control.[14]

However, such pronouncements failed to move the national governments. After two more months of Council inaction, Scelba repeated the Parliament's demands to Council President Luns on July 22. At the Council meeting that same day, the ministers instructed the Committee of Permanent Representatives to look into the matter of direct elections— thus avoiding any possible complications with the Court of Justice.[15]

During the four months leading up to The Hague conference, it became apparent from information emanating from the Council bureaucracy that the French position was unchanged, that is, that direct elections were to be the "culmination of European integration." According to the French view, the Parliament's legislative powers must be increased before direct elections could be held. Among other objections raised by the national experts was that the draft convention of 1960 was more than nine years old and portions of it had to be revised. (As previously noted, most of the members of the Parliament agreed that revision was necessary.)

Furthermore, "apart from questions of principle," the major problem involved the number of delegates allotted each state. The French government did not accept the 426-member figure or the distribution fixed by the 1960 draft convention. Rather, it preferred the size of each delegation to be based on population—hence EDU leader Habib-Deloncle's insistence on the principle of "one man-one vote" during the March 1969 European Parliament session on direct elections. (The Benelux states were naturally opposed to proportional representation. The Netherlands and Belgium, however, were willing to adopt this system at a later date when federalization had progressed to the point that a "Chamber of States" was established to balance a directly elected "People's Chamber.")[16]

Questions were also raised about the transition period which was outlined in the 1960 draft convention. Most of the national analysts were in favor of abolishing this innovation. Other technicalities of a non-serious nature were discussed, including the date on which the elections would be held. However, no date was recommended.[17]

Notwithstanding the pessimistic report of the Council experts, Federalists fully expected that direct elections and the entire issue of strengthening the Community's institutional structure would be a topic of discussion at the December summit meeting. Outwardly, the attitude of the six states toward further supranational development appeared to be positive if obscured by generalities and platitudes. What was apparent, however, was that neither France nor West Germany was willing to undertake immediate steps to strengthen the Community.

The French position was relatively clear. The West German attitude continued to be ambivalent. Further federalization of Western Europe was at odds with the Kiesinger-Brandt government's attempts to develop closer ties with the East European nations. Political cooperation and completion of the Common Market were desirable, but stronger Community institutions could prove a threat rather than a boon. In a journal article published in May 1969, Kiesinger maintained that economic and political union "must" remain separate:

> As things now stand, the Economic Community
> will and must be far wider in scope than the
> Political Community. Anyone, for example,
> who believes that the Economic Community will
> develop into a Political Community, automatically
> excludes the neutrals from possible participation
> since a political European Community must of
> necessity work out a common external policy
> and a common approach to matters of world
> policy. . . .

According to Kiesinger, although there was much to criticize in the Gaullist vision of Europe, the General's "basic idea was the right one:"

> If we really want a Political Community, then
> the large number of applicants of participants

> in widely differing political circumstances are
> bound to alter the nature of a Community re-
> garded by so many as the nucleus of a Political
> Community.

While claiming that in the future a "European Federal State" was "essential," Kiesinger described this system in the most nebulous terms as a
group of nations "arranged amicably" around a political mechanism in
a broad-based common European market.[18]

Foreign Minister Brandt, soon to be chancellor himself, voiced similar
views. On July 2 in an address before the WEU General Affairs Committee
and the chairmen of the foreign affairs committees of the WEU Assembly
and the European Parliament, Brandt stressed that the government was
not considering an ambitious "German initiative." "In future talks and
negotiations, European questions must be raised anew within the limits
of what is possible." According to Brandt, the Six should undertake three
principal aims—the fulfillment of economic union through the completion of the Common Market, the enlargement of the Community, and
the renewal of efforts toward "closer political cooperation." Although
he added that an attempt should be made to "extend the powers of the
European Parliament," the composition of his audience necessitated this
declaration.[19] On October 28, after his address to the Bundestag, the new
chancellor was criticized by CDU/CSU Chairman Rainer Barzel and,
ironically, former Chancellor Kiesinger for abandoning the Community
as a vehicle for political integration.[20]

Although West Germany and France continued to hold back on the
issue of strengthening the Community institutions, Federalists' expectations rose throughout the fall as the summit conference approached. The
clamor from all quarters demanding that the conference achieve dramatic
results rose also. Maurice Faure, former French foreign minister and
European Parliament member, claimed that progress toward political integration could not be revived without the adoption of majority voting in
the Council of Ministers and the consideration of a plan for direct election of the members of the European Parliament.[21] In late November,
the Socialist parties of the Six jointly called for a "positive outcome"
to the summit conference. The Socialists' definition of "positive outcome"
meant a commitment to expand the budgetary powers of the European
Parliament, to hold direct elections, and to reform the decision-making
authority of the Council to "bring it into line with the provisions of the

treaties."[22] The European Union of Christian Democrats also issued a declaration on the upcoming summit that echoed the demands of the Socialists:

> As long as Europe is not definitely on the path
> to political unification and as long as a United
> States of Europe has not been created, the
> nations of Europe will not be in a position to
> play their full part in international affairs.
> This conference at The Hague should lay down
> the basis for economic and political union.[23]

The Commission, for its part, recommended that the six governments review "the functioning of all Community institutions" as soon as possible or at least by the end of negotiations on enlargement of the Community.[24] The Commission also submitted an eight-point program of proposals designed to strengthen the Parliament's legislative and budgetary powers.[25] As for the Parliament itself, it held an extraordinary session in Luxembourg on November 3 to devise a resolution for consideration at the conference. The resolution ultimately adopted urged the national governments to "determine in an unambiguous manner" the goals of European integration. Among its recommendations, the Parliament called upon the governments "to make arrangements, on the basis of the draft presented by the European Parliament in 1960 for election of its members by direct universal suffrage, and in any case, to adopt a procedure whereby the Council and the European Parliament could come together to produce a definitive text."[26]

By December 1 when the six heads of state met at The Hague, it was mandatory that the meeting at least appear to fulfill all expectations. Symbolically, the site for the conference was the same hall in which the Congress of Europe had met more than two decades earlier. In the spirit of the occasion, the conference participants outdid themselves in making lofty statements on behalf of intergovernmental cooperation on all levels.[27] But the performances were lackluster. While Pompidou observed that economic union, enlargement of the Community, and the strengthening of its institutions were the "three problems" facing the states "at the present time," he was decidedly reticent on the last point.[28] Brandt's statement was little better. According to the chancellor, foreign policy was the chief consideration, that is, "the question of the peaceful organiza-

tion of Europe, negotiations with the countries of Eastern Europe and our
interests with regard to the conflict in the Middle East. . . .":

> While we concentrate on narrower issues, we can-
> not shirk the decisions which are needed if our
> fellow citizens are to appreciate once more that
> Europe is not merely a matter of market regula-
> tion. . . . We would all surely agree that our
> Community should not constitute another bloc
> but should rather be a model which could serve
> as a component of a balanced all-European peace
> order. It is in this spirit that the Federal Republic
> of Germany is seeking an understanding with
> the East in cooperation and agreement with its
> partners in the West.

In his lengthy, nine-part statement, Brandt devoted two brief paragraphs
to the institutional development of the Community. He recommended
that the "Council's method of working be tightened up, that the Commission's executive functions be widened where required (and) that the
powers of the European Parliament be broadened, particularly by giving
it budgetary control." Furthermore, he observed that "the structure of
the Community must be brought into line with the principles of parliamentary control. In doing this, we must not lose sight of the principle of
direct elections laid down by the Treaty."[29]

Italian Premier Mariano Rumor's reference to direct elections was
pointed but brief. Luxembourg Prime Minister Pierre Werner remarked
on the link between the direct election of the European Parliament and
the expansion of its powers but argued that the existence of this link
"should not prevent us from acting in either field."[30] Belgian Prime
Minister P. J. S. de Jong and his Dutch counterpart, Gaston Eyskens,
took a similar approach.

The final communiqué issued by The Hague summit belied the noncommital nature of the participants' statements. It sounded impressively
positive, noting that the Community had reached a turning point in its
history with the end of the transition period of the Common Market,
and that the six governments reaffirmed "their belief in the political ob-
jectives which give the Community its meaning and purport, their determination to carry their undertaking through to the end, and their confidence in the final success of their efforts." The communiqué also

reaffirmed the concept of intergovernmental cooperation ("political union") and the principle that the Community was and would remain "the original nucleus" of European integration. The six governments agreed to cooperate on economic and monetary matters, technological development, atomic research, social concerns, Community enlargement, and various other aspects. In the area of foreign affairs, the foreign ministers would investigate how cooperation could be achieved. On the matter of strengthening the Community institutions, the communiqué stated that "in due course" the financing of the Community's budget in accordance with Article 201 of the EEC Treaty would be achieved and the European Parliament's budgetary powers expanded. In addition, the communiqué stated that "the problem of the method of direct elections is still being studied by the Council of Ministers."[31]

For Federalists waiting for some clear-cut program of attack designed to accelerate quickly the sputtering unification process, the summit was a distinct disappointment. As Walter Hallstein later remarked, the conference had presented the Six with an invaluable opportunity. "What could be more appropriate, therefore, than to seize this moment to give 'political integration' a definite nudge? It did not happen."[32] Hallstein correctly placed the blame on Pompidou and Brandt. Both were willing to further the development of the Community and to pursue intergovernmental cooperation as long as such actions complemented rather than conflicted with national interests.

The reactions of the members of the European Parliament were mixed but, on the whole, dissatisfaction with the summit conference's "accomplishments" was the rule. At the annual joint meeting of the Parliament, Council, and Commission on December 11, the four political groups expressed their views. The Christian Democrats and Socialists cited the conference for providing political unification with a new impetus. But both groups disparaged the lack of emphasis on the strengthening of federal institutions. The Dutch head of the Liberal and Allied group, Cornelis Berkhouwer, spoke of the meeting as "an unfinished symphony." True to form, the European Democratic Union pronounced the summit results to be completely satisfactory. The Communists, as was becoming their custom, called for a total overhaul of the Rome and Paris Treaties to make the Community truly democratic.[33] Although few in number and not yet a political group, the representatives of the Italian Communist party made their presence known by taking an uncompromisingly radical, pro-federal stand that generally put them at odds with everyone else. With their penchant for jargon-laced declarations, they gave the impression of protesting too much.

Also during the joint meeting, Fernand Dehousse presented an interim report of the Political Affairs Committee on direct elections. He noted that "two major events would be certain to influence the development and solution of this problem"–the granting of, first, budgetary and, next, legislative powers to the Parliament and the enlargement of the Community. He recommended that the Council set up a liaison body with the Parliament to look into these matters.[34] (This view was indicative that Federalists still were unsure as to whether strengthening the Parliament should precede direct elections or vice versa. The old "chicken or egg" argument remained very much alive.)

By 1970, it appeared quite likely that at least budgetary powers for the Parliament were forthcoming. In late 1969, the Commission had drawn up proposals concerning increasing the Parliament's power over the Community's purse strings. The Parliament had revised these proposals to give them more teeth. It was these modified proposals that the Commission presented to the Council.[35] The transitional period had ended and on February 5-7, the Council met to agree on the formal legal terminology of the regulation for financing the common agricultural fund. The Community was to have its own resources. This meant that the Council had to agree on a formula for strengthening the Parliament's budgetary powers.[36] Meeting again in Luxembourg on April 22, the Council formally adopted amendments to the EEC Treaty modifying the budget process. This so-called Luxembourg Treaty allowed the Parliament to fix its own budget. During the "initial phase" until the end of 1974, the Parliament could propose modifications to the draft budget of the Community. These revisions could be rejected only by a majority of the Council members. After 1975, the Parliament would have control over the disposition of the available portion of the budget. Unfortunately, the Parliament would have authority over only the Community's administrative expenditure after 1975–or roughly 4 percent of the total Community budget! As the Luxembourg Treaty stated, "the Council retains full powers in respect to 'operational expenditure,' amounting to 96 percent of the budget."[37] There was no provision allowing the Parliament to reject the Community budget in its entirety–a legislative privilege that Federalists viewed as crucial to the Parliament's development.

Needless to say, the majority of the Parliament's members was not pleased with the arrangement. However, half a loaf was better than none. On May 13, the Parliament adopted a resolution which noted that it was willing to adopt a "highly conciliatory attitude" for the time being. The Council's budgetary provisions were seen only as "the first step towards the wider powers for the European Parliament in the spirit of The Hague conference."[38] Whereas the spirit of The Hague summit still appeared to be alive as far as cooperation on foreign policy and economic and monetary policy were concerned, on the issue of European elections, it was another matter.[39]

Leading Federalists continued to extol the necessity and the inevitability of direct elections. On March 3, Commission President Jean Rey told an audience at the University of Stuttgart Hohenheim that a directly elected European Parliament would be a reality by the end of the decade.[40] On March 27, French Senate President Alain Poher claimed that a "political Europe" would not exist "without a European Parliament elected by direct universal suffrage and endowed with real legislative powers."[41]

But the all-important position of the French government remained substantially unchanged. Speaking in Strasbourg on June 28, Pompidou sounded much like de Gaulle:

> Europe will be built with a respect for the personality of the states which belong to it, or else it will not be built at all. Europe can only be built if it maintains close and friendly relations with all countries and in particular with the Eastern countries in our own continent. Europe must not appear as a bloc, but as a powerful instrument for union, relaxation of tension and cooperation.[42]

At a press conference on July 2, Pompidou restated this view, and spoke of the desirability of a "European confederation," adding that "the best way to render such a confederation impossible is to try to move too quickly. . . . But we must also remember the hard legacy of the past and our present geography which cannot be eliminated and which has not made a united Europe over the centuries. . . . Patience and faith, that is my motto. . . ."[43]

The West German government's attitude toward further political integration—federal or confederal—remained decidedly reserved. Responding to a question on direct elections posed by a CSU representative to the

Bundestag, Parliamentary Secretary of State Ralf Dahrendorf responded that the Brandt government advocated European elections but "its attitude so far has not met with a favorable response from all the member states of the Community. At the conferences due to be held in the near future, we shall insist that the idea of Europe be given a further solid foundation through direct elections for the European Parliament."[44] In like manner, Foreign Minister Walter Scheel attempted to quiet the fears of the European Parliament. In an address before the Parliament in Strasbourg on September 16, Scheel denied that the Federal Republic's pursuit of détente with the Soviet Union would "hinder" political integration.[45] The Soviet-German non-aggression treaty of August 12 had intensified Federalists' fears that West Germany was abandoning political integration.

The other four EEC governments made occasional declarations in a similar vein. The Rumor government continued to maintain that direct elections were "Italy's main objective."[46] In the Parliaments of the six states, Federalists continued to introduce measures or amend existing bills on unilateral European elections. On June 10 in the Dutch Assembly, Theodorus Westerterp tabled a draft law on the direct election of Dutch representatives to the European Parliament.[47] On June 30, Francis Vals and Spénale and other French Socialists introduced yet another bill setting a new date (May 9, 1971) for French direct elections.[48]

However, although the topic of European elections was part of the agenda of the Council of Ministers on three different occasions in 1970, nothing transpired. Part of the problem remained the unwillingness of France and the disinterest of West Germany. But an additional factor was the preoccupation of the Six with discussions on intergovernmental cooperation in foreign affairs and economic and monetary policy and also with negotiations on enlargement of the Community.

With regard to foreign affairs, the Community states set up a committee headed by Belgian Etienne Davignon to draw up a report. This report, which was approved by the ministers on July 20, recommended that the foreign ministers meet twice a year. In emergency situations, the ministers or national leaders would meet in extraordinary session. These meetings would be prepared by a political committee (the Davignon Committee) at least four times a year. The committee could *invite* the Commission to participate when Community issues were on the agenda. Section 6 of the report dealt with the European Parliament's role in such a confederal framework. As the report noted, "public opinion and its spokesman (the Parliament) must be associated with the construction of the political union, so as to ensure that it is a democratic process." To this end, it recommended that the foreign ministers hold an informal meeting every six months with the European Parliament to facilitate an exchange of views. In addition, once a year the president of the Council would make a report to the Parliament.[49]

This weakened version of the old Fouchet Plan did not generate much excitement. Rather, it was the prospect of enlargement of the Community that was cause for considerable celebration on the part of the Federalists. British participation in the Community remained one of their chief goals from the origin of the European Coal and Steel Community. De Gaulle's resignation had finally opened the door. With the British economic picture brightening after several years of instability, Harold Wilson called for an election in June 1970. The EEC entry was a major campaign issue, but Wilson found himself in the peculiar position of curbing his former enthusiasm over joining the Community in order to appease left-wing members of the Labour party who had remained consistently anti-Common Market.[50]

Wilson was forced to fall back on the old "wait until the price is right" strategy. As it was, the 1970 election campaign revealed only the vaguest of distinctions between the Labour and Conservative positions on the Community. A cartoon in the *Birmingham Post* succinctly summed up the situation in its depiction of a buoyant Edward Heath and an equally enthusiastic Wilson standing on diving boards high above the "Common Market" swimming pool. Wilson, leaping from the board, was shouting, "I'm keener than you to keep out!" His rival, about to take the plunge himself, was crying, "I'm keener than you to go in."

To bolster his nebulous position, Wilson unexpectedly released in February 1970 a controversial White Paper. Titled "Britain and the European Communities, an Economic Assessment," the report attempted to analyze the cost of British entry into the EEC under certain assumptions. Citing that "new development" since 1967 would increase the cost of joining considerably, the White Paper avoided making any concrete conclusions on the basis that entry negotiations were not yet complete; it simply suggested that Britain's overall balance of payments costs for joining would range somewhere from 100 to 1,100 million pounds.[51] The White Paper was immediately assailed by Wilson's critics as confusing and completely worthless.

Despite the favorable upturn in the British economy, British voters—
in a remarkable upset—returned a Conservative government. Edward
Heath, the new prime minister, rested on a comfortable thirty-seat
majority. The Cabinet was comprised of firm pro-marketeers. The election was followed a few days later by the opening of serious British
negotiations with the Six in Brussels.[52]

With enlargement of the Community in the offing and the Council of
Ministers still indisposed toward direct elections, Federalists considered
the possibility of somehow coordinating the various existing unilateral
plans for European elections.[53] It was assumed that France would have
to be left out of such a scheme despite the introduction of several bills
on unilateral direct elections in the French Assembly. Pompidou appeared
unlikely to have a change of heart in the near future. During a press conference on January 21, 1971, the French president spoke of a future
"real European government" and observed that until this federal government was a reality, "speculations concerning the European Parliamentary
Assembly are in my mind quite pointless":

> One cannot imagine these powers being in-
> creased until there is a real executive power
> opposite it. As for designating its members,
> they are at the present time the representatives
> of various nations, nominated in random, almost
> arbitrary number. We can all, so long as we respect
> the Rome Treaty, have them designated as we see
> fit; nothing can be changed, neither the nature
> of their mandate nor the extent of their powers
> nor their limitation.[54]

Although unilateral elections appeared to be a viable way to circumvent French intransigence, the insurmountable technical problems posed
by such an approach were obvious—not to mention the inevitable question that would arise in regard to the legality of such a move. The treaties
specifically called for the Council of Ministers to approve unanimously
a "uniform electoral procedure" with elections held simultaneously in all
six states.

The only alternative was to wait until Britain, Ireland, and Denmark
joined the Community. In the meantime, on June 30, the Commission
established a fourteen-member special group of constitutional law experts to examine, among other institutional issues, the strengthening of

the powers of the European Parliament.[55] This committee submitted
its report at the end of March 1972. The so-called Vedel Report (named
after chairman Georges Vedel, dean of the Faculty of Law and Economic
Sciences at the University of Paris) was a lengthy document of 124 pages
and eight chapters.[56]

The section on strengthening the Parliament offered several ambitious
and highly controversial recommendations. Chief among these was the
assessment that "there is no need to wait until the Parliament is directly
elected before increasing its powers." For the first time, the "chicken-
egg" argument was firmly laid to rest. The report outlined a two-stage
program designed to provide the Parliament with greater authority. During the "first stage," which was to begin immediately, the Parliament
would achieve the power of "co-decision" with the Council of Ministers
over (1) revision of the treaties, (2) the use of Article 235 of the EEC
Treaty (extension of the treaty over areas not covered by it), (3) admission of new members to the Community, and (4) the ratification of the
Community's international agreements. Furthermore, the Parliament
would have the authority to make a "suspensive veto" (the power to
force the Council to review a decision) over a wide range of Community
activities including the common farm policy, transportation policy, short-
term economic policy, common trade policy, the European Social Fund,
special treatment of foreign nationals, and the working conditions of
Community officials. During "stage two," the Parliament would be given
an absolute veto and "the same power of co-decision" as over the first
four areas.

The report surmised that since this right of co-decision made parliamentary approval of Council decisions mandatory, the Parliament would
be consulted on a regular basis and might be asked to propose amendments to drafts of Community measures in advance. The report also
recommended that the Parliament approve the selection of the president
of the Commission.

The Vedel Committee saw the Parliament's lack of legislative powers
as the key to its continued ineffectiveness. According to the report, the
Parliament "has 'worked in a vacuum' and made almost no impact on
press, public opinion and the political parties" due to its lack of "real
power." In regard to budgetary control, the committee noted that the
Luxembourg Treaty of April 22, 1970, accomplished next to nothing as
the Parliament could do little more than check budget figures rather than

determine what these figures should be. To correct this oversight, the Parliament should have the right of co-decision over "adopting the budget itself."

Finally, in regard to direct elections, the committee advocated that unilateral direct elections should continue to be pursued in the national parliaments and suggested that the six governments agree on a system for European elections "as soon as possible" after January 1, 1973, when the delegates of the new Community members took their seats in the Parliament.[57]

In addition to the Vedel Report, other ideas were advanced as to how to increase the power and influence of the Parliament. One of the most counterproductive suggestions, although it was made in good faith, was put forward by *The Economist* and also by *The Times.* The former, in an article titled "Make It a Moving Circus," argued that there were two difficulties involved in strengthening the European Parliament—French opposition and the Parliament's chief meeting site of Strasbourg. Although little could be done to immediately eradicate the former, both problems eventually could be solved if the Parliament held its sessions in each of the nine national capitals. According to *The Economist,* the Parliament had to emerge from the "wilderness" if it were going to attract attention and high-caliber delegates:

> If Europe is a success, if these peripatetic parliamentary meetings are themselves a success, then a European capital with a stationary parliament holding real powers might one day emerge. But if they want to make that dream come true it is up to the "Europeans" to stop sitting so frightened, or in their fear so arrogant, in remote recesses like Strasbourg.[58]

The Times suggestion was along the same lines. In a piece titled "Parliament on the Move," *The Times* claimed:

> A peripatetic parliament as a transitional measure . . . is an attractive idea. It should further commend itself to the French if it were decided that Paris should be the seat of the Parliament, while still reserving to Strasbourg a share of the honors. . . . Paris would then be the political center of the

Community, and Brussels the economic center,
with London, as the natural bank, the financial
center.[59]

Federalists had high hopes that the Vedel recommendations, direct
elections, and other various proposals to strengthen the Parliament would
be discussed by a summit conference of the six heads of state and the
leaders of the three new Community members scheduled for October
1972. It was felt that a number of the Vedel proposals—such as parliamentary approval of the nomination of the Commission president—could
be easily implemented without any revision of the treaties. During its
July 5 session, the European Parliament adopted a resolution which expressed its expectation that the conference would "give a decisive drive
to the dynamic development of the Community." The resolution called
for expansion of the Parliament's powers along the lines of the Vedel
Report and demanded that the national governments carry out their
responsibility in regard to direct elections. The resolution also emphasized that the issue of direct elections was distinct from the question
of greater authority for the Parliament and that the latter could not be
deferred until European elections were held.[60]

However, the summit conference held on October 19-20 in Paris pre-
dictably resulted in much talk and little action. Pompidou originally had
called for the meeting to discuss economic and monetary policy. It was
doubtful for a time that the meeting would take place at all or if it did,
that nothing would be accomplished. The spirit of The Hague summit had
long since evaporated. Economic and monetary union had been undermined by a severe monetary crisis in May 1971 caused by a flood of surplus
dollars into West Germany. The Brandt government had chosen to resort
to unilateral corrective measures, much to Pompidou's irritation. The crisis
was exacerbated by the Nixon administration's August decision to impose
an import surcharge and to renounce the gold exchange for the dollar.
France and Germany responded with varying remedies. To compound the
problem, Britain floated the pound. Other disagreements surfaced.
Pompidou's suggestion that the Community's Political Secretariat be
located in Paris was not well-received by France's partners. Furthermore,
the Benelux states' desire to weaken the Council of Ministers was not welcomed by the French government.

However, to cancel the summit conference would have been political suicide for Pompidou since National Assembly elections were approaching in the spring. Thus, the conference was held although nothing was expected to be accomplished.[61] Strained relations notwithstanding, the addresses of Pompidou and Brandt echoed the cooperative tone of their statements at The Hague nearly three years earlier. On institutional matters, they remained as noncommital as ever. British Prime Minister Heath spoke of a "gradual evolution" of the role of the "Assembly" (the European Parliament).[62] The sixteen-point program issued by the nine governments at the end of the conference restated the usual goals for intergovernmental cooperation in various areas. Point 15 observed that the "Community institutions were proving themselves" but that they could be "improved to boost their efficiency" and called for the Council and the Commission to "implement promptly the practical measures to strengthen the Parliament. . . ."[63]

The Parliament responded to the summit conference communiqué during its November 15 session with a typical resolution commending the "resolve" of the nine governments to strengthen the Community and to hold eventual direct elections while deploring that no action had been taken in either instance.[64]

It was anticipated that the addition of the eighteen-member British Conservative party delegation to the European Parliament in January 1973 would act as a catalyst to hasten the Parliament's evolution into a genuine federal legislature. The Conservatives were outspokenly smug about Britain's history of strong parliamentary tradition and the "superiority" of the British Parliament—that predecessor of all legislatures—over its continental counterparts. The sixteen seats allotted the Labour party were to remain unfilled after Labour M.P.s overwhelmingly endorsed the party leadership's decision to boycott the Parliament by a vote of 140 to 55. Although a proposal to fill the Labour seats temporarily for a two-year "trial period" was considered, Harold Wilson bowed to the demands of left-wing party members. At the October annual party conference, 1,200 delegates had adopted resolutions demanding the "renegotiation" of the terms of British Common Market entry and the holding of a national referendum on renegotiation when Labour again headed the government.[65]

As if in preparation for the Conservatives' expected attempts to model the European "assembly" along the lines of the British Parliament, French Socialist Georges Spénale slapped the Commission with a motion of censure on November 16. Budget Committee chairman Spénale charged the Commission with "betraying its commitments" by not proposing ways to increase the Parliament's budgetary powers after 1975.[66] The unexpected motion—the first to be tabled by an executive of the Parliament and the first such motion in twenty years—shocked Spénale's colleagues. The Parliament had always outwardly supported the Commission despite occasional differences. Furthermore, the nine-man Mansholt Commission was a lame-duck executive which was to be replaced by the new fourteen-member enlarged Commission on January 1, 1973.[67] Having made his point, Spénale withdrew his motion of censure at the Parliament's December session. But his action indicated the beginning of a trend toward a more activist, less acquiescent Parliament.[68]

For two decades, *Europeans* had awaited the participation of Britain in the federal experiment. Now enlargement of the Community was to be a reality. Certainly, as far as institutional development and intergovernmental cooperation were concerned, little could be said for the three years since The Hague summit conference. Psychologically, the European Community had come a long way. From the December 1969 summit of the Six to the October 1972 conference of the Nine, there had been much said and negligible accomplishment. However, pronouncements of the national governments were positive if vague. January 1, 1973, marked the dawn of a new era. The road leading toward a federal Europe, so often blocked, now appeared free of major obstacles. Political integration was slowly gaining momentum. For supporters of a real European legislature, now was the time for action.

chapter 8

"SUCCESS" THE SECOND TIME AROUND

When the enlarged European Parliament met for the first time on January 16, 1973, the Conservative delegation did not disappoint those who expected a major shakeup in the Parliament's routine operation. The new British members along with the Irish delegates were outspokenly critical of the low-key style of the debates, the stress on unanimity for adopting resolutions, and the Parliament's willingness to support the Commission in order to present the Community's critics with a united front. The new members were also unfamiliar with the continental tradition of basing debates chiefly on reports compiled by special committees.[1] As Conservative delegation head Peter Kirk commented, "from a Westminster point of view," the weakness of the European Parliament's procedure lay in the "highly formalized" nature of the debates. "Most of the real discussion goes on in committee, and, in the plenary debate, priority is given to the official spokesmen of the party groups." According to Kirk, the result of this system was bland proceedings which lacked "spontaneity."[2] He also noted that there was "much less yahoo behavior than in Commons." The necessity for members to use headphones in the multinational Parliament added to the dullness of the debates. As Kirk observed, the "deadpan expressions" of the delegates under their headsets prompted speakers to "repeat their points three and four times to get them across."[3] According to Michael Yeats, one of the ten members of the Irish delegation, he and his colleagues were "shocked" by the subdued continental parliamentary style.[4]

Accordingly, the new delegations—particularly the British Conservatives—decided (as Kirk put it) "not to hide [their] light under a bushel."[5] To begin with, the British delegation decided not to lose its identity through merging with one of the already established political groups. The eighteen members joined with two Danish delegates to form a European Conservative group which boasted nearly as much unity as the old Gaullist European Democratic Union did in its heyday.[6] The mostly Italian Liberal group had wooed the British, but the Liberals were too "conservative" for many of the more progressive British members. The Christian Democrats were logical partners, but many of the Italian members, conscious of the Socialist-Communist challenge back home, did not wish to be associated with Britain's "big business" party. A marriage of convenience with the Gaullists was too farfetched.[7]

Second, the Conservatives immediately presented the Parliament's Bureau with a number of suggestions designed to make the Parliament more like its British ancestor. This so-called Kirk Memorandum proposed the creation of an hour-long "Question Time" on current issues and more vigorous use of the motion of censure.[8] Concerning the former proposal, Kirk felt that Question Time should be reserved for individual members and not be controlled by the political groups.[9] The memorandum also recommended the establishment of a special committee to examine the Parliament's procedure to see how the rules could be amended to improve their effectiveness. In addition, it suggested that a member should have the opportunity to request of the president at the beginning of each session that the Parliament hold an emergency debate on a particular issue. Such emergency debates would take place at the end of the session and would not last longer than three hours. Furthermore, the Parliament could set aside a thirty-minute to one-hour time slot for "backbenchers' " debates.

In regard to the committee system, the memorandum recommended that the committees ought to be smaller in size, meet less often for longer periods of time, and concentrate more on the long-range policies of the Council and the Commission. The committees would also hold hearings in the style of the United States Congress and delegate more technical matters to subcommittees.[10] On the Parliament's budgetary powers, the memorandum recommended that a permanent committee be established to examine the accounts of the Council and the Commission. This auditing body would have the power to demand evidence from top-ranking Community officials. Finally, the Kirk proposals observed that the Parliament should eschew the practice of unanimity to portray accurately the differences of opinion on European policy within its membership.[11]

The excitement generated by the reform-minded British lasted throughout 1973. Question Time was instituted in February and the Parliament stepped up its demands for increased budgetary and legislative powers. On February 14, the Conservatives lived up to their advance billing by winning the tabling of a motion which claimed that the Parliament should "examine major issues of foreign policy and propose common lines of action by member states and that debates on these issues be held in the presence of representatives of the Council and Commission."[12]

This new aggressive spirit led to a number of developments. On June 4, the Parliament instructed its Political Affairs Committee to draw up a new report on direct elections.[13] On June 22, the Political Affairs and the Budget Committees met in Brussels to analyze the Commission's proposals for strengthening the Parliament's financial authority. The Commission came under fire for its "inadequacies" in this area and for not incorporating the "explicit provision" that the Parliament be empowered to reject the entire draft budget.[14] On June 29, the Parliament adopted a resolution which demanded that it be given "real powers of decision and control" over the Community budget since the national parliaments were "losing all direct powers" over the Community's expenditures.[15] On July 11, the practice was started of having national ministers appear before Parliament committees. At a special meeting in London, the British ministers for industrial development and the transport industries answered questions posed by the Parliament's Regional Policy and Transport Committee.[16]

In the meantime, the Parliament's debates remained aggressive in tone. During the July session, Kirk threatened to propose a motion of censure after Commissioner Petrus Lardinois did not show up to answer questions on the Community's farm policy.[17] The July session also marked the first time that a French Communist delegation sat as members of the Parliament.[18] Although the French Communists ultimately joined with their Italian counterparts in a single group, they did not agree with the Italians on a variety of issues, especially on the concept of a federal Europe. The former retained a hard-line Leninist orientation and an anti-

supranational stance that long had been abandoned by the Italian Communists, whose fervent federalism and willingness to work with the existing
political system made them unique among the West European Communist
parties. The combined Communists, in addition to an Italian Independent
Socialist and a Danish left-winger, still totaled one less than the required
fourteen members needed to constitute a political group. However, on
October 16, the Parliament amended the rules of procedure on this matter.
While the fourteen-member minimum was maintained, in cases where the
group in question was comprised of members from at least two states, a
minimum of ten members was sufficient.[19]

However, despite the cosmetic changes and the new strident language
of its members, the Parliament's stature remained unchanged. The Community information service and the national presses continued to trumpet
that—as *The German Tribune* phrased it—"The sterile European Parliament
of the sixties no longer exists."[20] The unfortunate reality of the situation
was not yet apparent. In fact, one could argue that enlargement of the
European Community and its Parliament had considerably lessened the
chances of a federal system developing even in the distant future. The
British had always viewed a united Europe as a loose confederation based
on voluntary intergovernmental cooperation. Likewise the Irish and Danish
governments, while happy to reap the economic benefits of participation
in the Common Market, anticipated no sacrifice of national sovereignty
to the benefit of a supranational government based in Brussels.

Federalists had hailed the resignation of de Gaulle as the salvation of
the Schuman-Monnet experiment. But Pompidou's decision to revive
European economic and political integration and to allow British entry
had subtly altered the unification process. The French government no
longer had to suffer public and world displeasure due to its pursuit of an
anti-federal European policy. Britain had willingly taken over the job of
the Community's bugbear. This left France free to quietly mold European
integration along the old Gaullist lines first promoted by Debré in the
early 1950s and later by the Fouchet Plan in the early 1960s. The Hague
summit conference of December 1969 had been a tentative step in this
direction. The Paris summit of October 19-20 had begun to lay the
groundwork for what was soon to be termed "European Union" (a more
modern euphemism for 1960s-style "political union"). In the Paris
summit communiqué, the nine governments had determined that the
foreign ministers should meet four times a year and that they should

draw up a second report (to supplement the Davignon Report) on political cooperation by June 30, 1973. The communiqué had also set an ambitious timetable for the completion of economic and monetary cooperation (December 31, 1980), the creation of a European Monetary Cooperation Fund (April 1, 1973), and the establishment of a Regional Development Fund (December 31, 1973).[21]

However, such intergovernmental cooperation was theoretically premised on the assumption that all nine states would be willing to place the good of the whole before national interests. It was this false assumption that was slowly and effectively eroding the concept of a federal Europe. Very few of the old champions of a supranational Europe such as Schuman, Monnet, Spaak, or Dehousse were still alive or, if living, actively able to campaign for their ideals as they had once done. Many supporters of a directly elected European Parliament were new faces who could not be classified as "Federalists" in the old sense in that they envisioned a genuine European legislature governing an integrated Western Europe. Rather, they saw European elections as a necessary development in order to provide 260 million Europeans with some semblance of control over the enormous sums generated and spent by the European Economic Community.

For some of this new breed of *European,* a federal Parliament with real legislative authority over Community activities was seen as a threat to national interests and to the smooth operation of the anticipated European Union. Significantly, when the five Irish Fianna Fail members of the Parliament finally decided to join a political faction in mid-1973, their choice was none other than the Gaullists. The resulting supergroup of twelve Gaullists, a handful of Liberal defectors, and a few Belgian Independents made the newly christened "European Progressive Democrats" the third largest group in the Parliament. The pact greatly aided the Gaullists, who, since the disastrous March 1973 election, had been reduced to twelve members and therefore were not an official political group.[22] Although Fianna Fail members claimed that the new EPD was "left of center," this was a matter of semantics.[23] On the issue of political integration, their general approach was compatible with their French partners. As Fianna Fail member Michael Yeats observed, the old Gaullist Union of States concept was a viable path to European unification.[24]

The confederal approach to political integration progressed a step further with the release on July 23, 1973, of the foreign ministers' second report on political cooperation. The report proposed that the ministers meet four times a year or whenever necessary. A committee of national "political directors" would meet "frequently" to lay the groundwork for the ministerial meetings. In addition, a "Group of Correspondents" would be created to study "the implementation of political cooperation" as well as "problems of a general nature." In certain cases, this group would prepare the meetings of the Political Committee. Furthermore, "Working Parties" of senior officials of the ministries of foreign affairs would be established to deal with the specific tasks. A "Presidency" would oversee the implementation of directives of the ministers and of the Political Committee. On the subject of foreign policy, the report proposed that the governments consult each other on "all important foreign policy questions" and "work out priorities." No government would adopt a particular policy until it had consulted its partners.

✽   Not unexpectedly, the section of the report dealing with the European Parliament recommended no significant changes. It was proposed that the Parliament's Political Committee and the ministers would hold four colloquies a year. The president of the Council would "continue, as in the past, to submit to the European Parliament, once a year, a communication on progress made in the field of political cooperation." The last section of the report was devoted to a reassurance that the "political cooperation machinery" dealt with intergovernmental cooperation only and thus was "distinct from and additional to the activities of the Community. . . . Both sets of machinery have the aim of contributing to the development of European unification." The report noted that, whereas the proposed confederal system would deal with current problems and the formation of medium and long-range planning, in matters concerning Community affairs, "close contact will be maintained with institutions of the Community."[25]

The ministers' report raised more questions than it answered, particularly on the delicate issue of the Community's role in "European Union." De Gaulle had been forced to shelve the Fouchet Plan ten years previously when the Benelux states protested that the scheme would abandon the Community as the foundation of an integrated Western Europe. But Pompidou could compromise—at least on the surface—while de Gaulle could not. During a press conference on September 27, Pompidou was asked if the "European Union" was more than a community and if it was "a step toward a kind of European State with its democratic control, its government and its economic and political powers." The French president's vague response indicated to more astute listeners that France's position on a supranational development remained unchanged:

> It is a problem of adjectives: European Union and
> European Community could mean the same thing but
> it so happens that the Community is called economic
> and that the European Union which we defined
> in its broad outlines during the summit conference
> lacks this adjective. Consequently, this union goes be-
> yond, it wishes to go beyond, the economic issue. . . .
> In regard to control, well, it is a difficult question.
> Every time solutions are suggested we realize that they
> are not adequate. I will simply say that so long as
> there is no real European executive, there can be no
> real European Parliament. This does not detract
> from the parliamentary assembly in Strasbourg but
> it sets the limits within which this role cannot at
> present help being restricted.[26]

In the fall of 1973, the fate of direct elections appeared considerably more tenuous in light of Pompidou's position and the nebulous phrases of the ministers' report on political cooperation. In a question to the Council on October 17, an independent British member of the Parliament requested that the ministers explain whether they intended to "resume consideration" of direct elections or "do nothing." The Council's reply was evasive at best.[27] With no assurances, the Political Committee under the direction of Dutch Socialist Shelto Patijn continued to work on a new draft convention for direct elections.

Europeans had a golden opportunity to put West German Chancellor Willy Brandt on the spot when he addressed the Parliament in Strasbourg on November 13. But Brandt, displaying the usual pro-Federalist rhetoric, adroitly sidestepped any commitments. He repeated the old cautions that supranationalism would not develop overnight but only through evolution and proposed that the national governments "shorten the time tables" for economic and monetary, social, and political union. In regard to the latter, he maintained that a "proper sense of proportion" was necessary:

> After twenty years of efforts to achieve European
> integration we should all by now have learned that
> the functional rather than the constitutional method

> is more likely to get us home. I do not mind if one
> calls this pragmatism. The goal is clear. It is, as I
> have put it from time to time, a sensibly organized
> European government which in the fields of common
> policies will be able to make the necessary deci-
> sions and will be subject to parliamentary
> control. . . .

Brandt also took the opportunity to repeat the long-standing official West German policy on federalism:

> The European states will transfer to that govern-
> ment those sovereign rights which in the future
> can only be effectively exercised together; the
> remaining rights will stay with the member states.
> In this way we shall preserve both the national
> identity of our peoples which is the source of
> their strength and add the European identity
> from which fresh energies will ensue.[28]

Finally, the chancellor claimed that the European Parliament "must be given a real say in Community matters." He did not elaborate as to how this feat was to be accomplished. The reference to direct elections was, in a word, discouraging. While observing that the treaties called for direct elections, he also noted that "we have no right to lapse into paralysis as long as we have not reached this goal."[29]

If supporters of European elections had any hopes of pressuring the national governments into actually setting a future date, these hopes were dashed and further progress stymied by the October Arab-Israeli War and the resulting energy-related economic crisis.[30] To make matters worse, the British public appeared to be having second thoughts about participation in the Community. The Great Debate that raged in Britain prior to the vote in the House of Commons on British entry had intensified rather than abated. According to a poll published by *The Times,* the number of Britishers opposing EEC membership had doubled to 29 percent in the six months since January 1973. Pro-Community voters had decreased from 31 percent to 23 percent.[31] Rumors were afloat that a few of the senior officials in the British mission to the Community were claiming that membership might prove an economic disaster for Britain. Ominously, at the annual Labour party meeting in October, delegates voted by only a small margin against a resolution which opposed Britain participation in principle. In addition, the conference reaffirmed the Labour policy of

boycotting the European Parliament and the intention of holding a national referendum once a Labour government was back in power.[32]
    An additional unsettling factor was the negative attitude of the United
States toward the Community. The debacle in Vietnam and the Water-
gate imbroglio had turned the Nixon administration inward. A huge U.S.
balance of payments deficit, devaluation of the dollar, and increasing
protectionism in the Congress led to growing tension between the United
States and the Community states by 1973. Presidential National Security
Advisor Henry Kissinger had ruffled the feathers of the United States'
West European allies by calling for a reassessment of the Atlantic Alliance.
In an address on April 23 before Associated Press editors in New York,
Kissinger stressed that the status of Western Europe had changed dramatically from a position of total dependence on the United States in
the early postwar period to one of aggressive independence in the détente
era of the late 1960s and early 1970s. He noted that the United States
had supported and still did support European integration, but that this
very support had "produced new realities that require new approaches.
. . ." He accused the EEC nations of economic protectionism and of being
unfairly critical of U.S. defense, economic, and monetary policies.[33]
    President Richard Nixon's May 3 report to the Congress on "U.S.
Foreign Policy for the 1970s" was a restatement of the earlier Kissinger
address:

> Now, America and Europe are challenged
> to forge a more mature and viable partner-
> ship. . . . Throughout the postwar period, the
> United States had supported the concept of a
> unified Western Europe. We recognized that such
> a Europe might be more difficult to deal with
> but we foresaw manifold advantages. . . . We
> expected that unity would not be limited to
> economic integration, but would include a
> significant political dimension. We assumed,
> perhaps too uncritically, that our basic interests
> would be assured by our long history of coopera-
> tion, by our common cultures and our political
> similarities.[34]

    However, by the end of the year, Kissinger was bluntly expressing his
disapproval of the Nine's moves toward "European Union" without the
sanction of the United States. According to Kissinger, the "cumbersome

machinery" established to facilitate this cooperation—the European summit conferences—"highlighted" the differences among the nine states rather than otherwise. Specifically, he was annoyed at what he called the "recent practices" of the Community states to "present the decisions to us as a fait accompli not subject to effective discussion."[35]

These external and internal pressures put a tremendous strain on the Community states. On the one hand, the British vacillation and the Nine's dependence on the United States and on Arab oil fostered closer cooperation among the Community members while the same forces undermined the creation of common policies envisioned in the "European Union."

Needless to say, when the heads of state met at Copenhagen on December 14-15, direct elections were not on the agenda. (The European Parliament adopted one of its typical pre-summit resolutions during its December 12 session. As usual, the summit conferees ignored the Parliament's demands for speedy action on development of Community institutions. Yet, for *Europeans,* this was not unexpected, as it was becoming more and more common in the Parliament's debates for members to complain that the institutionalized summit meetings were beginning to replace the Community machinery.)[36] The crisis-permeated atmosphere of the two-day meeting was rendered more chaotic by the unannounced appearance of the foreign mininsters of several Arab states (Algeria, Tunisia, the Sudan, and the Emirates). The final communiqué issued at the close of the conference understandably did little more than restate the pledges of the two earlier summits. An annex to the communiqué dwelt on the necessity of concerted action to deal with the energy crisis.[37]

Indeed, in the following months, the term *crisis*—long a staple of Community vocabulary—dominated the prolific publications emanating from Brussels. As Peter Kirk wryly commented before the Parliament at the year's end, "a cynic" could conceivably claim "that the Community is in a permanent state of crisis and that it rather thrives on crises as a form of energy that drives it forward." "But," admitted Kirk, "I think few of us would deny that the crisis with which it is faced at the present moment is one of slightly greater proportions than those we have been accustomed to over the previous years."[38]

The critical economic situation was hampered by the domestic political instability of the Community members. Edward Heath's Conservative administration was trounced in shocking fashion in the February general election and a minority Labour government pledged to "renegotiation" now charted Britain's course. In Italy, the Christian Democratic-dominated government was forced to reshuffle yet again as Mariano Rumor constructed a three-party coalition that was Italy's thirty-sixth government in thirty years.[39] With French President Pompidou in ill health, leading politicians in France were jockeying for position. In Belgium, the Netherlands, and Denmark, coalition government was the rule while the West German Brandt government—the most economically and politically stable of the Community states—was plagued with increasing left-wing radicalism. Even in the legislatures of Ireland and Luxembourg no political party could claim a majority.[40]

As a result, the term *Community solidarity* replaced strengthening federal institutions in the pronouncements of the Commission and in the debates of the European Parliament. The twin dilemmas of inflation and recession and the continuing oil crisis took precedence over European elections and increased budgetary powers for the Parliament—although Federalists were quick to point out that political cooperation among the Nine could be aided only through stronger supranational institutions.[41] According to Altiero Spinelli, one of the last of the old-guard Federalists, the Community was little more than "the Europe of bureaucrats, the Europe of secret sessions, the Europe of perpetual intergovernmental negotiation, the Europe of the refusal of democratic participation. . . ."[42]

Many *Europeans* were becoming increasingly disenchanted with the confederal approach to political unification typified by an endless procession of fruitless summit meetings. During the May 14 session, the Parliament adopted a resolution which stressed that the root cause of the critical economic situation lay partly in the "excessively technical approach" of European economic integration and in the weakening of the Community's institutions. In addition, the failure of the national governments to carry out the promises made at the past three summit meetings had a deleterious effect on European public opinion. The Parliament called for a "fresh impetus" which would lead to the holding of direct elections, the restoration of the powers of the Council and the Commission which were being subsumed by the new confederal apparatus, economic and monetary cooperation, and closer intergovernmental cooperation.[43] During the July 9 and October 16 meetings, several of the more outspoken members of the Parliament assailed the governments over the direction of political integration. German Socialist Ludwig Fellermaier argued that the summit meetings resulted merely in declarations while the governments continued

to retard the Community's development.[44] Shelto Patijn, in charge of
the new convention on direct elections, complained about the tendency
of political unification to take two different routes. "We seem to have
reached a cross-roads in the development of the Community. One road
is the broad highway of political cooperation but the other, the Euorpean
Community, seems to be a dead end."[45]

By the autumn of 1974, however, there were some indications that
the national governments were finally going to take some tentative steps
in the direction of institutional reform. Both West Germany and France
had new heads of state who were eager to pose as champions of European
unification. On May 16, Helmut Schmidt succeeded Brandt as chancellor
when the latter resigned under fire after a top aide was arrested as an East
German spy. Three days later, Valery Giscard d'Estaing was elected president of France. As future events were to reveal, Schmidt and Giscard
d'Estaing were no more *European* than their predecessors. But this
was not apparent when the new French president invited the other eight
heads of state to Paris for a summit conference on December 9-10. The communiqué issued at the meeting's end contained a concrete pledge that the
states would hold European elections "at any time in or after 1978"
(point 12):

> The heads of Government note that the election
> of the European Assembly by universal suffrage,
> one of the objectives laid down in the Treaty,
> should be achieved as soon as possible. In this
> connection they await with interest the pro-
> posals of the European Assembly on which they
> wish the Council to act in 1976. . . . The com-
> petence of the European Assembly will be ex-
> tended, in particular by granting it certain
> powers in the Community's legislative process.[46]

The one sour note in the statement on direct elections was the reservations of the British and Danish governments inserted into the communiqué.
According to Harold Wilson, while Britain did not wish to prevent her
partners from holding European elections, Britain could not make a commitment before renegotiation of the British terms of Common Market
entry and the holding of a referendum on British participation in the
Community. The Danish government declined to explain its statement
that it could not be ready to hold the elections by 1978.[47]

In addition to point 12, the communiqué revealed the governments' intention of speeding up progress toward a confederal system. According to point 3, the nine heads of state would hold "Councils" three times a year or when necessary. An administrative secretariat would be established to handle the affairs of the "European Union." Lastly, because no one really knew what "European Union" would entail, Belgian Prime Minister Leo Tindemans was entrusted with the unenviable task of defining just what the term meant.[48]

In this more encouraging atmosphere, the Parliament met on January 14, 1975, to debate Patijn's draft convention for direct elections. The document was little more than an updated, revised version of the 1960 Dehousse plan. The number of delegates for the directly elected Parliament was set at 355. Belgium had 23 seats; Denmark, 17; Germany, 71; France, 65; Ireland, 13; Italy, 66; Luxembourg, 6; the Netherlands, 27; and the United Kingdom, 67 (Article 2).[49] The rationale behind this interesting figure was that too large a Parliament would be unwieldy and that strict proportional representation would discriminate against the smaller states. The 1960 draft convention had simply tripled the number of members of the original Common Assembly for a 426-member chamber. However, such an approach in 1975 would result in a 594-member Parliament. It was felt that the 355-member figure was a realistic one and that a Parliament of this size would be "large enough for the present."[50] The Political Committee adopted a complex formula based on population to come up with the distribution outlined in Article 2. According to the formula, based on the 1973 population of states:

a. Up to a population of 1 million each State receives 6 seats.
b. States with a population between 1 million and 2.5 million are given 6 further seats.
c. Up to a population of 5 million, each State receives 1 further seat for each additional 500,000 inhabitants.
d. For a population between 5 million and 10 million each State receives 1 further seat for each additional 750,000 inhabitants.
e. For a population between 10 million and 50 million each State receives 1 further seat for each additional 1 million inhabitants or part thereof.

      f. For a population exceeding 50 million, each
         State receives 1 further seat for each additional
         1.5 million inhabitants or part thereof.[51]

    The convention retained the "dual mandate," leaving it up to the individual member or the national parliament to decide whether a member of the national legislature could also be a delegate to the European Parliament. Article 7 specified that the Parliament would draw up a uniform electoral procedure by 1980. Until that time, however, the states would determine their own procedures. The states also were left to decide which political parties could participate in European elections (Article 8). (The Communists were opposed to this provision since they felt this would discriminate against the election of Communists to the Parliament.) Regarding the date for elections, Article 9 required that they be held on the same day in all the states but allowed some flexibility in that a state could spread the elections over two days or hold them one day earlier or later. The date for the first elections was set for "not later than the first Sunday of May 1978 (Article 13). It was felt this would allow enough time for ratification by the national assemblies. Notably, the controversial "transitional period" incorporated into the 1960 document was omitted since it was no longer necessary to retain links with the national legislatures through maintaining the appointment of a portion of the Parliament's membership.[52]

    The debate on the new draft convention was relatively more subdued than the final vote indicated. A total of 106 members voted for the convention with only 2 Danish Socialists opposed. Of those in favor, 35 were Christian Democrats, 33 were Socialists, 13 were Liberals, 17 were Conservatives, 6 were Progressive Democrats (5 of whom were Irish with one Dane), and 2 were Independents. Not unexpectedly, of the 17 abstentions, 9 were Communists, 6 were French Progressive Democrats, and 2 were Danish Liberals.[53]

    The size of the Parliament was a major sticking point. The Political Affairs Committee had originally proposed a 550-member figure but an amendment by the Legal Affairs Committee to cut this number to 355 barely passed over the opposition of the Conservatives, Liberals, and a number of Christian Democrats. The Socialists felt that the smaller figure was more realistic. Another controversial issue was the convention's failure to map out a uniform electoral procedure. The Communists in particular wanted the plan to incorporate a system based if possible on proportional representation. But most of the Parliament was willing to accept the convention, warts and all, in order to place it before the Council of Ministers as soon as possible. As Patijn remarked at the close of the debate, most of the twenty-five speakers who had voiced their views agreed with him that the convention was as realistic a plan as was possible under the circumstances. Of the seventeen amendments proposed, most were of a technical rather than a substantive nature with six of them dealing with Article 2, that is, the size and distribution of seats.[54]

However, with the Council of Ministers, it was a different story. A special "ad hoc group" was established under the direction of the Committee of Permanent Representatives to analyze the draft convention. The experts proceeded to compile a list of questions that they felt needed answers.[55] The most important of these naturally dealt with the number and distribution of seats. Another major concern involved the single election date. For example, France would have preferred to coordinate European and national elections. Britain and Denmark still viewed the 1978 election date as impractical and wanted the choice of the date to be left to the governments. They both were also concerned over the dual mandate issue, although for different reasons. The British saw joint membership in the national and European Parliaments as unrealistic from a work-load standpoint while the Danes saw the link as indispensable to insure that the party strength in the national assembly reflected that of the European body.[56]

If progress on the draft convention was slow, at least there were some positive developments on other fronts. Much to the *Europeans'* relief, the Wilson government approved the renegotiated terms of British entry into the Common Market in March and in June the British public voted to remain in the European Economic Community. This meant that the members of the Labour delegation could take their seats in the European Parliament. By joining the Socialists, the Labourites made this political group the largest in the Parliament (66 members). The Christian Democrats numbered 51; the Liberals, 25; the Conservatives, 17; the European Progressive Democrats, 17; the Communists, 15; and 7 members remained unaffiliated with any political group.[57]

Another encouraging sign was the ministers' approval on July 22, 1975, of a draft treaty which created a Court of Auditors and which gave the Parliament the right to reject the entire Community budget. (Earlier, on March 4, a conciliation committee comprised of representatives of the Council of Ministers and of the Parliament was established to iron out disagreements over the budget.)[58] The Parliament, while reluctantly accepting the new budget provisions, characteristically complained that the revisions in the treaties did not go far enough. Also, the Parliament was critical of the Council's tendency to consider supplementary budgets rather than lumping all expenditure in a single package since this weakened the Parliament's financial power.[59]

However, progress toward direct elections continued to plod along. During the July 16-17 Brussels summit meeting of the newly christened "European Council" (the new institutional term for the nine heads of state), the date for direct elections was reaffirmed and the Council of Ministers was instructed to present yet another report by the year's end.[60] In November, a delegation from the Parliament met with the ministers to defend the draft convention. At that time, the Danish government withdrew its general reservations to direct elections but maintained its opposition to a single election date and its support of the dual mandate.[61]

Meeting in Rome on December 1-2 for the third of the scheduled 1975 summit conferences, the European Council examined the ministers' report on the draft convention and announced that the elections would be held "on a single date in May or June 1978. Any country which at that date is unable to hold direct elections shall be allowed to appoint its representatives from among the elected members of its national parliament." The European Council accordingly instructed the ministers to "continue examination" of the convention and to submit another report so that the governments could approve the final plan for direct elections at the next European Council meeting.[62]

It was evident by late 1975 that British opposition would be the chief obstacle to holding European elections in the spring of 1978. On December 4, Harold Wilson announced the European Council's decision on direct elections to the House of Commons. While stating that he had "made it clear" at the December summit that Britain accepted "in principle the commitment to direct elections in the Treaty of Rome," he stressed that he had added "that we required a further period for consultations with political parties in this House and for consideration of the matter by Parliament before we could adopt a final position about holding direct elections ourselves as early as 1978."[63] The following February, the Labour government issued a Green Paper on direct elections that restated the official position while emphasizing that the British government "was not committed to any of the proposals made for holding European elections":

> Seven of the nine Member States have accepted
> a target date of May or June 1978 for the hold-
> ing of the first elections. HMG have some doubts
> about the practicability of so early a date. All
> nine Member States will require time to decide
> upon and make legislative provision for, the
> arrangements to be followed in each country
> and it remains to be seen whether this work can
> be completed in time for the elections to be
> held on the target date. HMG take the view
> that the necessary consultations and procedures
> must be carried out in an orderly way and
> should not be rushed. Nevertheless they believe
> that Parliament will wish the work to be com-
> pleted with all reasonable speed.[64]

The Green Paper, however, did little to quiet the fears of many Labourites who believed that a directly elected European Parliament was the first step toward a European federation that would hinder the implementation of future Labour programs in Britain.[65]

Supporters of the elections refused to be too discouraged by the balky British. As European Parliament President Spénale optimistically pointed out, Britain did not "oppose the principle of European elections" and it was quite probable that both Britain and Denmark would "come round" to the position of their seven partners by 1978.[66] But as the first months of 1976 passed by, it began to appear that the Council of Ministers would fail to agree on a finalized version of the draft convention, making ratification by the national parliaments by the spring of 1978 impossible. The major cause of the stalemate was the ministers' failure to agree on the composition of the directly elected Parliament. Compounding the dilemma were the different electoral systems of the nine states. In Belgium and Italy, for instance, the legal voting age was twenty-one (for the Italian Senate, twenty-five) while in France, Germany, Ireland, Luxembourg, the Netherlands, and Britain, the minimum age was eighteen. In Denmark, the voting age was twenty.

The system of voting for the lower chamber varied considerably. In

Belgium, Denmark, and Italy, voting was by party lists in multimember constituencies on a proportional basis. In Luxembourg, voting was by party list but in four electoral districts on a proportional basis. In the Netherlands, voting was also by party list but in a single national constituency on a proportional basis. Ireland used a single transferable vote system in multimember constituencies. In France, elections were by a single vote in a single-member constituency. If a candidate received no absolute majority, a second ballot was held between the leading candidates. A proportional vote was not assured in such a system. The German system was even more complex. Each citizen had two votes, one for a candidate in a single-member constituency and the second for a party list resulting in a proportional vote. Britain used a single vote-single constituency system requiring only one ballot. A candidate needed only a simple majority to win.

Of the nine states, only Britain and France did not follow a proportional system. However, for European elections France preferred a proportional system based on population since this would favor the larger states. Ireland, on the other hand, suggested a formula which would benefit the smaller states.[67] Thus, while the French plan envisioned a 284-member Parliament that, for example, gave West Germany 65 seats, France, 55 seats, Ireland, 6 seats, and Luxembourg, 3 seats; the Irish version projected a 384-member body with 74, 68, 18, and 9 seats respectively.[68]

Various compromise formulas were suggested to break the impasse on the size of the Parliament and the distribution of its seats. On February 9, the Italian government presented a 361-member plan that benefited the smaller states somewhat, especially Ireland and Denmark. Not unexpectedly, the Italian plan pleased no one. Britain preferred the French formula. British Foreign Minister James Callaghan dryly noted that if Ireland's scheme were adopted, a state of three million people would have greater representation than Scotland with its five million citizens or Wales with its population of four million. Denmark clung to the Irish plan while Ireland rejected the Italian formula as providing Luxembourg with special treatment which would not be extended to Ireland.[69]

In addition to the disagreement over the composition of the Parliament, the governments still could not agree on an election date or even whether the European Parliament should be designated as a "parliament" in the final convention or as the "European Assembly." (The latter term was ultimately chosen.) In the meantime, the Gaullists and Communists

in an unholy alliance were gearing up an anti-direct election campaign in
France while in Britain Foreign Minister Callaghan announced the creation of a special committee to investigate European elections—an action
which was seen as a "delaying tactic."[70]

Obviously, there was no chance that the European Council could approve
the draft convention at the April summit in Luxembourg as scheduled.
Even if the final document had been ready, direct elections would have
taken a back seat to more pressing matters. The Community was gripped
in a continuing monetary crisis that was undermining the EEC's own
currency system.[71] The failure of the much-publicized previous summit
meetings to produce many tangible results, especially in the economic
sector, had weakened the concept of intergovernmental cooperation as
a means of unifying Europe. The April summit conference proved no exception to this trend. Hoping to save face, at least on the direct election
issue, French President Giscard d'Estaing suggested as a last-minute expediency that the size of the 198-member Parliament be left as it was for the
time being. However, this "Giscard Plan," as it came to be known, did not
meet with an enthusiastic reception.[72]

Supporters of direct elections were once again plunged in gloom.
There was much grumbling over the ineptitude of the national governments. The European Parliament sent a special deputation of the heads
of its political groups to make its feelings known to the Council of Ministers.[73] During the April 7 session, spokesmen for the Socialists, Christian Democrats, Liberals, and Conservatives took turns castigating the
European Council. British Socialist Michael Stewart commented that
there was no longer any need to worry that this non-treaty institution
would usurp Community institutions since it obviously was too ineffective to do so. Dutch Christian Democrat Alfred Bertrand remarked that
the heads of state could not even agree enough to issue a final communiqué while British Conservative Tom Normanton charged that the European
Council's impotence had damaged the Community's world image. Characteristically, Italian Communist Fazio Fabbrini claimed that, unlike the
rest of the Parliament, the Communists were not surprised by the summit's
outcome, since they had always known that the European Council would
prove a failure. Only the French Communists and the Gaullists were pleased
with the turn of events.[74]

While the *Europeans* continued to complain and call for action, the
governments continued to thrash out a compromise. On May 4, the

Belgian government proposed a 401-member Parliament which would be partially based on a proportional system with special treatment for Luxembourg. According to this plan, half of the Community's population would continue to be represented by the present 198 members while the remaining 203 seats would be determined proportionally on a ratio of one seat per 654,051 votes.[75]

This plan proved to be unacceptable, as did the "Giscard Plan." The latter was withdrawn without fanfare after the French president visited Britain on June 21-25.[76] A compromise was finally attained on July 12 when the European Council settled the twin questions of the Parliament's size and the distribution of the seats. The directly elected Parliament would have 410 members. West Germany, France, Italy, and Britain would have 81 seats each; the Netherlands, 25 seats; Belgium, 24 seats; Denmark, 16 seats; Ireland, 15 seats; and Luxembourg, 6 seats.[77] The British and Danish governments took the opportunity at the meeting to reaffirm the reservations they had expressed at the December 1975 summit conference.[78]

Although the Council of Ministers was expected to sign the convention for direct elections on July 27, this deadline went unmet. Finally, on September 20, the ministers signed the official text. The act was comprised of sixteen provisions. Article 2 specified the Parliament's size and the distribution of the seats while Article 5 allowed for the dual mandate. Article 8 stipulated that each state could set the date for the elections provided that date fell within the same period, that is, from Thursday morning until the following Sunday evening. Other than these revisions, the Parliament's own provisions remained relatively intact.[79]

It now remained for the nine national parliaments to ratify the act and to draw up enabling legislation (providing electoral systems) by the spring of 1978—a formidable feat, indeed, considering the noisy opposition of the Gaullists and French Communists and the growing antipathy of the Labour party in Britain. A mere ten days after the ministers signed the act authorizing direct elections, the delegates of the annual Labour party conference in Blackpool voted in defiance of party leadership by a two-to-one margin to oppose European elections on the basis this might result in a "new superstate." According to the resolution, such a superpower would "further weaken the British people's democratic control over their own affairs" and make realization of the Labour party's "basic programs . . . increasingly remote."[80]

But for the moment, these ominous warnings were lost on the Federalists who had worked years—in some cases, decades—for a directly elected European Parliament. The chasm had been bridged and the road ahead appeared rocky but passable. The Community information services immediately began churning out all one needed to know and more about the Parliament and the May 1978 "Euro Elections." The date was accepted as gospel. Doubts were present but well hidden behind the determined optimism that so typified the dedicated *European*. Yet whether the Parliament had scored a tremendous victory or won a minor skirmish in its battle to evolve into a European legislature remained to be seen.

chapter 9

PANACEA OR PANDORA'S BOX?

The spring of 1978 came and passed.
The European Parliament still remained an assembly of 198 indirectly
chosen representatives. What happened? Ostensibly, the cause of the
postponement of European elections was the British failure to make
electoral arrangements in time for the elections to be held as scheduled.
However, it could easily be argued that the nine governments assumed—
or at least hoped—that Britain would be unable to make the necessary
preparations by May 1978.

France, Britain, and Denmark still looked askance at the entire concept of European elections. Significantly, both Britain and France ultimately incorporated clauses into their legislation for direct elections
curtailing further expansion of the powers of the European Parliament.
British Prime Minister James Callaghan had to mollify anti-marketeers
within his Labour party while Giscard d'Estaing was forced to deal with
the hostility of the Gaullists and Communists during the crucial months
preceding the March 1978 French national elections. With the French
Communists and Socialists threatening to make an alliance that would
all but insure a victory for the Left at the polls, Giscard needed to secure
and maintain a unified base of conservative support at all costs.

As far as the other Community states were concerned, deciding the
size and boundaries of the European constituencies were sticky problems. For example, in Belgium the projected European elections

threatened to aggravate age-old Flemish-Walloon antagonisms. Even in
Italy and West Germany, longtime supporters (at least in theory) of a
directly elected European Parliament, European elections were far down
on the list of governmental priorities. Italy's perennially unstable Christian
Democrat-led government was facing its most serious challenge since the
war from the Communist party. Boasting the support of roughly a third
of the electorate, the Communists sought to gain a corresponding role
in governing the country. Chronic economic instability and escalating
acts of terrorism added to the woes of a minority government which was
not in a position to deal with European elections.

West Germany, for its part, maintained a tolerant, rather cynical attitude toward the upcoming direct elections. The Schmidt government
dutifully voiced its support of the elections as its predecessors had done.
But economic considerations, the precarious situation in the Middle East,
and East-West relations continued to be primary concerns. European
elections were an additional complication which would force West Germany to devote a fair amount of time and energy to an endeavor which
was neither necessary, useful, nor desirable.

The obstinacy of the British Parliament, then, was more welcome than
not. However, this did not deter the eight other Community states from
condemning their reluctant partner for its "typical" British lack of commitment to a unified Western Europe. This criticism, if self-righteous,
was justified. By early 1977, when debate began on ratification of direct
elections and approval of enabling legislation in the national parliaments,
there were strong indications that the Labour party would throw a monkey
wrench into the entire operation. The controversy surrounding the choice
of the voting system for European elections offered foes of British EEC
membership an excellent opportunity to delay the ratification process.

Britain had traditionally employed the so-called first-past-the-post system for national and local elections. In such a system, the candidate who
won a majority of the votes was the victor. However, this method, if
utilized for European elections, would necessitate the creation of large
constituencies which would favor the dominant political parties—especially
the Conservatives. Proportional representation, on the other hand, would
benefit the smaller parties and also the Labour party. This factor notwithstanding, a large number of Labourites opposed proportional representation—not because it was alien to them, but for the reason that such a
system could be more quickly implemented than the simple majority

system, allowing European elections to be held on schedule.[1] (The rest
of the Community states, including France, were using proportional
voting for direct elections.)

In the spring of 1977, the Callaghan government issued a White Paper
which outlined three other electoral systems as alternatives to the traditional procedure: voting by party list with the seats distributed proportionally, a "single transferable vote" allowing a voter to select any number
of candidates according to preference, or a combination of these systems
with a candidate's membership in the House of Commons made a prerequisite for membership in the European Parliament.[2]

While the small Liberal party naturally favored proportional representation, such a system was rejected for obvious reasons by the Conservatives.
The Callaghan government supported proportional representation for
political reasons. Liberal party leader David Steel's nine-month pact with
Callaghan had enabled the prime minister to maintain a bare majority in
Commons and to avoid a general election until an opportune time arose.
But the outcome of the vote in Commons on the choice of electoral system on December 17, 1977, was never really in doubt. Only a small
majority of Labourites (32) supported the prime minister's proportional
representation bill while four cabinet members opposed it. Overall, only
147 Labourites voted for the measure with 115 opposed and 46 abstentions. A large majority—319 to 222—approved the "first-past-the-post"
system for European elections.[3] Since Commons had yet to give its final
approval to the electoral arrangements, to be followed by consideration
by the House of Lords and the delineation of the new constituencies,
Britain could not make the May 1978 deadline under any circumstances.

The outcome in Britain confirmed the worst fears of the *Europeans,*
who viewed postponement of the elections as a psychological defeat.
There was talk of holding European elections irregardless since the other
eight states had either completed ratification and had approved electoral
systems or were well enough along in the process to guarantee completion
prior to the deadline. However, France and the Netherlands officially refused to hold the elections without British participation.[4]

Contrary to expectations, ratification and approval of enabling legislation by the French Assembly was not particularly difficult. Some of the
steam was taken out of the vociferous Gaullist-Communist opposition by
Giscard's adroit decision to submit the act authorizing direct elections to
the French Constitutional Council for consideration prior to placing it

before the Assembly. The Constitutional Council put its stamp of approval on the plan on December 30, 1976, observing in its report that a directly elected European "assembly" posed no threat to French national sovereignty.[5] The French government further undercut the opposition through including a stipulation in the electoral bill that the new directly elected European Parliament could not demand any further increase in its powers. This action, however, did not appease the orthodox Gaullists. Led by federalism's most implacable foe, Michel Debré, they continued to attack direct elections as a threat to France. On May 4, 1977, Debré proposed that sessions of the directly elected Parliament be subordinate to the European Council. Under this scheme, the heads of state would decide the Parliament's agenda for the three times a year that it would meet.[6]

In early June, a week before the debate was to begin, Gaullist leader Jacques Chirac announced that his party—which comprised over one-third of the 490-seat National Assembly—would attempt to shelve the government bill by attaching an amendment securely protecting French sovereignty. Worried over the upcoming elections, Chirac hoped that by postponing the debate, he could circumvent a possible party split since certain moderates, such as Chaban Delmas, favored the bill. However, according to French law, a measure involving a foreign treaty could not be revised. With the failure of this tactic, Chirac fell back on the traditional Gaullist weapon of demanding a renegotiation of the Rome Treaty. However, with national elections less than a year away and amid rampant rumors of a Communist-Socialist alliance leading to a leftist triumph, unity among conservative political factions was paramount. Chirac was forced to abandon Debré and the diehard opponents of direct elections to support the government.

As for the French Communists, they were pressured not only by their Italian colleagues to drop their opposition but also by their prospective partners in electoral alliance—the Socialists—who saw the political virtues of a common European policy. Thus the legislation was adopted, but outside the normal parliamentary procedure. Despite the disintegration of the opposition, to insure that the bill passed, Premier Raymond Barre resorted to an obscure ruling that terminated debate on a measure and allowed it to be adopted without a vote.[7]

While the outcome of the French Assembly's debate on European elections was anticlimactic, in the other seven national parliaments approval of the elections and the electoral procedure was either completed or proceeding slowly in an inevitable fashion.[8] But since Britain obviously could not make the deadline, the nine governments would have a period of grace before facing the distasteful task of holding European elections. On April 7, 1978, when the European Council met in Copenhagen for the first summit conference of the year, the heads of state rescheduled the elections for June 7-10, 1979.

With much expansive oratory, spokesmen for the six European political groups hailed the governments' selection of June 1979 as evidence of the states' commitment to a strong and vital European Parliament. During the July 1978 session of the Parliament in Luxembourg, even the French Communists grudgingly endorsed the principle behind direct elections. Thus the Community's drum-beating on the election theme resumed, but initially in a much more subdued fashion.

It has been three decades since the early postwar Federalists launched the campaign to create a genuine European legislature. Despite tremendous obstacles, European elections are now past history. On June 7-10, 1979, following a massive European Community propaganda blitz, an estimated 110 million citizens of nine West European states elected 410 M.E.P.s (European Parliament members).

But after thirty years of struggle, achievement of the long-anticipated goal was, in a word, anticlimactic. Certainly, for a few short days, the Parliament and the multinational elections were front-page news in both the United States and Europe. However, the number of non-voters was extraordinarily high. Only just over half of the 180 million eligible voters went to the polls, ranging from an 85.9 percent turnout in Italy, where voting is compulsory, to a meager 31.3 percent in Britain.[9] While true that in the United States such a turnout would be considered a fair showing, in Western Europe, however, it was a positive embarrassment. The European elections were definitely upstaged by national elections held shortly beforehand in Italy and Britain.

Still analysts on both sides of the Atlantic hailed the strong showing by the conservative parties as evidence of a general West European swing to the Right. While the various Socialist parties previously held a third of the seats in the old appointed Parliament, in the directly elected body, Socialist strength had slipped to one-fourth.[10] Riding the coattails of Margaret Thatcher's newly established government, British Conservative candidates captured 60 of 81 seats. In Italy Communist support was slightly below the recent national election percentage at 29.6 percent (as compared to 30.4 percent). In the 1976 Italian elections, the Communists had reached an all-time high support of 34.4 percent.[11] The French Communists fared much worse, winning only 19 of France's 81 seats. However, the French voter turnout was only 61.2 percent. Along with the French Communists, the dismal showing of the Gaullists (15 seats) and the British Labour party (17 seats) encouraged integration advocates to view the results as a "vote for Europe," since the three parties were staunch opponents of federalism.[12]

There is great danger in making simplistic assessments and predictions based on instant analysis. The first European elections were a novelty. Many of the candidates, such as former West German Chancellor Willy Brandt, former French Health Minister Simone Veil, former Belgian Premier Leo Tindemans, and Italian statesman Emilio Colombo, lent an atmosphere of prestige and glamor to an otherwise inauspicious affair. Significantly, the American press made more fuss over the election of Otto von Hapsburg, oldest son of the last Austro-Hungarian emperor, than the elections of the Parliament. (Many of these celebrities who were elected fully intended to relinquish their seats to substitutes so as to avoid the mundane rigors of sitting as an M.E.P.).

Furthermore, one can hardly predict national political trends in the Community states from the European election results. A 60-percent voter turnout is not much basis for prediction, nor is it a mandate for further political integration or for expanding the European Parliament's powers. One conceivably could argue that those indifferent or opposed to increased federalism simply ignored the June elections.

The big question, then, remains: What does the future hold for political unity and the European Parliament? The *Europeans* have achieved their long-sought goal. The elections have been held, the small turnout rationalized by the determinedly optimistic supporters of political unity and the world awaits the impact of this "new" European Parliament. But the public rhetoric surrounding the elections masks a growing uneasiness on the part of the *Europeans*. The evolution of political integration has taken a distinct turn away from federalism toward old-style intergovernmental cooperation. The original conception of the so-called founding fathers of the Community was that the Council of Ministers would evolve into an upper chamber—a kind of European senate representing the states—while the Assembly would, through direct elections, become a "peoples' chamber." The abortive draft treaty for a European Political

Community embodied this concept. The ECSC High Authority and later the EEC Commission were envisioned as an embryonic federal executive. But the last twenty years—particularly the past decade—have witnessed a far different evolution for the Community. To be sure, the supranational economic apparatus has developed along the lines foreseen by Jean Monnet in the early 1950s. The nine-nation Common Market is a strong and ambitious trading competitor of the United States and Japan and is presently seeking to expand its economic ties with China and COMECON (the EEC's East European counterpart), as well as with the individual East European states. But this robust progress in the economic sector has failed to "spill over" into the political arena as the Functionalists of the 1950s predicted. Rather than diminish in authority, the Council of Ministers and its bureaucratic structure has grown and evolved into an ersatz executive for the Community. Periodic summit meetings of the heads of the Community states take place under the euphemistic title of "European Council" to sanction the decisions of the ministers or to issue vague directives. In fact, *Europeans* and the news media have come to expect little or no accomplishments from these meetings. The EEC Commission of the 1960s that so enraged General de Gaulle with its upstart ambitions has become more and more a mere secretariat for the states.

The national governments, for their part, have not been oblivious to the criticism engendered by this turn of events. As previously noted, the European Council requested Belgian Prime Minister Leo Tindemans to prepare a report on the progress and future of "European Union." Amid much fanfare, the Tindemans Report was placed before the Council at the end of 1975. The report was lauded for its realism and optimism. The late Anthony Crosland, British president of the Council of Ministers, claimed that the report rendered the debate between Federalists and Confederalists "irrelevant and unreal."

In reality, however, Tindemans's assessment represented little more than a capitulation to the Confederalist approach. While he chastised the states for their preoccupation with domestic affairs, Tindemans also observed that the European citizens and the Community itself were partially to blame for the sorry state of European Union—the former for lack of interest and the latter for "falling victim to its own successes" (that is, the reconciliation of formerly hostile nations, economic prosperity, and détente). The report went on to suggest means of revitalizing

European Union and in doing so tacitly accepted intergovernmental cooperation as the real basis of Western Europe's future. Calling for a "single
decision-making center" in the form of a streamlined Council of Ministers,
Tindemans stressed the need for the Nine to coordinate foreign, economic,
and monetary policy as well as other areas of common interest. But while
emphasizing that intergovernmental cooperation "would not help to solve
European problems," he advanced proposals for strengthening the Community's institutions that were discreetly modest. Arguing that direct
elections would give the Parliament "a new political authority," he proposed that the Council should "consider" the Parliament's resolutions—
a practice which "should be enshrined in a treaty amendment which
would accord to the Parliament a real right of initiative." In addition, the
Parliament should "focus public attention by holding large scale political
debates." The president of the European Council and other leading politicians could be "invited" to these sessions. Furthermore, the Parliament
should have the authority to approve the European Council's selection
of the president of the Commission.[13]

In summation, Tindemans noted that the "delegation of executive
power," particularly by the Council, was essential to the success of the
European Union. In his view, it was not a matter of revising the institutional framework of the European Union but improving upon it.

The Tindemans Report has effectively sanctioned the status quo. It
breaks no new ground. The national governments have been talking about
coordinating foreign policy, economic and monetary policy, and the like
for several years now with little to show for their efforts. Yet the talking
goes on. In the Parliament itself, the same platitudes are delivered with
the same lack of conviction. But as one high-ranking Parliament official
observes, behind the closed doors of the committee and political group
meetings, the sentiments expressed are quite the opposite.

The chief fear of those *Europeans* who have fought so long for direct
elections—Spénale, Patijn, Vredeling, Berkhouwer, Spinelli, and their colleagues—is that the elections might change nothing. For more than thirty
years, proponents of a European Parliament elected by universal suffrage
adamantly have held that direct elections would be Europe's salvation.
But in the 1970s, the national governments have taken firm control of
the Community. France and Britain have placed limitations on the further
development of the powers of the directly elected Parliament. The European public is ignorant or uninterested in the EEC and its political future

(although periodic Community polls—"Eurobarometers"—appear to indicate that the idea of a united Europe is alive and well).

More significantly, the old enthusiasm of the earlier *Europeans*—the Parliament's leadership in the 1950s and 1960s—is gone. The acquiescent tone of the Tindemans Report permeates the pronouncements of those who once agitated for a strengthened Parliament. Shelto Patijn (Dutch Socialist), a chief architect of the 1975 draft convention for direct elections, is among the more ambitious of the new generation of *Europeans.* Yet his assessment of the Parliament's future is pessimistic at best. According to Patijn, "if there is a development towards a more federal Europe, there is a chance that the Parliament will develop in that situation." But he admits that "for the time being this looks very unlikely." He predicts that the Parliament ultimately will gain the power of co-decision with the Council of Ministers and envisions a relationship between the two institutions comparable to that of the U.S. House and Senate. However, he concedes that any such development would "probably be very slow." Conservative leader Geoffrey Rippon, while viewing direct elections as a positive step, holds that the Parliament will not be given any significant measure of authority at the expense of the Council in the foreseeable future. One of the last of the old-guard *Europeans*, W. J. Schuijt, agrees. According to Schuijt, there is "no real prospect of the European Parliament developing into a real federal legislature. . . . There is a strong opposition to any increase in the powers of the Parliament in France and the United Kingdom." He echoes the assertion of many *Europeans* in his claim that the authors of the Paris and Rome Treaties never intended that the Parliament "govern" a supranational European state (a view that completely ignores the aspirations of the early postwar Federalists). Furthermore, he maintains that even without wider powers the Parliament could make its decisions carry more weight if it would "exercise its present advisory and supervisory functions more fully."[14]

Thus, with the exception of a handful of diehard Federalists and the Italian Communists, the prevalent attitude is one of resignation. Altiero Spinelli, still retaining the zeal that long has characterized his federalist views, argues that direct elections mark "not the point of arrival but the point of departure." But for the vast majority of *Europeans,* the elections mean a culmination rather than a prelude to greater things—an endorsement of the Parliament's *raison d'être* rather than an approval of its participation in the Community decision-making process. European Commission President Roy Jenkins warns against slipping into a state of euphoria over the holding of the elections while his British colleague on the Commission, Christopher Tugendhat, counsels the Parliament to content itself with making the most of its existing advisory and investigative powers.[15]

The British government is adamant about the permanency of British participation. As a Foreign Office spokesman put it, the great debate over Common Market entry was "resolved" by the referendum of 1975. "One cannot foresee any circumstances in which the United Kingdom would leave the Community."[16]

One who can visualize such a possibility is former Prime Minister Harold Wilson, who recently toured U.S. college campuses promoting his own view of the state of British-Community affairs. Wilson undoubtedly reflects the sentiments of a good part of the British Labour party and many grass-roots Conservatives in his criticism of what he terms "Eurocratic interference" and his refusal to bury the idea of British withdrawal from an "unstable" European Community. According to Wilson, an unstable EEC could result from the advent of a Communist government in one of the Community states or the domination of the European Parliament by a Communist-Socialist coalition.[17]

While Wilson's views are officially debunked by the Labour leadership and the British government, there is no evidence that the economic ties binding the nine states are sacred. Divorce is not unthinkable—as the British press periodically points out. *The Sunday Times* has observed that if most Britons ever think at all about the Community it is to "wish vaguely that this unloved body would somehow go away."[18] The average British citizen is convinced, with some justification, that Common Market membership has made everything from butter to bread more expensive. It is not uncommon to hear casual condemnations of the EEC at a country bus stop or on a city street corner. It is doubtful that the capricious English weather will be blamed on the Community, but the possibility remains. On the political level, the Labour party leadership is covertly lukewarm on the issue of continued EEC membership while a large portion of the party rank and file remain unalterably opposed to British participation.

The phenomenon known as "Eurocommunism," like the issue of irreversibility of Community membership, is another unknown factor. A legitimate reason for the indefinite postponement of European elections in the 1980s might be the emergence of a Communist government in one of the Community states. Italy, beset by chronic economic and political instability, is particularly vulnerable. If Communist participation in the Italian or French governments is indeed inevitable, as most analysts of European Communist parties have claimed, what would be its future impact on the Community and future European elections? Many *Europeans* are quick to point to the strong pro-federal track record of the Italian Communists since the late 1960s. In the debates of the European Parliament, the PCI delegates have been the most extreme in their demands for greater powers for the Community institutions and for limitations on national sovereignty. They have condemned the recent trend toward greater intergovernmental cooperation and disparaged the ineffectiveness of the European Council. Likewise, they have consistently voted against even the most ambitious of the Parliament's resolutions on political integration on the basis that these resolutions did not go far enough. It has already been noted that the Italian Communists rejected the 1975 draft convention for direct elections because the plan left electoral procedure for the first elections in the hands of the states.

There is much controversy over whether the Italian Communist leopard really has changed its spots. In the immediate postwar period, the Italian Communists remained unalterably opposed to European integration on the grounds that it was an anti-nationalist and a pro-capitalist tool of the United States and the Western European states it dominated. Although the PCI voted against the Rome Treaties, by November 1960 there was evidence of the beginning of a change of heart. At the 1960 party conference in Moscow, the Italian delegates officially raised the question of Communist participation in European Community institutions. According to their argument, the success of the EEC and its increasing independence from the United States negated the traditional Communist opposition. In September 1962, in its "Theses for the Tenth Congress," the PCI advanced the idea that Communist participation in the EEC was necessary to insure that the Community was reformed along "acceptable" economic and political lines. By the mid-1960s, it was strongly lobbying for Communist representation in the Italian delegation to the European Parliament.[19]

The new Italian Communist position was expressed in general terms by group leader Giorgio Amendola in his maiden speech to the Parliament in March 1969. According to Amendola, whereas the EEC was originally a product of the Cold War and perpetuated the division of Europe into

East and West, the 1960s had witnessed an increasing divergence between the policies of the United States and Western Europe (such as the de Gaulle-inspired NATO crisis). He argued that in order to achieve European unification, NATO and the Warsaw Pact had to be "liquidated" and replaced with cooperation among all European states regardless of political ideology. He also called for the left-wing political parties in all European nations to join to insure peace and social democracy through participating in a directly elected European Parliament.

Discussions with Parliament members and Community officials present a reassuring picture of the Italian Communists. A case in point is Altiero Spinelli, who left the European Commission in 1976 to run as an independent for the Chamber of Deputies on the Communist party ticket. According to Spinelli, when he first began talking of Communist participation in the Italian government, "it made everyone's hair stand on end." While he admits that many of his non-Communist colleagues still harbor "profound doubts" about the sincerity of the Italian Communists' conversion, there is a growing acceptance of the inevitability of their joining the government in the near future.[20] European Parliament member Michael Yeats (Irish European Progressive Democrat) is quick to scoff at any allegation that the Italian Communists—whom he considers to be political moderates—would jeopardize the present state of the Community if they were in a position of power. In Yeats's opinion, certain British Labour delegates of the European Parliament are to the left of the PCI members.[21] Likewise, Schuijt points out that the full participation of the Communist party in the Italian government would prove no threat to the existence or development of the Community. Although he recognizes the French Communists' opposition to the EEC, he dismisses their importance on the basis that they have "no prospects" of joining the French government until "at least" 1983 after their poor showing in the March 1978 elections.[22] In sum, the common refrain heard when the Communist question is posed is that the Italian variety is a breed apart. A related assertion is that European elections tend to benefit the moderate-conservative political groups rather than the Socialists or Communists. If a good many *Europeans* secretly are uneasy over the Eurocommunism issue, it is difficult to judge from their public statements.

The French Communists are another case altogether. Unlike their Italian colleagues, they remain opposed to the concept of European integration, adhering to the old Soviet position. The "future of the workers" is ostensibly their chief concern. This stance has precluded the development of a common Socialist-Communist position since the French Socialists have been supporters of the Community in the 1960s and 1970s.[23] Although they abandoned their unsuccessful struggle to block European elections, the French Communists are outspoken in their determination to impede further progress toward political integration. As European Parliament member Gérard Bordu bluntly claims, "We will make sure that the rights of the assembly (the Parliament) must not be surreptitiously increased against the democratic will of France."[24]

Ironically one could argue that the biggest threat to the new European Parliament and to the whole concept of supranationalism is not Eurocommunism or another internal crisis in the Community but the inevitable enlargement of the EEC itself by the inclusion of Spain, Portugal, and Greece. Greece is already scheduled to join the EEC in January 1981. The danger is all the more serious because, on the surface, the expansion of the Community from nine to ten or more states is welcomed by most *Europeans* as a catalyst to further political integration. Even the Italian Communists have spoken favorably of such an event. According to Renato Sandri, while enlargement could well weaken the Community's institutional structure, politically it could be a positive move.

However, in reality, a larger Community can only set back the federal evolution of Western Europe past the point of no return. While on the political level, the Community is gradually evolving into a loose confederation of sovereign states, on an economic plane the trend is toward the broad Free Trade Area formerly advocated by the British in the 1950s as an alternative to the unabashed federalism of the Schuman approach. The British government quite naturally is pleased with this turn of events, as is the French government, which has always looked with a jaundiced eye upon the growing power of the Community institutions. The German government, ever careful to assuage the fears of the *Europeans* through occasional pro-integration statements, has given no indication that it is not content with the present confederal direction of European union.

The addition of even one new member to the Community would wreak havoc upon future European elections. The electoral convention would have to be revised to provide for the new delegates to the Parliament. (This is assuming that the national governments agree on a common electoral procedure in time for the 1984 elections, which, considering past history, is unlikely.) The mere prospect of enlargement could be an excuse for the states to postpone successive elections.

There is no doubt that the European Community is a great economic success. All nine states have sacrificed at some time certain noncrucial interests for the collective good of the whole. The result is that the EEC is a formidable trading block—and enlargement might make it an even more potent force. With just nine states, the EEC boasts a population of more than 260 million—larger than the United States.

Yet, politically, the Community has progressed little in the twenty years of its existence. The Council of Ministers still runs the show while the Parliament agonizes sometimes for hours over whether to use the term *deplore* or *regret* in one of its countless resolutions. As Hans-August Lücker (German Christian Democrat) observes, the Community seems to be stagnating, even regressing into a confederal association reminiscent of the nineteenth-century Concert of Europe.[25]

In the midst of these tremendous doubts and hopes, the members of the Parliament go about their business as usual, shuffling between the assembly buildings at Strasbourg and Luxembourg with occasional side trips to Brussels, preceded by tons of paper and equipment and a host of parliamentary officials. The states have yet to choose a permanent site for the Parliament. The result is continual chaos and the expenditure of over a third of the Parliament's multimillion-dollar annual budget on moving expenses alone. Direct elections have further complicated the picture since the Parliament building in Luxembourg, conveniently across the parking lot from the European Center, is much too small for the 410-member Parliament. On the other hand, picturesque Strasbourg boasts a new large assembly building constructed to house the Council of Europe.

Both cities have a vested interest in winning the honor of official site for the Parliament. Luxembourg's stake in real estate and in existing and potential buildings, not to mention tourist revenue, is enormous. Along with the Parliament's Secretariat, the European Court of Justice, the European Investment Bank, and the Community Statistical Office are located there. The rolling hills beyond the city are dotted with huge sprawling glass and concrete examples of the most modern architecture. All about, towering yellow construction cranes desecrate the country-side and the roar of machinery in the early mornings competes with the music of the resident bird population.

Whether or not the Parliament is meeting in Luxembourg, the city is awash with Community bureaucrats and "consultants" of various professions and nationalities who are housed at Community expense for months at a time. Tour buses disgorge sightseers before the packed Holiday Inn adjacent to the European Center. On a given day when the Parliament is in session, its ushers, recruited from the national assemblies and resplendent in their different uniforms, may herd hundreds of disinterested spectators in and out of the small gallerys above the Assembly chamber. During the July 1978 session, for instance, the bulk of these tourists were Irish. (The Fianna Fail was sponsoring a "get-to-know-your-European Parliament" tour in collaboration with Aer Lingus, the Irish national airline.) The real VIPs among the spectators, however, were not the Irish but a delegation from the Japanese parliament. A handful of reporters sat impassively beneath their headphones in the press gallery, oblivious to the activity and confusion in the rest of the building.

Luxembourg, eager to present the Parliament with a fait accompli, has pushed ahead with its plans for the construction of an assembly hall for the 410-member Parliament. For its part, the Parliament has investigated the feasibility of relocating at least some of its operations in Brussels—a move which has roused the ire of both the Luxembourg and French governments (the latter on behalf of Strasbourg). (According to rumors, Luxembourg and France were thought to have made a "secret pact" in 1978 to block European elections unless the Parliament abandoned its interest in Brussels.)

Such is the dilemma of the European Parliament. Powerless, pushed about, ignored and shackled by its own timidity, the Parliament faces the prospect of gaining little from the long-anticipated European elections. Perhaps the chief responsibility for this dilemma and for the reorientation of the direction of political integration rests with the *Europeans* themselves. Ten years ago, in the midst of the crisis-filled 1960s, Altiero Spinelli criticized his colleagues for lacking what he called "the courage to wage an all-out battle" to increase the Parliament's powers. This same criticism has held true for the 1970s. European Commissioner Richard Burke aptly summarized this unhappy situation:

> The United States of Europe is still a dream
> cherished by many, but its attainment is no
> longer a matter of practical political effort in

the Community institutions. The grand design
of the founding fathers, the strategy for the
creation in stages of a European federation,
has effectively been set aside. No alternative
strategy has taken its place.[26]

Of course, it is easy to consign the federal ideal to the theoretical scrap
heap. If the evolution of the Community follows true to form, another
Cold War-related crisis like the invasion of Czechoslovakia in 1968 could
spark renewed interest in further federalization. On the other hand, a
crisis *within* the EEC could accelerate the present confederal trend of the
Community's evolution. Whatever the case, the future of the directly
elected European Parliament remains an enigma. Whether the elections
mark the beginning of a new impetus toward further political integration
or the gradual death of an unachievable ideal remains to be seen. *Europeans* can take great pride in the fact that after thirty years of struggle
for a directly elected European Parliament, they have achieved their goal.
The sobering thought is that it may take three more decades to reap the
rewards of this Pyrrhic victory.

APPENDIX

Results of the First European Elections, June 1979

FRANCE (81 seats)

Giscardists	25
Socialists	22
Communists	19
Gaullists	15

BRITAIN (81 seats)

Conservatives	60
Labour	17
Others	4

WEST GERMANY (81 seats)

Christian Democrats	42
Social Democrats	35
Liberals (Free Democrats)	4

ITALY (81 seats)

Christian Democrats	30
Communists	24
Socialists (two parties)	13
Liberals (two parties)	6
Others	8

NETHERLANDS (25 seats)

Christian Democrats	10
Socialists	9
Liberals	4
Others	2

BELGIUM (24 seats)

Christian Democrats	10
Socialists	7

Source: *The New York Times,* June 17, 1979 and *Europe,* no. 214, July-August, 1979, pp. 8-11.

| Liberals | 4 |
| Others | 3 |

DENMARK (16 seats)

Anti-Common Market	4
Liberals	3
Socialists	3
Conservatives	3
Communists	1
Others	2

IRELAND (15 seats)

Fianna Fail	6
Fine Gael	5
Labour	2
Others	2

LUXEMBOURG (6 seats)

Social Christians	3
Liberals	2
Socialists	1

NOTES

CHAPTER 1

1. Walter Lipgens, "European Federation in the Political Thought of Resistance Movements during World War II," in *European Integration,* ed. F. Roy Willis (New York: New Viewpoints, 1975). This study is part of a comprehensive assessment titled *Europa-Föderationspläne der Widerstandsbewegungen 1940-1945* (Munich: Oldenbourg, 1968). For further background see Charles F. Delzell, "The European Federalist Movement in Italy: First Phase 1918-1947," *Journal of Modern History* 32 (1960) : 241-50.

2. Paul-Henri Spaak, *The Continuing Battle: Memoirs of a European, 1936-1966,* trans. Henry Fox (Boston: Little, Brown, 1971), pp. 95, 105-16.

3. For a philosophical study of the concept of Europe from Europa's mythological rape to the federalism of the twentieth century see Denis de Rougemont, *The Idea of Europe,* trans. Norbert Guterman (New York: Macmillan, 1966). For the concept of Europe in this century see Hendrik Brugmans, *L'idée européene 1920-1970* (Bruges: De Tempel, 1970).

4. Adenauer remarked in his memoirs that he saw "in a future United States of Europe . . . the great hope of Europe and Germany" for these reasons. Konrad Adenauer, *Memoirs 1945-53* (Chicago: Regnery, 1966), p. 37.

5. Lipgens, "European Federation," p. 2.

6. Winston Churchill, "The United States of Europe" (speech to the States-General of the Netherlands, The Hague, May 9, 1946), in *Winston S. Churchill: His Complete Speeches 1897-1963*, ed. Robert Rhodes James, vol. 7 (New York: Chelsea House, 1974), pp. 7322-23.

7. Churchill, "The Tragedy of Europe" (Zurich University, September 19, 1946), in ibid., pp. 7379-81.

8. Churchill to Roosevelt, "Morning Thoughts: Note on Postwar Security," (February 2, 1943, Doc. 210), in *Roosevelt and Churchill: Their Secret Wartime Correspondence*, ed., Francis L. Loewenheim et al. (New York: Dutton, 1975), pp. 310-11.

9. For general background on the United States' relationship with Western Europe in the early postwar era see Max Beloff, *The United States and the Unity of Europe* (Washington, D.C.: The Brookings Institution, 1963); Lionel Gelber, *America in Britain's Place* (London: George Allen and Unwin, 1961); William C. Cromwell, *Political Problems of Atlantic Partnership* (Bruges: College of Europe, 1968); Ernst H. van der Beugel, *From Marshall Aid to Atlantic Partnership* (New York: Elsevier, 1966); Gerhard Mally, *The New Europe and the United States* (Lexington, Mass.: Heath, 1974); and Robert S. Jordan, ed., *Europe and the Super Powers* (Boston: Allyn and Bacon, 1971). The memoirs of Truman's various foreign policy advisors also offer an illuminating account of the American decision to espouse the cause of European federalism. See Dean Acheson, *Present at the Creation* (New York: Norton, 1969); George F. Kennan, *Memoirs, 1925-1950* (Boston: Little, Brown, 1967); Arthur W. Vandenberg, Jr., *The Private Papers of Senator Vandenberg* (Boston: Houghton Mifflin, 1952). Also see Harry S. Truman, *Memoirs*, vol. 1 (Garden City, N.Y.: Doubleday, 1955).

10. Max Beloff, *The United States*, p. 45.

11. Kennan, *Memoirs*, p. 337. Also Acheson, *Present at the Creation*, p. 228. Truman appointed a special Policy Planning Staff under Kennan to outline both a short- and a long-term European assistance program. The resulting plan proposed a "crash program" designed to relieve the fuel crisis then gripping Europe. In the long term, the report emphasized a jointly coordinated program initiated and implemented by the West European nations with "advice" from the United States. This concept of joint planning was reinforced by an influential memorandum written by Undersecretary of State for Economic Affairs William Clayton, who suggested a three-year U.S. grant coordinated by the "principal European nations" (Britain, France, and Italy). Clayton also recommended that a European customs union eventually be established. *Foreign Relations of the United States*, vol. 3 (1947), p. 230.

12. Ibid., pp. 237-39.

13. There was a general agreement among the Planning Staff, however, that the joint plan "must formally be a British one." Ibid., p. 227, and Acheson, *Present at the Creation*, p. 232.

14. Lipgens, "European Federation," p. 11.

15. Count Coudenhove-Kalergi, "Draft Constitution of the United States of Europe" (1944), rpt. in Arnold J. Zurcher, *The Struggle to Unite Europe, 1940-1958*, (New York: New York University Press, 1958) pp. 219-23.

16. *The Times*, January 18, 1947, and *Le Monde*, July 17, 1947. The British Committee's conception of a United States of Europe was based on the idea often expressed in Churchill's speeches—it would be a regional bloc under the UN Charter and would have close ties to the U.S. and the Soviet Union. The committee held that it was "premature" to envision what constitutional arrangement such a union would take.

17. Ibid.

18. Anthony Eden, *The Memoirs of Anthony Eden: Full Circle* (Boston: Houghton Mifflin, 1960), pp. 32-33.

19. Altiero Spinelli, *The Eurocrats: Conflict and Crisis in the European Community* (Baltimore: Johns Hopkins, 1966), p. 11.

20. Functionalists, however, had little faith in obviously confederal associations such as the Organization of European Economic Cooperation which was created in April 1948 to administer U.S. aid to Western Europe given through the European Recovery Act. Unlike Benelux, the OEEC did not involve the development of a common economic policy.

CHAPTER 2

1. Detailed descriptions of the proceedings may be found in Konrad Adenauer, *Memoirs 1945-53* (Chicago: Regnery, 1966), pp. 107-11; Paul-Henri Spaak, *The Continuing Battle: Memoirs of a European, 1936-1966*, trans. Henry Fox (Boston: Little, Brown, 1971), pp. 201-05.

2. Unfortunately, postwar Britain's foreign policy goals and her resources to carry out these goals did not prove complementary. By the war's end, Britain had lost nearly a quarter of her national wealth. Even before the abrupt termination of lend-lease on August 19, 1945, Churchill found himself forced to beg the United States for a no-strings-attached loan. British participation in the limited cooperative arrangement set up to administer the Marshall Plan (the OEEC) was a product of necessity. See D. Varga, "Anglo-American Rivalry and Partnership," *Foreign Affairs* 25 (July 1947) : 588.

3. Spaak, *The Continuing Battle*, pp. 204-5.

4. For general background see Arthur H. Robertson, *The Council of Europe: Its Structure, Functions and Achievements* (London: Stevens and Sons, 1961), and Robertson, *European Institutions* (New York: Matthew Bender, 1973). For a documentary history, see Howard Bliss, ed., *The Political Development of the European Community: A Documentary Collection* (Waltham, Mass.: Blaisdell, 1970).

5. Council of Europe, Consultative Assembly, *Official Report of Debates*, August 16, 1949, p. 75.

6. Consultative Assembly, *Documents*, Doc. 73, September 5, 1949, pp. 163-68.

7. In 1955, a NATO Parliamentarians' Conference was established, partly through the efforts of the Federalists and partly through the desire of member nations to provide a forum for public expression. In 1957, a Benelux Consultative Inter-Parliamentary Council was set up with functions and structure similar to that of the ECSC Common Assembly. The Benelux and NATO institutions were only two of six parliamentary bodies created in the 1950s. The others, apart from the Common Assembly (1952) and the Consultative Assembly (1949) already mentioned, were the Nordic Council (1953), established to promote Scandinavian unity, and the Western European Union Assembly (1954), designed as a poor substitute for the ill-fated European Political Community legislature. With the exception of the Common Assembly, none of these institutions developed into a European legislature even in the most limited sense of the word. For a comparative study see Kenneth Lindsay, *European Assemblies: The Experimental Period, 1949-1959* (New York: Praeger, 1960).

8. Even in the early sessions, this dichotomy was evident. See Council of Europe, Consultative Assembly, *Report of the Debates*, 1st sess., August 10-September 8, 1949.

9. Council of Europe, Consultative Assembly, *Documents*, Doc. 19, August 8, 1950, pp. 651-61.

10. Ibid., Doc. 105, pp. 955-87.

11. Acheson to the Consulate at Strasbourg, *Foreign Relations*, vol. 3, 1950, pp. 786-87.

12. According to Adenauer, Schuman wrote him explaining that the "purpose of his proposal was not economic but eminently political" in that it would calm French fears over a German resurgence while molding Europe along federal lines. Adenauer, *Memoirs*, p. 257. The Declaration is reprinted in Bliss, *Documentary Collection*, Doc. 1, pp. 31-33.

13. Great Britain, *Parliamentary Papers*, "Treaty Instituting the European Coal and Steel Community," Cmnd. 4863.

14. The Saar had been represented by a separate delegation in the Consultative Assembly of the Council of Europe. The Adenauer govern-

ment rejected separate status for the Saar in the ECSC Common Assembly. A compromise was reached in which it was agreed that West German membership in the new Community did not confer recognition on the Saar's current status. This important region was later returned to West Germany. For background on the problem see Hans A. Schmitt, *The Path to European Union* (Baton Rouge: Louisiana State University Press, 1962).

15. These ratification difficulties are recounted in lengthy detail in Henry L. Mason, *The European Coal and Steel Community* (The Hague: Martinus Nijthoff, 1955), pp. 2-33.

16. By and large, from an economic standpoint, the threat of recession at the end of the Korean War had much more to do with the speedy ratification than pro-federalist sentiment. Of the Six, only Italy was enthusiastically pro-federalist. The Dutch were favorable to the treaty because the Netherlands would benefit from the expansion of its steel sales and the availability of cheap raw materials. However, Belgium's poor coal-producing record and Luxembourg's reliance on the steel industry for its existence lessened the desirability of the ECSC for both these states. For further information see Robert Mowat, *Creating the European Community* (London: Blandford Press, 1973).

17. Lindsay, *European Assemblies,* pp. 228-29.

18. Schmitt, *The Path to European Union,* p. 135.

19. For a study of the functions, composition, and powers of the Assembly see P. J. G. Kapteyn, *L'Assemblée Commune de la Communauté Européenne du Charbon et de l'Acier* (Leyden: Sijthoff, 1962), and Pierre Ginestet, *L'Assemblée parlementaire européenne* (Paris: Presses universitaires de France, 1959).

20. Lindsay, *European Assemblies,* pp. 219, 228-29.

21. Schmitt, *The Path to European Union,* p. 153.

22. McCloy to Acheson, *Foreign Relations of the United States,* vol. 3, 1950, pp. 746-47.

23. For general background on the EDC see Willard N. Hogan, *Representative Government and European Integration* (Lincoln: University of Nebraska Press, 1967); F. Roy Willis, *France, Germany and the New Europe, 1945-1967* (Stanford: Stanford University Press, 1968), and Richard Mayne, *The Recovery of Europe, 1945-1973* (Garden City, N.Y.: Doubleday, 1973). Mayne notes that a European army had been proposed before but not in concrete terms. Adenauer, André Philip, and Churchill had put forth proposals at various times prior to Monnet's. See pp. 240-41.

24. See introduction to Ad Hoc Assembly, *Draft Treaty Embodying the Statute of the European Community: Information and Official Documents of the Constitutional Committee,* October 1952-April 1953, p. 21.

25. Common Assembly, *Debates,* September 11, 1962, pp. 21-23. Also Ad Hoc Assembly, *Draft Treaty,* Doc. 3 (resolution of September 10, 1952, adopted by the ministers at Luxembourg), p. 26.

26. Ibid., Doc. 4 (resolution by the Assembly on the invitation of the ministers), p. 30.

27. See Ad Hoc Assembly, *Report of the Constitutional Committee,* December 20, 1952, pp. 6-96 passim.

28. Ad Hoc Assembly, *Draft Treaty,* pp. 55-173. A list of members of the Ad Hoc Assembly and the various committees and subcommittees is appended to the treaty.

29. Consultative Assembly-Common Assembly, Joint Meeting of the Members of the Consultative Assembly of the Council of Europe and Members of the Common Assembly of the European Community of Coal and Steel, *Official Report of the Debates,* June 22, 1953, p. 122.

30. For an excellent report on the Assembly's deliberations see American Committee on United Europe, *Report from Strasbourg: The Draft Constitution for a European Political Community* (New York: May 1954), and Theodore H. White, "A New Europe Comes to Life," *Reporter,* April 28, 1953, pp. 28-32.

31. "Preliminary Draft of a Pact for a Union of European States," reprinted in Bliss, *Documentary Collection,* Doc. 22, pp. 220-26. Debré's proposal was overwhelmingly rejected by the Assembly.

32. Ibid.

33. Consultative Assembly-Common Assembly, Joint Meeting, *Official Report of the Debates,* pp. 38-41. Belgian Senator Fernand Dehousse, one of the foremost champions of European unity in the 1950s and 1960s and later a chief architect of the 1960 draft convention for the direct election of the European Parliament, rebutted Debré's confederalist arguments at the joint meeting of June 1953. Dehousse expressed the views of the Federalists in noting that "a confederation . . . would remain stillborn because M. Debré has left out one essential—that dynamic quality which our Political Community will derive through the actual process of election, from the peoples and the masses, and from which its main strength will spring." See ibid., pp. 90-93.

34. American Committee on a United Europe, *Report from Strasbourg,* pp. 15-16.

35. Spaak recounts the ratification dilemma in *The Continuing Battle,* pp. 154-75.

36. Ibid.

37. Zurcher, *The Struggle to Unite Europe,* (New York: New York University Press, 1958) pp. 115-16.

38. Spaak, *The Continuing Battle,* p. 156.

39. U.S., Department of State, *Bulletin*, vol. 31, no. 784-809, "Anglo-American Discussion/Statement of June 28," July 5-December 27, 1954, p. 49.

40. Anthony Eden, *The Memoirs of Anthony Eden: Full Circle* (Boston: Houghton Mifflin, 1960), pp. 37-38.

41. Spaak, *The Continuing Battle*, pp. 161-75.

42. Eden discusses his role in the development of the plan in *Full Circle*, pp. 39-45.

CHAPTER 3

1. *European Community*, no. 16, June 1956, p. 1. The Socialists were the most outspoken among the political groups in the Common Assembly. See Guy van Oudenhove, *The Political Parties in the European Parliament* (Leyden: Sijthoff, 1965), pp. 47-48.

2. *European Community*, no. 16, June 1956, p. 5.

3. Zurcher, *The Struggle to Unite Europe*, (New York: New York University Press, 1958) p. 97.

4. Common Assembly, *Official Reports*, May 1954, pp. 110-12.

5. *European Community*, no. 7, May 1955, p. 3.

6. See Common Assembly, *Debates*, December 2, 1954. Gaullists Debré and Vendroux opposed the resolution. Vendroux went so far as to request the French government to appeal to the Court of Justice to annul the resolution. However, this did not come about. Several members did abstain. The German Socialists were coming to support further integration. Oudenhove notes that the Messina Conference of June 1955 brought all factions within the three political groups into agreement on political integration. This left the Gaullists as the only opponents of supranationalism. See his *The Political Parties in the European Parliament*, pp. 106-7. See also Forsyth, *The Parliament of the European Communities* (London: Political and Economic Planning, 1964), p. 8. The resolution helped to revive the flagging spirits of the *Europeans* after the EDC failure. See also Consultative Assembly of the Council of Europe, *Report on the Activities of the Common Assembly of the European Coal and Steel Community from July 1, 1955 to June 1, 1956*, October 8, 1956, Doc. 523, p. 2.

7. Monnet resigned as president of the High Authority on November 11, 1954, to devote his entire attention to rejuvenating the move toward integration. On October 14, 1955, he created the Action Committee for a United Europe, an association of leading moderate political trade union figures which included the leader of the previously anti-Federalist

German Social Democrats. See Mayne, *The Community of Europe,* p. 110.

8. Robert Mowat, *Creating the European Community* (London: Blandford Press, 1973), pp. 128-29. Beyen had been among those who felt that the European Political Community had been too radical a step. Although he had participated in the negotiations that led to the creation of Benelux and was a supporter of integration, he nonetheless believed that economic union on a large scale was the best path to eventual political integration.

9. Willis, *France, Germany and the New Europe 1945-1967* (Stanford: Stanford University Press, 1968), p. 242. For the Federalists' rationale for turning to the functional approach see Spaak's speech to the Consultative Assembly in *Official Report of the Debates,* October 21, 1955, pp. 610-11. In May 1955, the Common Assembly joined the Benelux ministers in calling upon the Council to take the necessary steps to further European integration. A Working Party was appointed to study the Assembly's powers and several resolutions were adopted calling for expansion of the Assembly's control. See Consultative Assembly, *Second Report of the Common Assembly of the ECSC,* July 28, 1955, Doc. 396, p. 4.

10. "Memorandum of the Benelux Countries to the Six Countries of the ECSC," May 18, 1955, rpt. in Bliss, *Documentary Collection,* Doc. 2, pp. 34-39.

11. *European Community,* no. 8, June 1955, p. 1. Also, *Common Assembly Debates,* May 10-14.

12. Willis, *France, Germany and the New Europe,* pp. 228-29.

13. Mowat, *Creating the European Community,* p. 130.

14. "Resolution Adopted by the Ministers of Foreign Affairs of the Member States of the ECSC," in Bliss, *Documentary Collection,* Doc. 2, pp. 34-39.

15. The British government preferred to follow its own approach to economic cooperation, the Free Trade Area.

16. It was not unusual for a delegate to the Common Assembly to sit for another European body. For example, Belgian Senator Fernand Dehousse was president of the Consultative Assembly as well as a member of the Belgian delegation to the Common Assembly.

17. One of the reasons a fourth assembly had even been considered was that certain political parties in France would be more likely to ratify a treaty in which the Common Assembly—which they identified with supranationalism—played no part. See Robertson, *European Institutions,* p. 194.

18. Consultative Assembly, *Documents,* Doc. 568, October 19, 1956, pp. 1-15. The WEU Assembly adopted a similar recommendation. See Western European Union Assembly, *Proceedings,* Doc. 33, October 11, 1956, p. 137. Also ibid., May 9, 1957, p. 250.

19. Robertson, *European Institutions,* p. 195. In addition to the plan for a fourth assembly, a kind of "three-in-one" assembly in which the activities of the three communities would be compartmentalized was discussed and rejected. See European Parliament, *The First Ten Years, 1958-1968,* p. 18.

20. The stress on the economic aspect of the new Community—as revealed by the choice of its name—was deliberately done to deemphasize the political ramifications. See Willard N. Hogan, *Representative Government,* p. 162.

21. "Treaty Establishing the European Economic Community," rpt. in Bliss, *Documentary Collection,* Doc. 4, pp. 47-70.

22. John Fitzmaurice, *The Party Groups in the European Parliament* (Lexington, Mass.: Saxon House, 1975), p. 39. The dominant role of the Council generally has been obscured by EEC analysts who tend to focus on the activities of the Commission. Part of the reason for this rests on the Commission's extensive public relations efforts. See David P. Calleo, *Europe's Future: The Grand Alternatives* (New York: Horizon Press, 1965), p. 54.

23. Morgan, *West European Politics since 1945,* (London: Batsford, 1972) p. 148. The Council was further strengthened by the creation of a Committee of Permanent Representatives. These committee members had ambassador status and oversaw the Commission's activities between Council meetings.

24. For an assessment of the Council's powers relative to the Commission and the European Parliament, see Leon N. Lindberg and Stuart A. Scheingold, *Europe's Would-Be Polity* (Englewood Cliffs, N.J.: Prentice-Hall, 1970), pp. 86-87.

25. Sir Barnett Cocks, *The European Parliament: Structure, Procedure and Practice* (London: Her Majesty's Stationery Office, 1973), p. 13. Cocks's study offers a good, basic functional description of the Parliament and is especially useful for those unfamiliar with the EEC and its institutions.

26. Lindberg and Scheingold describe the Parliament as "little more than an onlooker" in the actual decision-making process. *Europe's Would-Be Polity,* p. 86. The Parliament, of course, feels its impact in the formation of policy is quite substantial. European Parliament, *The First Ten Years,* p. 23.

27. "Treaty Establishing the European Economic Community," in Bliss, *Documentary Collection,* Doc. 5, p. 50.

28. Ibid. The Euratom Treaty also had a direct election provision (Article 108,3) as did the ECSC Treaty (Article 21,3).

29. The Court of Justice was the fourth Community institution.

30. *European Community,* no. 12, January 1956, pp. 1-2. Also Common Assembly, *Debates,* November 22-25, 1956.

31. The European Parliament and the ministers instituted the practice of having an annual "colloquy" when they met for the first time in November 1957. European Parliament, *The First Ten Years,* p. 26.

32. *European Community,* no. 16, June 1956, p. 7.

33. Ibid.

34. ECSC *Bulletin* 15 (May 1956). Also *European Community,* no. 16, June 1956, p. 4.

35. Common Assembly, *Debates,* May 9, 1956, pp. 419-23, and June 22, 1956, pp. 835-36. The Socialists were the most cohesive group in the Assembly and were dominated by the German SPD. The Christian Democrats, while sharing the Socialists' pro-integration beliefs, were more moderate. See Political and Economic Planning, *European Political Parties* (New York: Praeger, 1970), pp. 487, 488-90. For an assessment of the confrontation see Oudenhove, *The Political Parties in the European Parliament,* pp. 53-54. According to Oudenhove, "the Socialists' violent criticism came very near, if not in form at least in substance, to a motion of censure." The episode followed months of increasing frustration over the limitations placed on the Assembly by the ECSC Treaty. See Consultative Assembly of the Council of Europe, *Common Assembly Report,* Doc. 523, pp. 3-37.

36. Altiero Spinelli has noted that the Parliament "is probably the institution which has suffered the most from the imprecise definition of its function." *The European Adventure: Tasks for the Enlarged Community* (London: C. Knight, 1972), p. 173.

37. The Assembly also used written and oral questions (chiefly to the Commission, rarely to the Council) to influence a piece of legislation. Stephen Holt, *The Common Market: The Conflict of Theory and Practice* (London: Hamish Hamilton, 1967), pp. 81-82.

38. David Coombes, *Politics and Bureaucracy in the European Community* (London: George Allen and Unwin, 1970), p. 315.

39. The negotiators had rushed to complete the treaties partly due to fear of a possible oil crisis because of the Suez dilemma and also due to fear that the present pro-European governments in France and Germany would be replaced by anti-unity regimes. See *Bulletin from the European Community for Coal and Steel* 22 (February-March 1957): 1. Also,

Mowat, *Creating the European Community*, pp. 138-39. There was no
assurance that the EEC Treaty would be ratified. The Dutch were upset
over what appeared to them to be a favorable French trade position.
In West Germany, Finance Minister Ludwig Erhard's opposition was well-
known. In France, the government had difficulty securing a majority because of the strength of the Communists, right-wing Poujadists, and the
Mendès-France wing of the Radical Socialists in the National Assembly.
Furthermore, *Europeans* in all six nations were disenchanted over the
limited supranationalism of the treaties.

40. *Journal Officiel des Communautés Européenne,* "Assemblée Parlementaire Européenne," Procès-verbaux (June 23, 1958) : 213-16. Also
European Community, no. 31, May-June 1958, p. 6, and no. 31, August-
September, pp. 4-5. The issue was referred to a six-nation committee. The
Parliament recommended Brussels as the headquarters of the Community
executives and even recommended the creation of a "European District"
(like the U.S. District of Columbia). But the opinion of the states was
another matter. As Schuman noted at the time, they would have the
final say. *Bulletin from the European Community for Coal and Steel* 29
(March-April 1958) : 2-3.

41. Ibid., pp. 1-3. The new EEC Assembly included among its membership three ex-premiers, Pinay, Pleven, and Schuman, and two Italian ex-
foreign ministers, Martino and Piccioni. All members of the Common
Assembly, including the three presidents of the European political
groups, were reelected to similar offices in the European Parliament.

42. European Parliament, *The First Ten Years*, p. 22.

43. Within each group, members sat in alphabetical order with the
group's bureau at its head.

44. *Journal Officiel,* "Assemblée Parlementaire Européenne," Session
constitutive (March 1958) : 18-19.

45. Ibid., Procès-verbaux (March 19, 1958) : 1. Also *Bulletin from the
European Community for Coal and Steel* (March-April 1958) : 1.

46. *Journal Officiel,* Session constitutive (March 20, 1958) : 4.

47. Ibid., Composition du bureau, des commissions et des groupes
politiques (March 21, 1958) : 12. At the end of the constitutive session
of the European Parliament, Robert Schuman held a press conference and
discussed the issue of European elections, noting that "it was partly a
problem of psychological preparation in forming public opinion and later
parliamentary opinion." He claimed that direct elections could become
"a matter of real urgency within two years." *Bulletin from the European
Community for Coal and Steel* (March-April 1958) : 2.

48. The Rules of Procedure have been continuously amended over the
years to adjust to the Parliament's slowly increasing role within the EEC.

49. *Journal Officiel,* Règlement de L'Assemblée Parlementaire Européenne (June 23, 1958) : 223-24.
50. Ibid., pp. 227-33.
51. Mowat, *Creating the European Community,* p. 143.
52. De Gaulle, certainly no supporter of federalism, also rejected the Free Trade Area as a British attempt to undercut the EEC, which he considered to be of far more benefit to France than the former.
53. Mayne, *The Recovery of Europe, 1945-1973,* pp. 316-17. Despite de Gaulle's claim, the theme of a revitalized preeminent France reappears continuously throughout his memoirs. See Charles de Gaulle, *The War Memoirs of Charles de Gaulle,* vols. 1 and 2 (New York: Viking Press, 1959).

CHAPTER 4

1. Eric Stein, "The European Parliamentary Assembly: Techniques of Emerging 'Political Control,' " *International Organization* 13, no. 2 (1969) : 233.
2. The other eight members were André Boutemy, Enrico Carboni, Edouard Corniglion-Molinier (later replaced by René Pleven in January 1959, who was replaced by Maurice Faure in March 1959), J. van der Goes van Naters, Ludwig Metzger, Maria Probst, Natale Santero, and W. J. Schuijt. Four additional members were later added to the subcommittee: Herman Kopf, Jean Legendre, Nicolas Margue, and Gaetano Martino.
3. The Working Party had no guidelines for direct elections. The Rome Treaties, unlike the Paris Treaty, were by and large (with the exception of the Common Market provisions) a statement for action rather than a detailed set of rules. Roy Pryce, *The Politics of the European Community* (Totowa, N.J.: Rowman and Littlefield, 1973), p. 12.
4. Oudenhove, *The Political Parties in the European Parliament, The First Ten Years, 1952-62* (Leyden: Sijthoff, 1965), pp. 226-27. As of October 1958, there were 65 Christian Democrats, 41 Liberals, and 34 Socialists in the Parliament.
5. Fernand Dehousse, "General Report on the Draft Convention on the Election of the European Parliament by Direct Universal Suffrage," April 30, 1960. The entire draft convention and accompanying reports and resolutions in addition to the debates on the convention of May 10, 11, and 17 are available in a separate documentary collection: European Parliament, *The Case for Elections to the European Parliament by Direct*

Universal Suffrage, 1969. The above can also be found in Parlement Européen, *Débats,* May 10, 11, and 17, 1960, pp. 19-156.

6. Eric Stein, *Integration, Unification, Harmonization and the Politics of the Possible: The Convention on European Elections* (Leyden: Sijthoff, 1961), p. 511. Also, Oudenhove, *The Political Parties in the European Parliament,* p. 227.

7. Holt, *The Common Market; Conflict of Theory and Practice* (London: H. Hamilton, 1967), pp. 86-87.

8. *Journal Officiel,* "Assemblée Parlementaire Européenne," Procèsverbaux (December 17, 1958) : 15-17. For an account of the growth of "extra-treaty" institutions and their effect on early EEC operations see Leon N. Lindberg, *The Political Dynamics of European Integration* (Stanford: Stanford University Press, 1963), pp. 62-65.

9. Motion for a resolution on the adoption of a draft convention on the election of the European Parliament by direct universal suffrage, *The Case for Elections,* p. 62.

10. Initially, the Working Party attempted to take into account the minimum voting requirements of all six states. The Parliament ultimately settled on twenty-one years.

11. This circumvented the problem of Communist representation posed by the West German exclusion of the Communist party from national politics. It did, however, make possible an eventual French-Italian Communist bloc within the Parliament.

12. Dehousse saw the molding of public opinion as all-important, since he viewed direct elections as the only means to administer a "salutary shock" to the national governments which would force them to expand the Parliament's powers.

13. Dehousse, "General Report," *The Case for Elections,* pp. 35-36.

14. Maurice Faure, "Report on the Composition of the Elected Parliament," ibid., p. 43.

15. Ibid., p. 46.

16. Ibid., p. 42.

17. W. J. Schuijt, "Report on Questions Relating to the Electoral System," ibid., pp. 50-51.

18. Ibid., p. 51.

19. Dehousse, debates of May 10, 1960, ibid., p. 75.

20. Metzger, debates of May 11, 1960, ibid., p. 93.

21. Battista, ibid., p. 147.

22. Martino, debates of May 17, 1960, ibid., p. 150.

23. Oudenhove, *The Political Parties in the European Parliament,* p. 228.

24. Although Metzger demanded to know exactly how the votes were divided, he was refused on the grounds that no roll call vote was taken and that "there was a very large majority in favor . . . , few abstentions and no objections." Eric Stein hazards an estimate of fifteen. See *The Convention on European "Elections,"* p. 513. *The European Community Bulletin* (July 1960) : 4 puts the number of abstentions at twelve.

25. Final text of the draft convention, debates of May 17, 1960, in *The Case for Elections,* pp. 238-45.

26. Schuijt, debates of May 17, 1960, ibid., p. 233.

27. Political and Economic Planning, *Direct Elections and the European Parliament,* occasional paper no. 10 (London: October 24, 1960), p. 18.

28. De Gaulle was to claim later when the Union of States scheme was rejected by the Benelux states that the plan was Debré's and not his.

29. Willis, *France, Germany and the New Europe, 1945-1967* (Stanford: Stanford University Press, 1968), p. 293.

30. The German acquiescence to the French plan was reaffirmed by Adenauer after a meeting with French Premier Debré in Bonn on October 8, 1960. For the text of the communiqué issued after the meeting see Western European Union Assembly, *The Political Union of Europe,* 1964, pp. 50-51. See also Pryce, *The Politics of the European Community,* p. 15. According to Pryce, "although from the beginning the Dutch were distinctly nervous," they and the other four states felt they could successfully handle French ambitions.

31. "Press Conference by President de Gaulle," September 6, 1960, rpt. in WEU Assembly, *Political Union of Europe,* 1964, pp. 49-51.

32. Political and Economic Planning, *Direct Elections,* p. 19. Miriam Camps notes that Peyrefitte was alleged to have written a cynical memorandum in the summer of 1960 on "how to sell the Gaullist conception of a European confederation . . . by exploiting the hopes and making use of the forms and language of the 'Europeans' to attain Gaullist ends. . . ." The memorandum was published in June 1962 by the Agence Internationale d'Information pour la Presse in Luxembourg. See Camps, *Britain and the European Community 1955-1963* (Princeton: Princeton University Press, 1964), p. 500.

33. European Economic Community, *Fourth General Report* (the Parliament), 1961, pp. 229-33.

34. Ibid., pp. 235-37. A minority of the members were either for the French plan without reservations or committed to the Schuman approach to political integration.

35. Ibid., pp. 251-52.

36. "Communiqué Issued after the Second Meeting of Heads of State,"

Bad Godesberg, July 18, 1961, rpt. in WEU Assembly, *Political Union of Europe,* 1964, pp. 51-55.

37. The whole idea of intergovernmental cooperation came under a considerable amount of fire, particularly the proposed establishment of a permanent body of national civil servants (the Political Commission) to aid the Council. European Parliament, Doc. 110 (December 21, 1961). See also Walter Hallstein, *Europe in the Making* (New York: Norton, 1972), p. 297.

38. Ibid., p. 298.

39. WEU Assembly, *Political Union of Europe,* 1964, "Text proposed by the French delegation" p. 67-8.

40. Robert Mowat, *Creating the European Communities* (London: Blandford Press, 1973), p. 165.

41. "Draft Treaty for the Establishment of a European Union," January 18, 1962, rpt. in WEU Assembly, *Political Union of Europe,* 1964, pp. 58-62.

42. Willis, *France, Germany and the New Europe,* pp. 297-98. Italian Premier Fanfani attempted to mediate. Attilio Cattani, who had headed the Italian delegation to the Spaak Committee, replaced Fouchet as head of the Study Committee. See Willis, *Italy Chooses Europe* (New York: Oxford University Press, 1971), pp. 93-95. The German Social Democratic party and the French Socialists also opposed the French plan as a threat to European integration. See William Patterson, *The SPD and European Integration* (Lexington, Mass.: Lexington Books, 1974), p. 142. Also, Ellen M. Charlton, *The French Left and European Integration* (Denver: University of Denver Press, 1972), p. 56.

43. Parlement Européen, *Débats,* May 9, 1962. Spaak suggested that the Dehousse-Duvieusart plan should be debated further since it was a praiseworthy although a flawed attempt at solving the impasse surrounding the Union of States. Council of Europe, Consultative Assembly, *Official Report of Debates,* May 15, 1962, pp. 31-39.

44. "Press Conference by President de Gaulle," May 15, 1962, rpt. in WEU Assembly, *Political Union of Europe,* 1964, pp. 81-84.

45. "Press Conference by President de Gaulle," January 14, 1963, ibid., pp. 85-89. De Gaulle resorted to the excuse that Britain was an unsuitable partner for the Six because she was an insular, maritime, chiefly industrial nation with worldwide commercial ties. In addition, he claimed that Britain was too dependent on the United States (as revealed by the Nassau meeting between Macmillan and Kennedy in December 1962).

46. In 1960, Dehousse had projected direct elections for 1962. By 1963, even the most diehard optimists could visualize direct elections

being held no earlier than 1966 or 1967—if at all. Michael Steed, "The European Parliament: the Significance of Direct Elections," in *The New Politics of European Integration,* ed. Ghita Ionescu (London: Macmillan, 1972), p. 140.

CHAPTER 5

1. By 1963, because of the anticipated fusion of the EEC, ECSC, and Euratom, the three communities had come to be referred to as simply "the Community" in parliamentary debates.

2. *Official Gazette of the European Communities,* no. 63, April 20, 1963. On July 10, 1961, after meeting in Bonn, the ministers had issued a statement which noted that although "five delegations consider it possible . . . to make a decision right away to consider action to be taken on the Parliament's proposals concerning its election . . . the French delegation considers that the time has not yet come to embark on this course." On November 21, 1962, Italian Foreign Minister Piccioni, president of the Council, had noted that "the election of the European Parliament by universal suffrage was not apparently a matter of pressing urgency." European Parliament, *The Case for Elections,* p. 253.

3. Altiero Spinelli has criticized the Parliament for not pursuing two possible directions in its struggle to increase its powers: closer relations with the national assemblies and closer collaboration with the EEC Commission. Whereas he feels the Commission is more to blame in the latter instance, in regard to the national bodies he charges that the Parliament has not bothered to "nurture" this relationship, preferring to maintain a "disinterested" attitude. See *The Eurocrats* (Baltimore: Johns Hopkins, 1966), pp. 164-72.

4. Michael Niblock, *The EEC: National Parliaments in Community Decision-Making,* European series no. 17 (London: Chatham House/ Political and Economic Planning, 1971), pp. 75-76.

5. See Parlement Européen, *Débats,* March 27, 1963, pp. 60-102.

6. Ibid., pp. 120-21. For text of the resolution see *Bulletin of the European Communities,* May 1963, annex, p. 60. The Gaullists left the Liberal group after the November 1962 French elections increased their number within the European Parliament to fifteen. Although they lacked the necessary seventeen minimum members to form a political group, they managed to get the Parliament to agree in January 1965 to decrease the minimum number needed to fourteen. The Gaullists then formed the European Democratic Union group. They were consistent opponents of strengthening the Parliament. See Political and Economic Planning, *Euro-*

pean Political Parties (London: George Allen and Unwin, 1970), pp. 478-79.

7. "Speech by Walter Hallstein, President of the EEC Commission, at Columbia University, New York, March 4, 1963," rpt. in WEU Assembly, *Political Union of Europe 1963-1973,* pp. 13-14.

8. Furler, Parlement Européen, *Débats,* June 27, 1963, pp. 156-61. See also ibid., "Resolution sur les compétences et les pouvoirs du Parlement Européen," pp. 185-86.

9. Ibid., p. 186.

10. Ibid. For a full account of the debates see pp. 161-84.

11. Illerhaus, ibid., pp. 173-74.

12. The Parliament's critics have claimed that it has lacked the will to really force the states to take its demands seriously and to actively lobby for its goals. Yet perusal of the parliamentary proceedings of the mid-1960s does not substantiate this charge.

13. Wolfram E. Hanrieder, *The Stable Crisis: Two Decades of German Foreign Policy* (New York: Harper and Row, 1970), pp. 60-61.

14. The solution to the potential problem of German nuclear armament, as far as U.S. policymakers were concerned, was to have West Germany join an integrated nuclear force. De Gaulle, intent on developing an independent French nuclear capability, accused Erhard of violating the Franco-German Treaty. The United States exacerbated the already testy relations between de Gaulle and Erhard by supporting the West German rejection of a lower price for French agricultural products while negotiations were proceeding on the common farm policy. Although the MLF proposal was withdrawn by the Johnson administration in December 1964, the damage was done.

15. "Speech by Chancellor Erhard in the Bundestag, Bonn, January 9, 1964," rpt. in WEU Assembly, *The Political Union of Europe,* pp. 29-30.

16. Ibid., p. 30.

17. Council of Europe, Consultative Assembly, *Official Report of the Debates,* January 14, 1964, pp. 593-600.

18. "Press Conference by President de Gaulle, Paris, January 31, 1964," rpt. in WEU Assembly, *The Political Union of Europe,* pp. 32-33.

19. *European Community,* no. 70, April 1964, p. 1.

20. Ibid. The Council was unable to agree on the size of the single Commission. Of the two proposals under consideration, one called for a nine-member commission and the other for fourteen members. In regard to the council voting procedure, according to the EEC Treaty, the Council decided most policy matters by a unanimous vote while the ECSC Council under the Paris Treaty was required to decide most matters by a qualified

majority (five-sixths) vote. France was opposed to majority voting. In early 1964, it appeared possible that the French government would try to change or omit the majority voting provisions from the Paris and Rome Treaties when the communities were merged. See *Le Monde,* May 10-11, 1964.

21. Parlement Européen, *Débats,* May 12, 1964, pp. 28-43.

22. "Communication from the EEC Commission to the EEC Council and Governments, Brussels, October 2, 1964," rpt. in WEU Assembly, *Political Union of Europe,* pp. 38-45.

23. Parlement Européen, *Débats,* October 21, 1964, pp. 109-16.

24. For a list of the fifteen questions with Hallstein's answers see *Bulletin of the European Communities,* December 1964, pp. 53-58.

25. For the text of the West German and Italian proposals see WEU Assembly, *Political Union of Europe,* pp. 45-55. For a contemporary account of European political union in the 1960s see Susanne J. Bodenheimer, "The 'Political Union' Debate in Europe: A Case Study in Intergovernmental Diplomacy," *International Organization* 21 (Winter 1967) : 24-54.

26. Although there is no official text of Saragat's address, his statement on the meeting is reprinted in EP, *The Case for Elections,* pp. 250-51. Saragat noted that, although five of the states gave the proposal a "favorable reception," France insisted that even partial direct elections were conditional on the successful completion of a plan for political union.

27. Edward T. O'Toole, "The Ambitious Men of Europe House," *Reporter,* February 25, 1965, pp. 21-26.

28. *The Times,* February 14, 1965.

29. For text of the resolution see *Bulletin of the European Communities,* March 1965, annex 2, p. 71.

30. O'Toole, "The Ambitious Men of Europe House," p. 26.

31. Françoise de la Serre, "La Communauté économique européene et la crise de 1965," *Revue Française de Science Politique* 2 (April 1971): 402-20.

32. While Hallstein was supported by Mansholt, a third member of the Commission, Robert Marjolin, correctly surmised that the plan would never be accepted by de Gaulle and that it was a mistake. Miriam Camps, *European Unification in the Sixties* (New York: McGraw Hill, 1966), p. 47.

33. John Newhouse, *Collision in Brussels* (New York: Norton, 1967), pp. 56-57. Both Newhouse and Camps provide comprehensive assessments of the crisis.

34. The provisions of Article 201 were as follows: "The Commission

shall study the conditions under which the financial contributions of Member States provided for in Article 200 may be replaced by other resources available to the Community itself, in particular by revenue accruing from the common customs tariff when finally introduced. The Commission shall for this purpose submit proposals to the Council. The Council may, after consulting the Assembly as to these proposals, unanimously determine the provisions which it shall recommend the Member States to adopt in accordance with their respective constitutional requirements." *Treaty Establishing the European Economic Community,* HMSO, 1962.

35. Camps, *European Unification in the Sixties,* p. 45.

36. For the text of the Commission's proposals on the Parliament's budgetary powers see *Bulletin of the European Communities,* June 1965, annex, pp. 56-59.

37. Parlement Européen, *Débats,* March 24, 1965, pp. 149-55.

38. According to Camps, the French government had not objected when the Commission had presented French-supported proposals before the Parliament prior to their submission to the Council of Ministers. See *European Unification in the Sixties,* p. 49.

39. Parlement Européen, *Débats,* March 24, 1965, pp. 149-55. The Parliament was scheduled to debate the plan in its May session.

40. Ibid., p. 154.

41. The size of the single Commission was set at nine members *after* the merger of the three communities. Until that time, the new Commission would have fourteen members.

42. See *Le Monde,* March 27-April 1, 1965.

43. *Verhandlungen des Deutschen Bundestages,* Doc. 4/2338. See also EP, *The Case for Elections,* pp. 16, 280-81.

44. Hallstein, Parlement Européen, *Débats,* May 11, pp. 76-77. Hallstein was quick to abandon his "imperative and unavoidable" aim to strengthen the Parliament in the months that followed. For entire debate see pp. 58-88.

45. For a comparison of the Commission text and the Parliament's amended version see *Bulletin of the EC,* June 1965, annex, pp. 56-59. The final vote on the resolution was 76 to 0 with 10 Gaullist abstentions. For a synopsis of the debates including the Gaullist views see *European Community,* no. 82, June 1965, p. 3. Also, European Parliament, *Working Documents,* "The Activities of the European Parliament from 1 May 1965 to 30 April 1966," Doc. 93, July 1, 1966.

46. Pleven, Parlement Européen, *Débats,* May 12, 1965, p. 104.

47. This did not mean that the Five agreed on how this was to be

accomplished. For a concise assessment of the positions of the German, Belgian, Italian, and Dutch governments see Hanrieder, *The Stable Crisis,* pp. 66-68.

48. European Parliament, *Monthly Bulletin of European Documentation* (July 1965) : 8.

49. See Parlement Européen, *Débats,* June 15, 1965, pp. 60-61.

50. EP, *European Documentation* (July 1965) : 4. The resumption of talks on political union were also discussed. According to a statement issued by the French government on the meeting, only the decisions made by the Council in the coming weeks would determine "under what conditions such a conference could be held." *Le Monde,* June 16, 1965.

51. Press accounts of the Brussels negotiations indicated that France was willing to extend the deadline past June 30 or to make a temporary agreement by that date. See *Le Monde,* June 15, 1965; *The Financial Times,* June 14-15, 1965; and *The Observer,* June 13, 1965.

52. *Le Monde,* June 17, 1965.

53. EP, *European Documentation* (August 1965) : 49-51. See also Patterson, *The SPD and European Integration,* p. 145.

54. *Le Monde,* July 2, 1965.

CHAPTER 6

1. Although French technical experts continued to participate in routine Community operations, France did not take part in Council meetings or other top-level activities. This so-called empty-chair policy paralyzed the Community decision-making process.

2. See Willis, *France, Germany and the New Europe, 1945-67* (Stanford: Stanford University Press, 1968), pp. 312, 322-23. According to Willis, de Gaulle's January 1963 press conference was the "opening salvo" in this campaign.

3. Camps, *European Unification in the Sixties* (New York: McGraw Hill, 1966), pp. 16, 35. Camps also holds that the crisis was a "logical consequence" of de Gaulle's failure to "wean" West Germany from its close ties with the United States.

4. Newhouse, *Collision in Brussels* (New York: Norton), pp. 20-21.

5. EP, *European Documentation* 9 (September 1965) : 17-20. Hallstein also pointed out that the European Parliament's demands were— when compared to the Commission's proposals—"decidedly further-reaching."

6. *European Community,* no. 86, October 1965, p. 2. For proceedings and resolution see Parlement Européen, *Débats,* September 24, 1965, pp. 7-9. The resolution also emphasized that no state had the right to refuse

to discharge its obligations under the treaties. The European Democratic Union abstained on the grounds that the crisis concerned the governments only.

7. EP, *European Documentation* 10 (October 1965) : 3-6. Also, *Le Monde*, September 11, 1965.

8. Parlement Européen, *Débats*, October 20, 1965, pp. 57-117 passim. Also *European Community*, no. 87, November 1965, p. 2, and EP, *European Documentation* 11 (November 1965) : 45-54.

9. Ibid., p. 47.

10. Ibid., p. 49.

11. Ibid., pp. 80-88. Also, *Le Monde*, October 22, 1965.

12. Parlement Européen, *Débats*, October 21, 1965, pp. 161-62.

13. Editorializing on the state of the Community, *The Times* bleakly remarked: "The crisis . . . must be seen for what it is: yet another upheaval in the continuous effort to create a new political entity in the heart of Europe. As virtually every issue from now on will involve some loss of sovereignty . . . the crises are bound to get bigger and noisier. Each crisis may be the last, leading to the breakup of the whole experiment." *The Times*, July 2, 1965.

14. For the initial West German reaction to the crisis see *Frankfurter Allgemeine Zeitung*, July 2-3, 9, 12, and 16, 1965. See also de la Serre, "La Communauté économique européenne et la crise de 1965," p. 145. The Council met on October 26.

15. De la Serre argues that de Gaulle's planned assault on NATO and his fear of a "rapprochement" between Britain and the Five led him to resolve the crisis. Ibid., p. 145.

16. De Gaulle wished to wait until after the French presidential elections. The results of the elections weakened rather than strengthened his bargaining position since he was forced to face a runoff election.

17. This facetiously termed "gentleman's agreement to disagree" amounted to a French capitulation. De Gaulle did not obtain a clearcut rejection of the principle of majority voting.

18. Hallstein, in the manner of a head of state, had "received" delegates of foreign nations on behalf of the EEC.

19. For text of the agreements see WEU Assembly, *Political Union of Europe, 1963-1973*, pp. 62-63.

20. EP, *European Documentation* 1 (January 1966) : 41-50.

21. Rey had distinguished himself as the negotiator for the Common Market in the "Kennedy Round" tariff-cutting discussions.

22. See Proceedings of the Second Chamber of the Dutch States-General, December 2, 1965, condensed in EP, *European Documentation* 1 (January 1966) : 46.

23. *Verhandlungen des Deutschen Bundestages*, Doc. 4/2338 and Doc.

4/3130. Also EP, *European Documentation* 9 (September 1965) : 43-48, and EP, *The Case for Elections,* pp. 281-88. For texts of the numerous Italian bills on direct elections from 1961 to 1970 see ibid., pp. 294-312.

24. EP, *European Documentation* 1 (January 1966) : 44-46. Vredeling proposed linking the majority vote principle with the strengthening of the Parliament but Foreign Minister Luns considered this "too radical a tactic."

25. Ibid., 2 (January 1966) : 33-47.

26. See Parlement Européen, *Débats,* Poher, March 8, 1966, pp. 14-17; Metzger, March 9, 1966, "Report on the Current Political Situation in the Community," Doc. 18, 1966-1967, pp. 108-13; Pleven, March 9, 1966, pp. 122-24; Marjolin, May 11, 1966, pp. 106-12, and Illerhaus Report, October 20, 1966, pp. 138-41 (for subsequent debates and resolution, pp. 141-62 passim). Also EP, *Working Documents,* Doc. 93, July 1966, "The Activities of the European Parliament from May 1, 1965 to April 30, 1966," pp. 23-24. Also ibid., Doc. 94, June 22, 1967, "The Activities of the European Parliament from May 1, 1966 to April 30, 1967," pp. 19, 71-72. Also "Discussion between Parliament, the Councils and Executives" in EP, *European Documentation* 7 (July 1965) : 63-67.

27. The Parliament had stepped up its submission of written questions to the commissions over the years. Whereas in 1958 only 29 questions were submitted, by 1966 the number had risen to 129 for that year. The Socialists were responsible for the majority of these questions (575 of the total 1,030 questions submitted from 1958 to 1966). Verbal questions were rarely used. See Gerda Zelletin, "Form and Function of the Opposition in the European Communities," *Government and Opposition* 2 (April-July 1967) : 430-31.

28. W. Hartley Clark describes the European Parliament at mid-decade in *The Politics of the Common Market* (Englewood Cliffs, N.J.: Prentice-Hall, 1967), pp. 80-84.

29. The Dutch government continued to be the most outspoken among the Six on the issue of strengthening the Community. See "Memorandum Submitted by the Dutch Government in Reply to the Interim Report on the Merger of the Executives" in EP, *European Documentation* 5 (May 1966) : 62-63.

30. *Le Monde,* February 23, 1966. Also EP, *European Documentation* 3 (March 1966) : 24-27.

31. In a matter of weeks after the June 30, 1965, crisis had been resolved, de Gaulle plunged Western Europe into another crisis by announcing that he would gradually end France's military association with the Atlantic Alliance between 1966 and 1967. This decision had a definite negative effect on Franco-German relations. For a brief survey of Italian

attempts to resurrect the issue of a Fouchet-style political union see
Bodenheimer, "The 'Political Union' Debate," pp. 29-30.
   32. Great Britain, *Parliamentary Debates,* Commons, 746 : 311-12.
   33. Wilson had campaigned in the 1964 election on the issue of Britain's
"stop-go" economy. However, once in office he found himself no more
able to deal with the chronic problem than his Conservative predecessor.
Throughout most of 1966, Britain was forced to buoy the sinking pound
with U.S. loans. In the summer of 1966, Wilson resorted to wage and
price controls—a move which alienated the Labour party and trade unionists.
Furthermore, Britain could not control either her Commonwealth or
EFTA partners. In announcing the second British entry bid, Wilson
claimed that the negotiations could be held *after* Britain joined the EEC.
See Uwe Kitzinger, *The Second Try* (London: Pergammon Press, 1968),
p. 49. Also Andrew Roth, *Can Parliament Decide . . . About Europe . . .
or About Anything . . . ?* (London: MacDonald, 1971), p. 93.
   34. "Press Conference by President de Gaulle," Paris, May 16, 1967,
rpt. in WEU Assembly, *The Political Union of Europe,* pp. 70-71.
   35. Parlement Européen, *Débats,* May 9, 1967, pp. 47-61.
   36. EP, *European Documentation* 4 (April-September 1967) : 57-58.
   37. EC, *Bulletin* (July 1967) : 29.
   38. Ibid., p. 24.
   39. *European Community,* no. 101, March 1967, pp. 21-22.
   40. EC, *Bulletin* (July 1967) : 5-7, 23. Also Hallstein, Parlement Européen, *Débats,* June 21, 1967, pp. 88-94.
   41. Ibid., July 21, 1967, pp. 118-30.
   42. *Le Monde,* November 29, 1967. Not unexpectedly, when the Council of Ministers met on December 19, it failed to approve the British request for negotiations.
   43. EP, *European Documentation* 5 (October-December 1967) : 36.
   44. Patterson, *The SPD and European Integration* (Lexington, Mass.:
Lexington Books, 1974), pp. 144-46.
   45. See Anthony Sampson, *The New Europeans* (London: Hoddert
and Stoughton, 1968), pp. 20, 28-55.
   46. J. L. Heldring, "No Unity for Europe," *Interplay,* October 1968,
p. 41.
   47. Spinelli, *The Eurocrats: Conflict and Crisis in the European Community* (Baltimore: The Johns Hopkins Press, 1966), p. 139.
   48. Hans Herbert Götz, "Nothing Has Changed or Has It?" *European
Community,* no. 118, November 1968, p. 7.
   49. Ibid. See also Parlement Européen, *Débats,* November 27-Decem-
ber 1, 1967, passim.
   50. EP, *European Documentation* 2 (April-June 1968) : 23-24.

51. *Verhandlungen des Deutschen Bundestages,* sess. 221, March 19, 1969.

52. EP, *European Documentation* 2 (April-June 1968) : 38-42.

53. Ibid., 4 (October-December 1968) : 64. In early 1969, some 200,000 Italians signed a "people's initiative bill" calling for direct elections. See Michael Steed, "The European Parliament: The Significance of Direct Election" in *The New Politics of European Integration,* ed. Ghita Ionescu, pp. 140-41. Yet another direct election bill was introduced in the Chamber of Deputies on June 27, 1968. This Socialist-sponsored measure designated May 9, 1969, as the date for Italian European elections. The bill was referred to the Foreign Affairs Committee and the Constitutional Affairs Committee. For texts of the October 7, 1968, motion and the June 1968 bill see EP, *The Case for Elections,* pp. 308-10.

54. EP, *European Documentation* 1 (January-March 1969) : 58-64.

55. Bills no. 679 (May 28, 1968) and 688 (April 5, 1968) reprinted in EP, *The Case for Elections,* pp. 291-92. The 1968 bills were identical to a bill (no. 391) introduced in the National Assembly by the *Rassemblement Démocratique* and allies on June 12, 1963. This bill had scheduled the elections for May 9, 1965, and had required the government to make known the electoral procedure by December 31, 1963. The measure had been buried in the Foreign Affairs Committee for nearly five years.

56. See Gordon Wright, *France in Modern Times* (Chicago: Rand McNally, 1974), pp. 432-35, and Mayne, *The Recovery of Europe,* p. 343.

57. "Benelux Memorandum on the Situation in the Community," January 19, 1968, rpt. in WEU Assembly, *The Political Union of Europe,* p. 71. Also Bliss, *The Political Development of the European Community,* Doc. 26 (the Benelux Plan), pp. 251-53.

58. For various excerpts of press statements of Brandt and other members of the West German government see EP, *European Documentation* 2 (April-June 1968) : 12-21. Although West Germany continued to stress the need for a "political community," the Czech crisis of August 1968 substantially weakened Franco-German relations. De Gaulle accused Kiesinger and Brandt of encouraging the crisis through courting Czechoslovakia, while the latter claimed that the French president was partly to blame for pursuing détente with the Soviet Union. See Hanrieder, *The Stable Crisis,* pp. 76-77.

59. EP, *European Documentation* 4 (October-December 1968) : 77. Luns first made his announcement at the WEU foreign ministers' meeting at The Hague. He repeated the invitation at an EEC meeting in Brussels (from which France was absent).

60. EC, *Bulletin* 1 (April 1968) : 8-15. Also Parlement Européen, *Débats,* March 12, 1968, pp. 2-4.

   61. Rey, ibid., May 15, 1968, pp. 119-29.

   62. The exchange was sparked by an oral question addressed to Mansholt by the Gaullists. Ibid., July 3, 1968, pp. 158-65. The June election was a triumph for the Gaullists and their allies who won 358 of 485 seats. Pierre Mendès-France and 117 members of the opposition lost their seats. Morgan, *Western European Politics since 1945,* pp. 162-63.

   63. Until 1969, the Italian Chamber and Senate had refused to replace delegates to the European Parliament who had died or failed to be re-elected in order to avoid nominating Communists. However, in the face of Socialist pressure, the Italian delegation was finally selected. Among these new members were seven Communists, one Monarchist, and one neo-Fascist. See F. Roy Willis, *Italy Chooses Europe* (New York: Oxford University Press, 1971), pp. 99-100. The French Assembly had avoided nominating Communists to the European Parliament by using party lists of candidates rather than proportional representation.

   64. EC, *Bulletin* 2 (May 1969) : 5-7.

   65. Ibid., pp. 79-81. Also *European Community,* no. 122, April 1969, p. 19.

   66. Dehousse Report, Doc. 214/69 (March 12, 1969), in European Parliament, *The Case for Elections to the European Parliament,* 1970, pp. 252-55. For the English translation of following debates see pp. 256-77.

   67. Ibid., pp. 252-53.

   68. For resolution see ibid., p. 258.

   69. The Gaullist proposal was merely a stalling tactic since there was no possibility of the Six agreeing on a "real European Constitution"—especially France. The Gaullists continued to base their opposition on their allegation that an "assembly system" of government was Europe's "incurable disease." See Ribère, ibid., pp. 263-64.

   70. Bermani, ibid., pp. 264-65.

   71. Romeo, Westerterp, ibid., p. 267.

   72. Ibid., p. 276. The Gaullists abstained.

CHAPTER 7

1. *Le Monde,* March 5, 1969. The French government's status as champion of détente in Europe was adroitly usurped by Brandt on behalf of West Germany.

   2. Ibid., March 16-17, 1969. It appeared that de Gaulle's opposition to enlargement of the Community (that is, British entry) was weakening

as his popularity diminished. In February 1969, he had informed the British ambassador, Christopher Soames, that he could accept British participation in a loosely knit free trade area. However, the president's suggestion that Britain and France hold secret discussions on the matter was viewed warily by the Wilson government, which informed France's Community partners of the scheme—much to de Gaulle's great irritation. See Mowat, *Creating the European Community*, pp. 200-201.

3. Maurice Schumann replaced Debré as foreign minister. However, the latter continued his hard-line Gaullist policies as minister of defense. Independent Giscard d'Estaing became finance minister and moderate Gaullist Jacques Chaban-Delmas was appointed prime minister.

4. EP, *European Documentation* 2 (April-June 1969) : 35. See also *Le Monde*, May 24, 1969.

5. Mowat, *Creating the European Community*, p. 202.

6. EP, *European Documentation* 2 (April-June 1969) : 38-40.

7. Morgan, *West European Politics since 1945* (London: Batsford, 1972), p. 212.

8. EC, *Bulletin* 3 (January 1970) : 7.

9. Ibid., 2 (July 1969) : 25-30.

10. EP, *European Documentation* 2 (April-June 1969) : 67-69. For the English translation of the debates see EP, *The Case for Elections*, pp. 314-19.

11. Ibid., pp. 310-12.

12. For text of the bill see ibid., pp. 278-79. Also see EP, *European Documentation* 3 (July-September 1969) : 2-5.

13. "Declaration on Europe by the Government of the United Kingdom and the Government of the Republic of Italy," April 28, 1969, rpt. in WEU Assembly, *The Political Union of Europe*, pp. 82-85.

14. *The Times*, May 7 and 21, 1969.

15. European Parliament, press release, July 22, 1969. Also see Michael Steed, "The European Parliament: the Significance of Direct Election," in Ionescu, *The New Politics of European Integration*, pp. 140-41.

16. *Agence Europe International d'Information pour la Presse*, no. 441 (new series), November 3, 1969.

17. Ibid.

18. EP, *European Documentation* 2 (April-June 1969) : 12-15.

19. Excerpt of the address is reprinted in WEU Assembly, *The Political Union of Europe*, p. 85.

20. *Verhandlungen des Deutschen Bundestages*, 6th legislative period, sess. 6 and 7, October 29-30, 1969.

21. *Le Monde*, September 6, 1969.

22. EP, *European Documentation* 4 (October-December 1969) : 33-34.
23. Ibid., pp. 34-35.
24. EC, *Bulletin* 2 (September-October 1969) : 32-33.
25. Ibid., 2 (December 1969) : 5-7.
26. Ibid., pp. 91-96.
27. The participants were Pompidou, Brandt, Belgian Prime Minister Gaston Eyskens, Italian Premier Mariano Rumor, Luxembourg Prime Minister Pierre Werner, and P. J. S. de Jong, the Dutch prime minister.
28. EC, *Bulletin* 3 (February 1970) : 38-40.
29. Ibid., p. 40.
30. Ibid., pp. 43-47.
31. EP, *European Documentation* 4 (October-December 1969) : 55-58. Also see *The Times,* December 3, 1969.
32. Walter Hallstein, *Europe in the Making,* (New York: Norton, 1972), pp. 298-99.
33. EC, *Bulletin* 3 (February 1970) : 111-13.
34. Ibid., p. 113.
35. European Parliament, "Information Memo," November 1969, p. 1. The Council at its December 22 meeting had appeared to accept the Parliament's two key points: first, that the ministers immediately set a date by which the Community would be financed completely by its own resources; second, that the Parliament should ultimately (under certain conditions) be allowed to overrule the Council on budgetary matters. See Michael Niblock, *The EEC: National Parliaments in Community Decision-Making,* European series no. 17 (London: Chatham House, 1971), pp. 89-90.
36. *European Community,* no. 131, February 1970, p. 3.
37. European Parliament, *The European Communities' Own Resources and the Budgetary Powers of the European Parliament,* selected documents (October 1972), pp. 14-20.
38. For the text of the resolution see ibid., pp. 144-45. Budget Committee Chairman Georges Spénale emphasized that the Parliament must at least have the right to reject the entire Community budget as a whole. *Agence Europe,* no. 568 (new series), May 13, 1970.
39. Special committees had been established to investigate governmental cooperation in economic and monetary matters (the Werner Committee) and in foreign affairs (the Davignon Committee).
40. EP, *European Documentation* 1 (January-March 1970) : 149.
41. *Le Monde,* May 9, 1970. Also, EP, *European Documentation* 2 (April-June 1979) : 20-21.
42. Ibid., pp. 28-29.

43. *Le Monde,* July 4, 1970.

44. *Verhandlungen des Deutschen Bundestages,* 6th legislative period, sess. 53, May 27, 1970.

45. Parlement Européen, *Débats,* September 16, 1970, pp. 105-11.

46. EP, *European Documentation* 2 (April-June 1970) : 57-58.

47. *Agence Europe,* no. 590 (new series), June 15, 1970.

48. National Assembly Bill no. 1356 reprinted in EP, *European Documentation* 3 (July-September 1970) : 8-10.

49. For the full text of the report see EC, *Bulletin* 3 (November 1970) : 9-14.

50. Throughout the 1960s Wilson had been forced to deal with left-wing critics. Before assuming the leadership of the Labour party, Wilson himself had been an outspoken activist, advocating nuclear disarmament in opposition to Hugh Gaitskell in the 1950s and allying with anti-government radicals on other issues. Prior to his selection as party leader, Wilson was able skillfully to manipulate left-wing activists to enhance his own standing in the party. However, once firmly entrenched as party chief after the 1966 election, he abandoned his receptive attitude toward the activists for one of ambivalence. The second British bid to enter the Community, handled by Wilson in what appeared to be a hasty and high-handed manner, alienated a sizable number of the moderate and conservative anti-Common Market Labourites, who joined with the left-wingers in a broad-based "supergroup." Shortly after the disastrous June 1970 election, the trade unions began to shift from a position of guarded support to an anti-Community stand. See Roth, *Can Parliament Decide . . . ?,* p. 173.

51. Great Britain, Parliament, *Command Papers,* 4289:21.

52. Until the publication of a White Paper on July 7, 1971, the Heath government had taken the official position that Britain would join the Community only if the terms were acceptable (essentially the Labour position). However, unlike the vague, philosophical Labour White Paper of the previous year, the Conservative document called unequivocally for Britain to "seize the opportunity and join the European Community." Great Britain, Parliament, *Command Papers,* 4715:2.

53. *Agence Europe,* no. 755 (new series), February 20, 1971. The SPD was split over the issue of West German unilateral direct elections. By late 1971, the party had dropped unilateral elections in favor of working toward Community-wide European elections. See Patterson, *The SPD and European Integration,* p. 146.

54. "Press Conference by Mr. Pompidou," January 21, 1971, rpt. in WEU Assembly, *The Political Union of Europe,* pp. 93-95.

55. *Agence Europe,* no. 859 (new series), July 29, 1971.

56. Ibid., no. 673 (new series), April 19, 1972.

57. European Community Press and Information, "Background Note," June 27, 1972. For a lengthy critical analysis of the report see Federal Trust for Education and Research, The Center for Contemporary European Studies and the University of Sussex Institute for the Study of International Organization, *Parliamentary Aspects of the Enlarged European Communities* (report of a joint meeting held June 2-4, 1972).

58. *The Economist* 243 (June 10, 1972) : 17-18.

59. *The Times,* June 10, 1972. Both *The Economist* and *The Times* dismissed the upcoming summit meeting of the Nine as a waste of time.

60. For the debate on the progress of the Community and the development of the Parliament see Parlement Européen, *Débats,* July 5, 1972, pp. 125-92 passim. For the text of the resolution see EC, *Bulletin* 5 (August 1972) : 30-33.

61. Morgan, *West European Politics since 1945,* pp. 224-25. Also "Vertigo before the Summit," *The Economist* 243 (June 10, 1972) : 32-35.

62. For the texts of the addresses of the heads of state see EC, *Bulletin* 5 (November 1972) : 9-47.

63. Ibid., pp. 22-23.

64. For the text of the resolution see ibid., pp. 67-71. Also, Parlement Européen, *Débats,* November 15, 1972, pp. 89-110.

65. *Baltimore Sun,* December 14, 1972.

66. The Luxembourg Treaty of April 22, 1970, had specified that the Commission should submit proposals to the Council to this effect within two years.

67. Parlement Européen, *Documents de Séance,* motion de censure, Doc. 204, November 16, 1972. Also *Agence Europe,* no. 1133, November 16, 1972.

68. Parlement Européen, *Débats,* December 11, 1972, pp. 7-16, and December 12, 1972, p. 51.

CHAPTER 8

1. EP, London Information Office, *European Parliament Report,* "How Is It Working?" (April 1973) : 7.

2. Peter Kirk, Christopher Soames, and John Davies, *Three Views of Europe* (London: Conservative Political Center, 1973), p. 26.

3. "Letter from Strasbourg," *The New Yorker,* September 15, 1975, p. 96.

4. Personal interview, 1978.

5. Kirk, *Three Views of Europe,* p. 27.

6. *European Parliament Report,* April 1973, p. 7. The Irish delegation remained unaffiliated while continuing to negotiate with the political groups. See also EC, *Bulletin* 2 (February 1973) : 5.

7. *European Community,* December 1972, p. 6.

8. *Agence Europe,* no. 1204 (new series), January 19, 1973, pp. 7-8. The Parliament's Legal Affairs Committee had investigated the creation of a Question Time in 1972. European Parliament, *Working Documents,* Doc. 252 (January 10, 1972). For Kirk's maiden speech to the Parliament see Parlement Européen, *Débats,* January 16, 1973, pp. 13-14.

9. *Agence Europe,* no. 1204, pp. 7-8.

10. Ibid.

11. Ibid. Kirk originally attached a draft motion to his memorandum demanding that these reforms should be introduced within three months. However, he soon realized that the European Parliament could hardly metamorphose into a British-style legislature overnight.

12. European Parliament, *Working Documents,* Doc. 306 (February 14, 1973).

13. Ibid., Explanatory Statement, Doc. 386 (January 14, 1975), p. 37.

14. European Parliament, "Information," June 22, 1973, pp. 1-2.

15. European Parliament, *Working Documents,* Doc. 131 (July 2, 1973).

16. European Parliament, "Information," July 11, 1973.

17. Kirk, European Parliament, *Debates,* July 3, 1973, pp. 16, 18-19.

18. *European Community,* no. 169, October 1973, p. 6.

19. Ibid., p. 6. Also European Parliament, *Working Documents,* Doc. 190 (October 1973).

20. *The German Tribune,* no. 579, May 17, 1973, p. 6.

21. *European Community,* no. 161, December 1972, p. 8.

22. Polls preceding the election had indicated that the French public was eager to have new leadership. The Socialists and Communists agreed to an uncomfortable alliance for the election. The result was a precipitous drop in support for the Gaullists and their allies, who managed to retain a clear majority but one that was reduced by nearly a hundred seats. See Wright, *France in Modern Times,* p. 437.

23. *The Irish Times,* June 23, 1973.

24. Personal interview.

25. WEU Assembly, *Political Union of Europe,* "Second Report on European Political Cooperation on Foreign Policy Approved by the Nine Foreign Ministers," Copenhagen, July 23, 1973, pp. 106-25.

26. Ibid., "Press Conference by Mr. Pompidou," Paris, September 1973, pp. 112-13.

27. EC, *Bulletin* 10 (October 1973) : 78-79.

28. Brandt, European Parliament, *Debates,* November 13, 1973, pp. 20-25.

29. Ibid.

30. The critical oil situation quickly replaced other issues as the major topic of Community concern.

31. *The Times,* July 6, 1973.

32. *The Times,* October 1, 1973. See also *European Community,* no. 171, December 1973, pp. 20-21. The British public tended to blame the Community for inflation, especially rising food prices.

33. U.S., Department of State, *Bulletin,* vol. 68, no. 1766, pp. 593-95.

34. Ibid., no. 1771, p. 755.

35. WEU Assembly, *Political Union of Europe,* "Address by Mr. Kissinger to the Pilgrims' Society," London, December 12, 1973, pp. 120-21.

36. The accompanying debate was riddled with members' complaints that summit meetings were coming to replace Community institutions. See European Parliament, *Debates,* December 12, 1973, pp. 145-63, especially Lange, pp. 161-62; Giraudo, p. 146; Bertrand, p. 148; and Romualdi, p. 158. For the resolution see EC, *Bulletin* 12 (December 1973) : 6-7.

37. WEU Assembly, *The Political Union of Europe,* "Communiqué Issued after the Nine-Power Conference," Copenhagen, December 15, 1973, pp. 124-25. Also EC, *Bulletin* 12 (December 1973) : 9-12.

38. Kirk, European Parliament, *Debates,* December 12, 1973.

39. *European Community,* no. 176, May 1974, pp. 16-17.

40. Ibid.

41. See European Parliament, *Debates,* "Debate on the General Report of the Commission for 1973," May 14, 1974, pp. 69-96.

42. *European Community,* no. 176, May 19, 1974, p. 16. Spinelli was later to resign his post as a member of the Commission to take a seat in the Italian Parliament and become affiliated with the Italian Communist party.

43. EC, *Bulletin* 5 (May 1974) : 72.

44. Fellermaier, European Parliament, *Debates,* July 9, 1974, pp. 104-5.

45. Patijn, ibid., October 16, 1974, pp. 135-37.

46. EC, *Bulletin* 12 (December 1974) : 8.

47. Ibid., pp. 8-9.

48. Ibid.

49. European Parliament, *Working Documents,* Doc. 368, "Elections to the European Parliament" (January 14, 1975), p. 6.

50. Ibid., p. 14.

51. Ibid., p. 15.

52. See "Explanation," ibid., p. 19.

53. See European Parliament, *Debates,* January 14, 1975, pp. 55-93 passim. For a breakdown of the vote see European Parliament, "Direct Elections" (informational pamphlet), 1977, p. 4. Also European Community Information Service, "Background Information," no. 32, October 29, 1975.

54. Patijn, European Parliament, *Debates,* January 14, 1975, p. 77.

55. *Agence Europe,* no. 1820 (new series), September 18, 1975.

56. Ibid., no. 1854 (new series), November 6, 1975.

57. *European Yearbook,* 23, 1975 (The Hague: Martinus Nijhoff, 1977), p. 633.

58. Ibid., pp. 633-34. Also *Official Journal of the European Communities,* no. C89, April 22, 1975, pp. 1-2. Also see European Parliament, *Working Documents,* Doc. 483 (February 17, 1974). The Parliament had agreed to support the Council's April 1970 financial provisions in return for the Council's pledge to investigate further EEC treaty revisions to give the Parliament greater budgetary powers. For background information see ibid., Doc. 175 (October 3, 1973), and ibid., Doc. 166 (July 9, 1975).

59. *European Yearbook,* 1975, p. 337.

60. Ibid., p. 635.

61. European Parliament, "Direct Elections," pp. 4-5.

62. *European Yearbook,* 1975, p. 635.

63. Great Britain, *Parliamentary Debates,* Commons, December 4, 1975, 901:1931.

64. Great Britain, Cmnd. 6399:5. See also *The Economist* 258 (February 21, 1976), p. 57.

65. *The Times,* February 27, 1976.

66. EC, *Bulletin* 11 (November 1975) : 10.

67. Ben Patterson, *Direct Elections to the European Parliament* (London: British Council of the European Movement, 1974), p. 2.

68. *Agence Europe,* no. 1915 (new series), February 9-10, 1976.

69. Ibid. For additional background on the various plans see *The Times,* March 30, 1976.

70. *Agence Europe,* no. 311, March 18, 1976. Also *The Guardian,* March 31, 1976, and *The Times,* March 30, 1976.

71. *The Guardian,* March 27, 1976.

72. European Parliament, "Direct Elections," p. 5.

73. *Euroforum,* no. 15, April 13, 1976, annex 1, pp. 1-3. Also European Parliament, *Debates,* April 5, 1976, p. 7.

74. Ibid., April 7, 1976, pp. 86-116 passim.

75. *Agence Europe,* no. 322, May 4, 1976, p. 4, and ibid., no. 1979 (new series), May 10-11, 1976.

76. European Parliament, "Direct Elections," p. 5.

77. *Agence Europe,* no. 341, July 14, 1976. The compromise grew from a Dutch proposal to give 80 seats to the four large states, 25 to Belgium and the Netherlands, 15 each to Ireland and Denmark, and 6 to Luxembourg. But the British wanted 82 seats to facilitate distribution to Wales, Scotland, Northern Ireland, and England.

78. EC, *Bulletin* 7-9 (July 1976) : 5-7.

79. Council of the European Communities, press release, September 20, 1976. Also *Europolitique Report,* no. 357, September 25, 1976.

80. *The Baltimore Sun,* September 30, 1976. Also *The Guardian,* September 18, 1976.

CHAPTER 9

1. The daily releases of the *Agence Europe* throughout 1977 and early 1978 provide a highly detailed account and are the best source of information on the activities of the national parliaments concerning direct election legislation, especially the British ramifications. For background information on the British electoral system see European Parliament, *Electoral Laws of Parliaments of the Member States of the European Communities,* August 1977.

2. Great Britain, Cmnd. 6768, April 1, 1977. Also British Information Services, Policy and Reference Division, "Methods of Direct Elections to the European Community" (New York: April 6, 1977), pp. 1-4.

3. *The New York Times,* December 14, 1977. The Liberal party was sorely disappointed by the result of the vote and threatened to withdraw its support from the Labour government. *The Guardian,* December 25, 1977, and *The Christian Science Monitor,* December 16, 1977. The Conservatives were more than 30 seats short of a majority with the smaller political parties so divided as to make their support impossible to obtain. The 13 Liberals were enough to keep the 308 Labour M.P.s in the majority in the 635-seat Commons.

4. *Agence Europe,* no. 2287 (new series), September 2, 1977.

5. *Financial Times,* October 12, 1976, and November 11, 1976. Also, *Agence Europe,* no. 2124 (new series), January 3-4, 1977.

6. EC Commission, *European Report,* no. 415, May 5, 1977.

7. *The Economist* 263 (June 18, 1977) : 65.

8. For a table outlining the progress of direct election legislation in the various national parliaments see *Courier,* no. 48, March-April 1978, p. 62. In regard to the special problem of West Berlin, the United States, Britain, and France on September 1, 1977, approved the selection of delegates to the European Parliament by the West Berlin Diet rather than by direct election in order to avoid antagonizing the Soviet Union.

9. See Appendix for a synopsis of the election results on a state-by-state basis; see *Europe* (formerly *European Community*) no. 214, July-August 1979, pp. 6-11.

10. *The New York Times,* June 12, 1979. For other press accounts of the elections see ibid., June 11, 1979; *The Washington Post,* June 11-12, 1979 and *The Guardian,* June 17, 1979.

11. *Europe,* no. 214, July-August, 1979, pp. 10, 42.

12. Ibid., pp. 9-10.

13. EC Commission, "European Union: Report to the European Council by Leo Tindemans," 1976.

14. Viewpoints expressed are distilled from personal interviews and/or personal correspondence.

15. Jenkins has reiterated this warning on various occasions, most recently before the Parliament on July 4, 1978, during the discussion of the European Council's choice of June 1979 for the elections. Tugendhat spoke in a similar vein before a meeting of the Conservative group on July 1. See *The Sunday Times,* July 2, 1978.

16. Personnel correspondence from the Foreign Office, April 27, 1978.

17. Excerpts from Wilson's address delivered at Florida State University, October 1, 1977.

18. *The Sunday Times,* June 25, 1978.

19. For background on the PCI and its changing attitude toward the Community see John Foster Leich, "The Italian Communists and the European Parliament," *Journal of Common Market Studies* 9 (June 1971) : 271-81. Also, Fitzmaurice, *The Party Groups in the European Parliament* ("The Communist and Allies Group"), pp. 129-44. A good supplement to the above is James O. Goldsborough, "Communism in Western Europe," *European Community,* no. 194, April-May 1976, pp. 3-6.

20. *European Community* interviewed Spinelli on the issue of Eurocommunism. See no. 202, July-August 1977, pp. 7-10.

21. Personal interview, 1978.

22. Personal correspondence, 1978.

23. A good assessment of the history of French Communist attitudes toward the Community is Sue Ellen Charlton, *The French Left and European Integration* (Denver: University of Denver Press, 1972).

24. Bordu spoke on behalf of the French Communists during the July 4 debate on the new election date.

25. Lücker was one of the few to voice his doubts during the Parliament's July 4 debate.

26. Address to the European Democratic Forum, Brussels, September 29, 1977.

BIBLIOGRAPHY

UNPUBLISHED SOURCES, PRINTED DOCUMENTS, AND GOVERNMENT PUBLICATIONS

Action Committee for the United States of Europe. *Statements and Declarations 1955-67,* 1969.

Ad Hoc Assembly. *Draft Treaty Embodying the Statute of the European Community.* October 1952-April 1953.

———. *Report of the Constitutional Committee.* December 20, 1952.

———. *Summary Report of Debates, 1952-53.*

American Committee on United Europe. *Report from Strasbourg.* New York: 1954.

Council of Europe, Consultative Assembly. *Official Reports,* 1949- .

Council of Europe. *European Yearbook,* 1955- .

———. *Official Report of Debates of the Joint Meeting of the Members of the Consultative Assembly of the Council of Europe and the European Parliament,* 1958- .

European Coal and Steel Community, Common Assembly. *Débats,* 1953-1958.

———. *Journal Officiel* (seven volumes), December 30, 1952-April 19, 1958.

European Economic Community. *Bulletin of the European Economic Community,* 1958- .

———. Commission. *Action Programme of the Commission for the Second Stage,* 1962.

——. *The Common Market Ten Years On* (1958-67), 1969.

——. *European Union: Report to the European Council by Leo Tindemans*, 1976.

——. *The First Stages of the Common Market 1958-1962*, 1964.

——. *General Report on the Activities of the Commission*, 1968.

——. *Strengthening of the Budgetary Powers of the European Parliament (Bulletin of the European Communities*, supplement), September 1973.

European Movement. *Direct Elections to the European Parliament* (report of an all-party study group commissioned by the European Movement). London: 1974, pp. XI-83.

European Parliament. *Colloque parlementaire européen*, 1972.

——. *Council's Draft Treaty . . . establishing a Single Council and a Single Commission*, July 9, 1975.

——. *Débats*, March 1958-1973.

——. Debates, 1973- .

——. *Documents du Séance*, 1958-1973.

——. *Le Dossier de l'Union politique*, 1964.

——. *Elections to the European Parliament by Direct Universal Suffrage* (draft convention–368/74), 1975.

——. *Electoral Laws of the Parliament of the Member States of the European Community*, August 1977.

——. *European Documentation: A Survey*, 1965-1971.

——. *Guide to Documentation on the European Parliament*, August 1965.

——. *Minutes of the Proceedings*, 1973- .

European Parliament Report (issues 1-4 published as *European Parliament Newsletter*), 1971.

European Parliament. *The Activities of the European Parliament from 1 May 1967 to 30 April 1968*, 1968.

——. *The Case for Elections to the European Parliament by Direct Universal Suffrage* (selected documents), 1970.

——. *The European Communities' Own Resources and the Budgetary Powers of the European Parliament* (selected documents), 1972.

——. *The Evolution of Political Groups in the European Parliament and their Future Prospects*, 1975.

——. *Role and Function of Parliamentary Control of Community Resources and Expenditures* (report drawn up for the Committee on Budgets), 1976.

——. *Setting up of a Public Accounts Committee in the European Parliament*, June 20, 1974.

——. *The Sittings* (after January 1975 called *The Information Series*), 1967-1975.

———. *Strengthening of the Budgetary Powers of the European Parliament*, October 3, 1973.

———. *Strengthening of the Budgetary Powers of the European Parliament*, August 12, 1974.

———. *Terminology of the Rules of Procedure of the European Parliament*, 1973.

———. *Toward Political Union: A Selection of Documents with a foreword by Mr. Emilio Battista* (Community Topics no. 25), January 1964.

———. *Working Documents* (originally *Documents du Séance*), 1973- .

Federal Trust for Education and Research. *Parliamentary Aspects of the Enlarged European Communities* (report of a joint meeting held June 2-4, 1972.)

Foreign Relations of the United States, vol. 3, 1947.

Great Britain. "Direct Elections to the European Assembly," Cmnd. 6399, 1976.

Great Britain, "Direct Elections to the European Assembly. Cmnd. 6768, 1977.

Great Britain. *Parliamentary Debates* (Commons), selected volumes, 1967-1978.

Labour Party, Great Britain. *Labour and the Common Market* (report of a special conference of the Labour party), April 1975.

Official Journal of the European Communities (special English edition), 1952- .

United States, Department of State. *Bulletin,* vol. 31, no. 784-809, July 5-December 27, 1954.

United States, House, Committee on International Relations. *Assessing the New Political Trends* (report on the ninth meeting of members of Congress and the European Parliament), 1976.

Western European Union. Assembly. *Proceedings, 1955-*

———. General Affairs Committee, *Political Unification of Europe 1963-73,* 1974.

Western European Union. Assembly. *Proceedings, 1955-* .

MONOGRAPHS, SPECIALIZED PUBLICATIONS, AND GENERAL STUDIES

Acheson, Dean. *Present at the Creation.* New York: Norton, 1969.

Adenauer, Konrad. *Memoirs, 1945-53.* Chicago: Henry Regnery, 1966.

Armand, Louis. *The European Challenge.* New York: Atheneum, 1970.

Association des instituts d'Études Européennes. *Les Partis Politiques et L'Intégration Européenne.* Colloque de Bruges, Annuaire 1969/70. Geneva: 1970.

Barber, James, ed. *European Community: Vision and Reality.* London: Croom Helm, 1973.

Beloff, Max. *Europe and the Europeans: an International Discussion.* London: Chatto and Windus, 1957.

——. *The United States and the Unity of Europe.* New York: Random House, 1963.

Birke, Wolfgang. *European Elections by Direct Suffrage.* Leyden: Sythoff, 1961.

Bliss, Howard. *The Political Development of the European Community – a Documentary Collection.* Waltham, Mass.: Blaisdell, 1970.

Bowie, Robert R., and Geiger, Theodore. *The European Economic Community and the United States.* Washington, D.C.: U.S. Government Printing Office, 1961.

Boyd, F. *British Politics in Transition, 1945-63.* New York: Praeger, 1964.

Bracher, Karl. *The German Dilemma: The Relationship of State and Democracy.* New York: Praeger, 1974.

Broad, Roger. *Community Europe Today.* London: Oswald Wolff, 1972.

Brugmans, Hendrik. *L'ideé européene.* Bruges: De Tempel, 1970.

Calleo, D. P. *Europe's Future.* New York: Horizon Press, 1965.

Calmann, John. *The Common Market: The Treaty of Rome Explained.* London: Blond, 1967.

Camps, Miriam. *Britain and the European Community.* Princeton: Princeton University Press, 1965.

——. *European Unification in the Sixties.* New York: McGraw Hill, 1966.

Chapman, David. *The European Parliament: The Years Ahead.* London: The European Movement, 1973.

Charlton, Sue. *The French Left and European Integration.* Denver: Social Science Foundation, 1972.

Churchill, Winston. *Winston S. Churchill: His Complete Speeches, 1897-1963,* Robert R. James, ed. New York: Chelsea House, 1974.

Clark, W. Hartley. *The Politics of the Common Market.* Englewood Cliffs, N.J.: Prentice-Hall, 1967.

Cocks, Bennet. *The European Parliament: Structure, Procedure and Practice.* London: H.M.S.O., 1973.

Coombes, David L. *Politics and Bureaucracy in the European Community.* London: George Allen and Unwin, 1970.

——. *The Power of the Purse in European Communities.* London: Chatham House, 1972.

Cornelis, Petrus-Arsène. *Europeans about Europe.* Amsterdam: Swets and Zeitlinger, 1970.

Cosgrave, Carol Ann. *The New International Actor: The United Nations and the European Economic Community.* New York: St. Martins, 1970.

Curtis, Michael. *Western European Integration.* New York: Harper and Row, 1965.

De La Mahotière, Stuart. *Towards One Europe.* Harmondsworth: Penguin, 1970.

Delzell, Charles. *Mussolini's Enemies: The Anti-Fascist Resistance.* Princeton: Princeton University Press, 1961.

Deniau, J. F. *The Common Market.* London: Barrie and Rockleff, 1967.

de Rougemont, Denis. *The Idea of Europe.* New York: Macmillan, 1966.

Eden, Anthony. *The Memoirs of Anthony Eden.* Boston: Houghton Mifflin, 1960.

European Yearbook, 1975. The Hague: Martinus Nijhoff, 1977.

Farr, Walter. *Daily Telegraph Guide to the Common Market.* London: Collins, 1973.

Federal Trust for Education and Research. *Electing the European Parliament.* London: Federal Trust, 1972.

Fitzmaurice, John. *The Party Groups in the European Parliament.* Westmead, England: Saxon House, Heath, 1975.

Forsyth, Murray. *The Parliament of the European Communities.* London: Political Economic Planning, 1964.

Friedrich, Carl J. *Europe: An Emergent Nation?* New York: Harper and Row, 1969.

Galtung, Johan. *The European Community: A Superpower in the Making.* Oslo: Universitetsforlaget, 1973.

Gatzke, Hans. *The Present in Perspective.* Chicago: Rand McNally, 1970.

Ginestet, Pierre. *L'Assemblée parlementaire européenne.* Paris: Presses universitaires de France, 1959.

Goodman, Elliott R. *The Fate of the Atlantic Community.* New York: Praeger, 1975.

Goodwin, Geoffrey. *European Unity: A Return to Realities?* Leeds: Leeds University Press, 1972.

Grosser, Alfred. *The Foreign Policy of the Fifth Republic.* Boston: Little, Brown, 1967.

———. *Germany in Our Time.* New York: Praeger, 1971.

Haas, Ernst. *The Uniting of Europe: Political, Social and Economic Forces 1950-1957.* Stanford: Stanford University Press, 1968.

———. *The Web of Interdependence: The United States and International Organizations.* Englewood Cliffs, N.J.: Prentice-Hall, 1970.

Hallstein, Walter. *Europe in the Making.* New York: Norton, 1972.
——. *United Europe: Challenge and Opportunity.* Cambridge: Harvard University Press, 1972.
Hanrieder, Wolfram F. *The Stable Crisis: Two Decades of German Foreign Policy.* New York: Harper & Row, 1970.
——. *West German Foreign Policy, 1949-1963.* Stanford: Stanford University Press, 1967.
Hartley, Anthony. *Gaullism: The Rise and Fall of a Political Movement.* New York: Outerbridge and Dienstfrey, 1971.
Haviland, H. Field, Jr., ed. *The United States and the Western Community.* Haverford, Pa.: Haverhill College Press, 1967.
Heidelberg, Franz C. *Das Europäische Parlament.* Bonn: 1959.
Henig, Stanley, ed. *European Political Parties: A Handbook.* New York: Praeger, 1970.
Hogan, Willard Newton. *Representative Government and European Integration.* Lincoln: University of Nebraska Press, 1967.
Holt, Stephen. *The Common Market: Conflict of Theory and Practice.* London: H. Hamilton, 1967.
——. *Six European States—Countries of the European Community and Their Political Systems.* New York: Taplinger, 1970.
Hovey, J. Allan, Jr. *The Superparliaments: Interparliamentary Consultation and Atlantic Cooperation.* New York: Praeger, 1966.
Ionescu, Ghita. *Between Sovereignty and Integration.* New York: Wiley, 1974.
——, ed. *The New Politics of European Integration.* New York: Macmillan, 1972.
Jennings, W. Iver. *A Federation of Western Europe.* London: Cambridge, 1940.
Kaiser, Karl. *Europe and the United States: The Future of the Relationship.* Washington, D.C.: Columbus Books, 1973.
Kennan, George F. *Memoirs, 1925-1950.* Boston: Little, Brown, 1967.
Kerr, Henry Hampton. "The European Parliament and European Integration: The Effects of Participation in an International Parliamentary Assembly." Ph.D. dissertation, University of Michigan, 1970.
Kitzinger, Uwe. *Britain, Europe and Beyond.* Leyden: Sythoff, 1964.
——. *The Challenge of the Common Market: The Politics of European Integration, Britain, Europe and the United States.* New York: Praeger, 1963.
——. *Diplomacy and Persuasion: How Britain Joined the Common Market.* London: Thames and Hudson, 1973.
——. *The Second Try: Labour and the European Economic Community.* New York: Pergammon Press, 1968.

Kjekshus, Helge. "The Parties Against the States: Pre-Federal Party Alignments in the European Community." Ph.D. dissertation, Syracuse University, 1966.

Krause, L. B., ed. *The Common Market—Progress and Controversy*. Englewood Cliffs, N.J.: Prentice-Hall, 1964.

Lambert, John. *Britain in a Federal Europe*. London: Chatto and Windus, 1968.

Lichtheim, G. *The New Europe—Today and Tomorrow*. New York: Praeger, 1963.

Lindberg, Leon N. *The Political Dynamics of European Economic Integration*. Stanford: Stanford University Press, 1963.

Lindberg, Leon, and Scheingold, Stuart A. *Europe's Would-Be Polity*. Englewood Cliffs, N.J.: Prentice-Hall, 1970.

Lindsay, Kenneth. *European Assemblies, the Experimental Period, 1949-1959*. London: Stevens and Sons, 1960.

———. *Towards a European Parliament*. Strasbourg: Secretariat of the Council of Europe, 1957.

Lipgen, Walter. *Europa-Föderationspläne der Widerstandsbewegungen 1940-1945*. Munich: R. Oldenbourg, 1968.

Lister, Louis. *Europe's Coal and Steel Community*. New York: Twentieth Century Fund, 1960.

Loewenheim, Francis L., ed. *Roosevelt and Churchill: Their Secret Correspondence*. New York: Dutton, 1975.

Lutz, Christian. *The Road to European Union: A Plea for a Constitutional Revolution*. London: Atlantic Institute of International Affairs, 1976.

Macmahon, Arthur W. *Federalism, Mature and Emergent*. Garden City, N.Y.: Doubleday, 1955.

Mally, Gerhard. *The European Community in Perspective: The New Europe, the United States and the World*. Lexington, Mass.: Heath, 1973.

Manzanarès, Henri. *Le Parlement européen*. Paris: Berger-Levrault, 1964.

Mayne, Richard. *The Community of Europe*. New York: Norton, 1963.

———. *Institutions of the European Community*. London: Chatham House, 1968.

———. *The New Atlantic Challenge*. New York: Wiley, 1975.

———. *The Recovery of Europe, 1945-73*. Garden City, N.Y.: Doubleday, 1973.

———, ed. *Europe Tomorrow: Sixteen Europeans Look Ahead*. London: Fontana, 1972.

Monnet, Jean. *Les États-Unis d'Europe ont Commencé*. Paris: 1955.

Morgan, Roger P. *West European Politics since 1945.* London: Batsford, 1972.

Mowat, Robert. *Creating the European Community.* London: Blandford Press, 1973.

Newhouse, John. *Collision in Brussels.* New York: Norton, 1967.

———. *De Gaulle and the Anglo-Saxons.* New York: Viking Press, 1970.

Niblock, Michael. *The European Economic Community: National Parliaments in Community Decision-Making.* London: Chatham House, 1971.

Northrop, F. S. C. *European Union and United States Foreign Policy.* New York: Macmillan, 1954.

Oudenhove, Guy van. *The Political Parties in the European Parliament, The First Ten Years, 1952-62.* Leyden: Sythoff, 1965.

Patterson, Ben. *Direct Elections to the European Parliament.* London: European Movement, 1974.

Patterson, William E. *The S.P.D. and European Integration.* Lexington, Mass.: Lexington Books, 1974.

Political and Economic Planning. *Budgetary Control in the European Economic Community.* London: PEP, 1960.

———. *Direct Elections and the European Parliament.* London: PEP, 1960.

———. *European Unity: A Survey of the European Organizations.* London: PEP, 1968.

———. *Negotiations on Political Union.* London: PEP, 1962.

———. *The Parliament of the European Communities.* London: PEP, 1964.

Prittie, Terence. *Willy Brandt: Portrait of a Statesman.* New York: Schoken Books, 1974.

Pryce, Roy. *The Political Future of the European Community.* London: Marshbank for the Federal Trust, 1962.

———. *The Politics of the European Community.* Totowa, N.J.: Rowman and Littlefield, 1973.

Renouvin, Pierre. *L'idée de fédération européenne dans la pensée politique du XIXe siècle.* Oxford: Oxford University Press, 1949.

Reynaud, Paul. *Unite or Perish.* New York: Simon and Schuster, 1951.

Robertson, Arthur Henry. *The Council of Europe; Its Structure, Functions and Achievements.* New York: Praeger, 1961.

———. *European Institutions: Cooperation, Integration, Unification.* New York: Matthew and Binder, 1973.

Rosenthal, Glenda. *The Men Behind the Decisions: Cases in European Policy-Making.* Lexington, Mass.: Heath, 1975.

Sampson, Anthony. *The New Europeans.* London: Panther, 1971.

Schmitt, Hans A. *The Path to European Union: From the Marshall Plan to the Common Market.* Baton Rouge: Louisiana State University Press, 1962.

Schonfield, Andrew. *Europe—Journey to an Unknown Destination.* London: Allen Lane, 1972.

Soames, Sir Christopher; Kirk, Peter; and Davies, John. *Three Views of Europe.* London: Conservative Political Center, 1973.

Spaak, Paul-Henri. *The Continuing Battle,* Henry Fox, trans. Boston: Little, Brown, 1971.

Spinelli, Altiero. *European Adventure.* London: C. Knight, 1972.

Thomas, Hugh. *Europe: The Radical Challenge.* New York: Harper and Row, 1973.

Truman, Harry S. *Memoirs.* Garden City, N.J.: Doubleday, 1955.

Urwin, Derek W. *Western Europe since 1945.* London: Longmans, 1972.

Wall, Edward H. *European Communities Act.* London: Butterworth, 1973.

Wallace, Helen. *National Governments and the European Communities.* London: Chatham House, 1973.

Walsh, A. *Into Europe: The Structure and Development of the Common Market.* London: Hutchinson, 1972.

Wanke, Otto. *Das Europäische Parlament.* Vienna, 1965.

Warnecke, Steven. *The European Community in the 1970s.* New York: Praeger, 1972.

Watson, Alan. *Europe at Risk.* London: Harrad, 1972.

Wighton, Charles. *Adenauer: A Critical Biography.* New York: Coward-McCann, 1964.

Williams, Shirley. *The Common Market and its Forerunner.* London: Fabian Research, 1968.

Willis, F. Roy. *France, Germany and the New Europe 1945-1967.* Stanford: Stanford University Press, 1968.

———. *Italy Chooses Europe.* New York: Oxford University Press, 1971.

Wright, Gordon. *France in Modern Times.* Chicago: Rand McNally, 1974.

Young, Simon Z. *Terms of Entry: Britain's Negotiations with the European Community.* London: Heinemann, 1973.

Zurcher, Arnold. *The Struggle to Unite Europe, 1940-1958.* New York: New York University Press, 1958.

ARTICLES

Albertini, Mario. "Le Parlement européen: profil historique, juridique et politique." *Fédéraliste* 15 (December 1973) : 94-121.

Allcott, Philip. "The Democratic Basis of the European Communities."

Common Market Law Review 11 (August 1974) : 298-326.

Aron, Raymond. "The Crisis of the European Idea." *Government and Opposition* 11 (Winter 1976) : 5-19.

Bangemann, Martin. "Europa und die Liberalen." *Liberal* 18 (1976) : 27-42.

Beaudry, Yvonne. "Jean Monnet: Europe's Hyphenator; the Common Market–A United States of Europe?" *Michigan Quarterly Review* 7 (Spring 1968) : 75-80.

Beesborough, Frederick. "The Parliament and European Unity: Learning from the American Experience." *European Community* (1976) : 7-10.

Bernick, Mike. "Britain's Experiment in Direct Democracy: How the E.E.C. Vote Worked." *New Leader* 58 (July 7, 1975) : 12-14.

Blaker, Peter. "Labour's Renegotiation Policy: A Conservative view." *World Today* 30 (August 1974) : 319-26.

Bodenheimer, Susanne J. "The 'Political Union' Debate in Europe: A Case Study in Intergovernmental Diplomacy." *International Organization* 21 (Winter 1967) : 24-54.

Bonham, G. Matthew. "Scandinavian Parliamentarians: Attitudes toward Political Integration." *Cooperation and Conflict* 4 (1969) : 149-61.

Bordu, Gerard. "Parlement européen: L'activité des Députés Communistes." *Cahiers du Communisme* 50 (February 1974) : 94-102.

Burban, Jean Louis. "Les Gaullistes et l'Élection du Parlement européen au suffrage universel direct." *Revue du Marché Commun* (February 1976) : 75-85.

———. "Relations entre Parlement européen et parlements nationaux." *Revue du Marché Commun* (December 1972) : 789-90.

Bywater, Marion, and Kemezis, Paul. "The Parliament Today: A Week in the Life of the Community's Legislature." *European Community* (September 1976) : 14-17.

Calleo, David P. "The European Coalition in a Fragmenting World." *Foreign Affairs* 54 (October 1975) : 98-112.

Dehousse, Fernand. "La contribution des assemblées européennes à l'unification politique de l'Europe." *Europe en Formation* 15 (January 1974) : 9-16.

Delzell, Charles L. "The European Federalist Movement in Italy, First Phase, 1918-1947." *Journal of Modern History* 32 (1960) : 241-50.

Economist. "Britain's Great Euro-Election Mystery," 21 February 1976, p. 57.

———. "Europe's Talking Shop," 3 April 1976, pp. 87-88.

———. "More Things than Are Dreamt of in Your Psephology," 24 January 1976, pp. 59-60.

———. "Oh To Be in Europe Now that the Voting's Near," 9 April 1977, p. 41.

———. "One Man's Europe," 24 May 1969, pp. 13-15.

———. "On Eurelection Day," 17 January 1970, pp. 14-15.

———. "On from Nine," 19 February 1977, pp. 16-17.

———. "The Perfect Result; Referendum Votes British Membership in the Common Market," 14 June 1975, p. 18.

Ehlermann, C. D. "Applying the New Budgetary Procedures for the First Time." *Common Market Law Review* 12 (August 1975) : 325-43.

European Community. "The Tindemans Report," March 1976, pp. 3-8.

European Review. "Bureaucracy or Community? The Political Development of the E.E.C." 23 (Winter 1973) : 14-16.

Feidt, Jean. "L'activité du Parlement européen en 1975." *Revue du Marché Commun,* July/August 1976, pp. 330-45.

———. "L'activité du Parlement européen pendant l'année 1972." *Revue du Marché Commun,* February 1973, pp. 59-65.

Feld, Werner. "The Federation of Europe: Creating the Political Will." *Interplay* 2 (March 1969) : 17-20.

Fontaine, E. "The 'Father of Europe' Defends His Problem Child." *Réalites,* September 1967, pp. 23-25.

Gati, Charles. "The 'Europeanization' of Communism?" *Foreign Affairs* 55 (April 1977) : 539-53.

Gazzo, Lidia. "Universal Vote for Miss Europe." *Vision,* January 1977, pp. 23-26.

Gordon, Lincoln. "Myth and Reality of European Integration." *Yale Review* 45 (1955) : 80-103.

Government and Opposition. "European Integration and the Future of Parliaments in Europe" 9 (Autumn 1974) : 460-91.

Heidelberg, Franz C. "Parliamentary Control and Political Groups in the Three European Regional Communities." *Law and Contemporary Problems* 26 (Summer 1961) : 430-37.

Hopkins, Michael. "The Bibliographical Resources of European Documentation Centers." *Journal of Librarianship* 7 (April 1975) : 84-99.

Hulle, Karel van. "The Institutions of the European Communities in a Changing Political Climate." *Marquette Law Review* 58 (1975) : 589-608.

Inglehart, Ronald. "Changing Value Priorities and European Integration." *Journal of Common Market Studies* 10 (September 1971) : 1-36.

Irving, R. E. M. "Italy's Christian Democrats and European Integration." *International Affairs* 52 (July 1976) : 400-416.

Jenkins, Roy. "The United States and a Uniting Europe." *European Community,* January/February 1977, pp. 17-23.

Kapteyn, P. J. G. "The European Parliament, the Budget and Legislation in the Community." *Common Market Law Review* 9 (November 1972) : 386-410.

Karp, Basil. "The Draft Constitution for a European Political Community." *International Organization* 8 (1954) : 102-35.

Kerr, Henry H., Jr. "Changing Attitudes through International Participation: European Parliamentarians and Integration." *International Organization* 27 (Winter 1973) : 45-83.

Koever, J. F. "The Integration of Western Europe." *Political Science Quarterly* 69 (1954) : 354-73.

Kolinsky, Martin. "Parliamentary Scrutiny of European Legislation." *Government and Opposition* 10 (Winter 1975) : 46-69.

Kotov, Yuli. "Unseemly and Dangerous Scheme." *New Times,* August 1976, pp. 14-15.

Krenzler, Horst Günter. "Europäische Direktwahlen and die Chancen der Liberalen." *Liberal* 18 (1976) : 180-86.

Krosigk, Fredrich von. "A Reconsideration of Federalism in the Scope of the Present Discussion on European Integration." *Journal of Common Market Studies* 9 (March 1971) : 197-223.

Kyle, Keith. "The European Parliament: The Need to Strengthen Democratic Controls." *World Today,* December 1972, pp. 530-37.

Laurent, Pierre-Henry. "The Benelux States and the New Community." *Current History* 64 (April 1973) : 166-71.

Lazer, Harry. "British Populism: The Labour Party and the Common Market Parliamentary Debate." *Political Science Quarterly* 91 (Summer 1976) : 259-77.

Leich, John Foster. "The Italian Communists and the European Parliament." *Journal of Common Market Studies* 9 (1971) : 271-81.

Leigh, Michael. "Germany's Changing Role in the E.E.C." *World Today,* December 1975, pp. 488-97.

———. "Giscard and the European Community." *World Today,* February 1977, pp. 73-80.

Lodge, Juliet. "The Organization and Control of European Integration in the Federal Republic of Germany." *Parliamentary Affairs* 28 (Autumn 1975) : 416-30.

———. "Reform of the European Parliament." *Political Science* 25 (July 1973) : 58-78.

———. "Toward the European Political Community: E.E.C. Summit and European Integration." *Orbis* 19 (Summer 1975) : 626-51.

May, James. "Is There a European Socialism?" *Journal of Common Market Studies* 13 (June 1975) : 492-502.

Mayne, Richard. "The Role of Jean Monnet." *Government and Opposition* 2 (April/July 1967) : 349-71.

Merkl, Peter H. "European Assembly Parties and National Behavior." *Journal of Conflict Resolution* 8 (March 1964) : 50-64.

Noel, Emile. "The Commission's Power of Initiative." *Common Market Law Review* 10 (May 1973) : 123-36.

O'Toole, Edward T. "The Ambitious Men of Europe House." *Reporter,* 25 February 1965, pp. 24-26.

Palmer, Michael. "The Role of a Directly Elected European Parliament." *World Today,* April 1977, pp. 122-30.

———. "Strengthening the Presidency." *New Europe* 4 (Summer 1976) : 38-41.

Patijn, Schelto. "European Elections." *New Europe* 4 (Summer 1976) : 32-37.

Pendergast, William R. "Role and Attitudes of French and Italian Delegates to the European Community." *International Organization* 30 (August 1976) : 669-78.

Pfisterer, Hans. "Das Europäische Parlament." *Sparkasse* 88 (July 1971) : 211-14.

Politische Studien. "Die politische Einigung des Freien Europas" (three articles and excerpts from declarations of West German political parties). 27 (March/April 1976) : 119-71.

Pridham, Geoffrey. "Transnational Party Groups in the European Parliament." *Journal of Common Market Studies* 13 (March 1975) : 266-79.

Prinsky, Robert. "A United Front: Europe Is in Disarray, but to the Outside It's a Formidable Force." *Wall Street Journal,* 26 November 1976, p. 1.

Rieber, Roger. "The Future of the European Community in International Politics." *Journal of Political Science* 9 (June 1976) : 206-26.

Robinson, Mary T. W. "The Political Implications of the Vedel Report." *Government and Opposition* 7 (Autumn) : 426-33.

Rocard, Michael. "French Socialism and Europe." *Foreign Affairs* 55 (April 1977) : 554-60.

Salpeter, Eliahu. "The E.E.C. Is Alive and Plodding: Moving toward Political Unity." *New Leader,* 2 August 1976, pp. 9-11.

Sanderson, Fred H. "The Five-Year Experience of the European Coal and Steel Community." *International Organization* 2 (Spring 1968) : 193-200.

Shlaim, Avi. "The Vedel Report and the Reform of the European Parliament." *Parliamentary Affairs* 27 (Spring 1974) : 159-70.

Shuster, Alvin. "Britain Says 'Yes.' " *European Community,* June 1975, pp. 3-7.

Sidjanski, Dusan. "Partis politiques en face de l'integration Européene." *Res Publica* 3 (1961).

Socialisme. "Des leaders socialistes évoquent l'avenir de l'Europe." 20 (February 1973) : 3-84.

Spaak, Paul-Henri. "The New Europe." *Atlantic Monthly,* September 1958, pp. 37-41.

Spek, Peter G. van der. "The Old and the New European Community: France l'Enfant Terrible." *Aussenwirtschaft* 27 (June 1972) : 167-84.

Steed, Michael. "The European Parliament: The Significance of Direct Election." *Government and Opposition* 6 (Autumn 1971) : 462-76.

Stein, Eric. "The European Parliamentary Assembly, Techniques of Emerging Political Control." *International Organization* 13 (1959) : 233-54.

Stevens, Anne. "Problems of Parliamentary Control of the European Community Policy." *Millennium* 5 (1974) : 269-81.

Stewart, Michael. "Direct Elections to the European Parliament." *Common Market Law Review* 13 (August 1976) : 283-99.

Streiff, Gérard. "L'affaire du Parlement européen." *Cahiers du Communisme* 52 (1976) : 90-100.

Tatu, Michael. "The Devolution of Power: A Dream?" *Foreign Affairs* 53 (July 1975) : 688-92.

Taylor, Paul. "The Politics of the European Communities: The Confederal Phase." *World Politics,* April 1975, pp. 336-60.

Thorn, Gaston. "The Meaning of the Tindemans Report on the European Union." *Intereconomics,* May 1976, pp. 130-32.

Urwin, Derek W., and Rose, Richard. "Persistence and Change in Western Party Systems Since 1945." *Political Studies* 18 (September 1970) : 287-319.

Weissberg, Robert. "Nationalism and Integration, and French and German Elites." *International Organization* 23 (Spring 1969) : 337-47.

Werner, Pierre. "The Identity and Role of Luxembourg within the European Parliament." *Journalism Today* 3 (Autumn 1972) : 5-9.

Z. "What Jean Monnet Wrought." *Foreign Affairs* 55 (April 1977) : 630-35.

Zelletin, Gerda. "Form and Function of the Opposition in the European Communities." *Government and Opposition* 2 (April/July 1967) : 416-35.

NEWSPAPERS AND OTHER INFORMATION SOURCES

Agence Europe
The Baltimore Sun
The Christian Science Monitor
European Community Information Service
European Parliament London Information Office
Journal of Commerce
Le Monde
The Financial Times (London)
The German Tribune
The Irish Times
The Manchester Guardian Weekly
The New York Times
The Sunday Times
The Times (London)
The Wall Street Journal
The Washington Post
The Washington Star

INDEX

Council of Ministers of the European Economic Community: functions and powers, 38, 152-54, 160; voting procedure, 74, 181-82 n.20
Crisis of 1965, 77-83, 85

Davignon Report, 116-17, 129
Debré, Michel, 22, 42, 45, 47-48, 58, 62, 105, 150; Union of States, 27-28
de Gasperi, Alcide, 6, 24, 29
de Gaulle, Charles, 6; Crisis of 1965, 79-80, 82-83; European Defense Community, 29; formation Fifth French Republic, 47-48; second British EEC entry attempt, 93-95; Union of European States, 59-66; views on European integration, 59-61, 73, 85-88, 92, 105-6, 109, 153; waning popularity, 98, 100, 103-6. *See also* Intergovernmental cooperation
Dehousse, Fernand, 34-37, 45-47, 50, 54, 56-57, 61, 65, 68, 101, 114, 172 n.16, 177 n.12
Direct Elections: inclusion in European Coal and Steel Community Treaty, 18-19. *See also* European Parliament, direct elections
Draft Constitution of the United States of Europe, 9-10
Draft Convention of 1960, 10-12, 67, 90, 108-11, 137-38; attitude of states toward, 58-59, 61, 66; background and provisions, 50-56; debate and approval by European Parliament, 56-58

Eden, Anthony, 11
Electoral Systems of the European Economic Community states, 141-42
Empty-Chair policy, 85-90. *See also* Crisis of 1965
Erhard, Ludwig, 71-72, 175 n.39
Eurocommunism, 127, 156-59
European Coal and Steel Community, general, 11, 35; national attitudes towards, 20, 169 n.16; ratification of treaty establishing, 20; structure and functions, 18
European Council, 140, 143-44, 150-51, 153-54, 157
European Defense Community, background, 22-23; French failure to ratify treaty, 29-31; provisions and reactions of states towards, 23-30
European Economic Community, n. 11; Rome Treaty provisions, 37-41; Rome Treaty ratification considerations, 44, 174-75 n.37; stagnation of late 1960s, 96-104
European elections, 147. *See also* European Parliament, direct elections
European Free Trade Association, 47, 59-60
European Parliament, 5-6, 9-12, 44-45; attitude of states towards, 44, 71, 76, 90, 92, 95-99, 107, 110-13, 115-16, 122-23, 128-29, 132, 134-35, 136, 139-44, 147, 154, 156; British EEC membership issue, 69; campaign to strengthen powers, 1963-66, 68-71, 73-

ABOUT THE AUTHOR

Paula Scalingi is an analyst of West European politics for the federal government. Her articles have appeared in *The Historian* and in the *Biographical Dictionary of Modern British Radicals.*